The Roya

Dedicated to

my Community at Belmont Abbey, Hereford

and

El Monasterio de la Encarnacion, in Peru

and

the Sisters of Charity of Fort Leavenworth, USA

The Royal Road to Joy

The Beatitudes and the Eucharist

David Bird OSB

GRACEWING

First published in 2003

Gracewing
2 Southern Avenue, Leominster
Herefordshire HR6 0QF

ISBN 0 85244 573 3

Typeset by Action Publishing Technology Ltd,
Gloucester GL1 5SR

Printed in England by
Antony Rowe Ltd, Eastbourne BN23 6QT

Contents

Part II: The Mass

Foreword

by The Right Reverend Mark Jabalé OSB,
Bishop of Menevia

I have known Father David Bird since the early fifties when we were at school together. A couple of years older than him, I joined the Monastery at Belmont Abbey ahead of him; but I was at Fribourg University at the same time as he was, and later was teaching at and Headmaster of the Abbey School when he was its Chaplain. I am therefore delighted that he asked me to write a foreword to this book.

These days, in England and Wales, the Catholic Church can seem very establishment, very much constrained by old customs. What is written here powerfully evokes the kingdom-living, which has inspired the Church, and enabled her again and again to draw new life, new freshness, from the authentic tradition entrusted to her. We are more used, perhaps, to being inspired by the way the Gospel finds its expression in the new movements in the Church.

In Dom David's book a member of one of the oldest religious orders in the Western Church shares what inspires his mind and heart. The reader will find that one of the book's great strengths is its passion; he or she will hear something of the prophet in the way that David beckons us from going through the motions into a new and committed engagement of life as a disciple, united with Christ, learning from Christ. The vision here is not of religion institutional or stale, but of a conviction which is fresh, enriched, ennobled, charged with faith, to help us as we journey on the 'royal road to joy'. I found that journey a very moving one, particularly the first part which deals with Beatitudes.

These earlier chapters, although grounded on biblical scholarship, make easy and interesting reading; they tell everyday Catholics what they need to know; and the reader does not need to be a theologian to follow the arguments. David's use of stories from his own experience – especially in Peru, which for me ring so true, as I spent three years there at the same time as Father David – and the two chapters which give a short introduction on the lives of two saints on the Royal Road to Joy, are particularly helpful in making this book relevant to every ordinary Catholic who is looking to live the life of the Gospel. The second part may arouse some disagreement from some readers; but then, the Liturgy is probably the one topic on which there is most controversy in the Church. Father David, in this part, tells us how the living of the Beatitudes is not only relevant, but actually helps in a deeper understanding of what is celebrated at the Altar. A Church living the Beatitudes is best-placed to celebrate the outward sign of that Mystery of Christ's suffering, death and resurrection.

This book has a great deal to say to the ordinary Catholic as much as to the more educated theologically. Reading the book in preparation for this foreword, I found myself strangely drawn to reading on; it is eminently readable and has that quality of touching the reader personally. I hope you enjoy reading it as much as I did.

✠ Mark Jabalé OSB
Bishop of Menevia

Preface

This book began as a personal quest for the roots of my own spirituality, written for my own benefit while I was holed up in my parish house in San Miguel de Pallaques, 2,650 metres above sea-level in the Peruvian Andes. It was summer according to the textbooks; and that is a time of thick mists, an incredible amount of rain, and unsafe mud roads winding their way round mountains, where car wheels are always too near the precipice for comfort. Rather than looking at the four walls of my room for the months of the rainy season, without very much to do because the weather brought most pastoral work to a halt, I decided to write down all the various strands and sources and experiences which contributed to my personal religion, and then to form them into a coherent whole. In this way I would be able to examine, develop and criticize my spirituality. I thought I was in charge of the book; but it developed its own logic and soon took charge of me. I was still writing three years later when I was in another parish, Tembladera, where the weather is more tropical and the Andes melt into the coastal plain. This book is part of what I wrote.

Here was I in a secular parish, a Benedictine monk, who, due to circumstances, was thousands of miles away from my monastery in Hereford, and hundreds of miles from our house in Peru, trying to preach the Gospel. As an English Benedictine, I had the help of Jean Pierre de

Caussade, a French Jesuit, whose classic work, *Abandonment to Divine Providence*, has aided many monks to live, sometimes in their monastery, sometimes on the mission, with a certain amount of spiritual coherence and continuity. He taught that we should seek God's presence in the concrete circumstances of our lives, in what he called 'the sacrament of the present moment', and that the obstacle to seeking God is our own self-will. This is completely in keeping with the Rule of St Benedict; yet he generalizes the teaching and makes it applicable to any situation, including mine. Nevertheless, I wanted to explore further; and the rain gave me the opportunity to do so. However, as though with a will of its own, the book turned away from my narrow little life and opened up horizons big enough to share with others.

I started with the Beatitudes, and I soon found that they are as full of surprises as the roads round San Miguel. It had never occurred to me before that they are a complete spiritual programme which shows us the various stages of Christian conversion, and that their teaching is identical to that found in the Desert Fathers, in the Patristic Tradition and in the Rule of St Benedict. Read in another way, they show us the permanent ingredients of Christian holiness.

In a previous parish called Negritos, on the Pacific coast in northern Peru, I had had the privilege to work with the American Sisters of Charity of Fort Leavenworth; and they had so impressed me that I went into the spirituality of St Vincent de Paul. Reading the Beatitudes, I now see how they impregnated his teaching with their light. The Beatitudes are basic to all Christian spiritualities.

Not only did I come to see the Beatitudes as a description of the process of Christian conversion, of our way to God; I also saw the connection between the Beatitudes and the Mass. Both, at different levels, bring us through the death and resurrection of Christ into the presence of the Father. It is an important characteristic of Benedictine experience that spirituality and liturgy are intimately connected as two dimensions of the same reality. It was this insight that led to the liturgical movement, which began in monasteries as a monastic concern and then spilled out into the Church at large and produced such tremendous results during and after the Second Vatican Council.

I suppose the difference between a monk in a monastery and any Christian outside is the difference between a plant in a greenhouse, and a plant growing wild. The greenhouse provides all that is necessary to make the plant prosper, while the wild plant has to do its best in the environment where it finds itself. To live his baptism is the monk's exclusive profession. If monastic life is contemplative, it is because Christianity is contemplative; if it is communal, it is because Christianity is communal; if it is liturgical, it is because Christianity is liturgical; if it is scriptural, it is because Christianity is scriptural. 'Work and Prayer' in obedience to God's will are the two basic Christian activities, whatever our vocation. The monastic charism is to live that which is common to all Christian vocations, as fully and as sanely as possible.

A monastery does not exist for any reason other than the Christian life. As Abbot Cuthbert Butler said, monastic life is its own justification: seeking God together is inherently good. Of course, seeking God in certain concrete circumstances may oblige a community to practise an active apostolate; but seeking God, not the apostolate as such, is the reason for its existence. God is both the source and the goal of all Christian life; and, in the monastery, this priority of God is built into the very timetable.

This is the basis of our apostolate to the Church as a whole, and our witness to the world. A monastic life, properly lived, is a challenge to the individual monk as well as to the rest of the Church to put God first, and not to put secondary aspects of Christianity in God's place, however important and essential they may be. This is an underlying theme of this book. It also should be a witness, to the Church and the world, of Christ's presence wherever people are gathered together in Christ's name, so that people may find peace and then become more aware of Christ's presence in their own communities. There are also many by-products of a community's quest for God, like liturgical expertise and the fruit of monks' reading, which can enrich the Church.

Many people regard Benedictines as liturgical experts, even though very few of us are scholars. I suppose that, if a liturgical form is used every day by a highly critical group of men or women, then it is being tested indeed. Moreover, most monasteries are made up of 'conservatives', 'progressives' and everything else in between; and in a community, people are stuck with each other. Thus, in the changes that came about after Vatican II, monks with different attitudes and persuasions have combined in each house to form the kind of liturgy, which is suitable to all. Generally speaking, this has led to a certain balance. We are only experts in the sense that someone who constantly drives a car becomes an expert driver. He may not be an expert mechanic; and the monk may not be a liturgical scholar.

Uniting spirituality with liturgy for reasons I shall explain in the first chapter, I decided to combine a commentary on the Beatitudes with a commentary on the Mass. It was only when I returned to Belmont for my holidays that a monk of the monastery who celebrates the Byzantine Rite told me of the important place the Beatitudes have in the Byzantine Liturgy of the Eucharist.

I had a limited number of books to consult; but I found this contributed to my purpose by narrowing my focus. I also had a number of quotations from past copies of *Worship* and *Cistercian Studies* which had impressed me at different times. I have quoted from *The Roots of Christian Mysticism*, by Olivier Clement, published by New City in 1993; and *Beatitudes* by Simon Tugwell OP, published by Templegate; and *The Eucharist*, by Louis Bouyer, published by the University of Notre Dame Press, Notre

Dame, Indiana; and *Catholic Rites Today*, edited by Alan Bouley OSB, and published by the Liturgical Press, Collegeville, Minnesota, 1992; and *The Church at Prayer* Vol. II, by Robert Cabie, published by Geoffrey Chapman, 1986. I took the whole of my information on the life of St Seraphim of Sarov from two books: *Flame in the Snow*, by Iulia de Beausobre, Templegate, 1996; and *St Seraphim of Sarov* by Valentine Zander, from St Vladimir's Press, 1985. The life of St John Mary Vianney is from *Curé d'Ars* by Henri Ghéon. I have also quoted from *Contemplative Community*, edited by Basil Pennington OCSO; Cistercian Studies Series; Cistercian Publications, Consortium Press, Washington DC, 1972. All scriptural quotations are from the New Revised Standard Version. Apart from the Bible, my most constant companion has been *Abandonment to Divine Providence* by Jean Pierre de Caussade, published by Fontana Library of Theology and Philosophy, Collins.

I wish to thank Dom Luke Waring, Dom Dyfrig Harris and Abbot Alan Rees from my monastery. Fr Luke and I have kept up regular contacts; and his profound knowledge of Scripture has always been at my disposal. He advocated a 'chiastic' reading of the 'Our Father', and I advocated a straight reading; and each decided the other was right, without abandoning his own position. Having come to the conclusion that it should be read both ways, we then did the same with the Beatitudes, also with success. Dom Dyfrig is studying the Gospel of St John in the light of the Mishnah and other early Jewish literature. He filled in many gaps in my knowledge about Temple worship, and introduced me to the work of Margaret Barker. This was very helpful because it complemented what I had written, much of which was based on my reading of the Letter to the Hebrews and the Book of Revelation. Abbot Alan Rees helped me with my remarks about church music in 'Good Liturgy: Bad Liturgy'. I also wish to thank Dom Simon McGurk, Prior of the Monastery of the Incarnation, for reading through and criticizing what I had written, and my Abbot, Dom Paul Stonham, for his kindness and encouragement. Finally, I would like to thank my friends in Peru, among whom I wish to give a very special thanks to the members of my ex-parish of Negritos and the young people of the parish I have quoted in the book.

David Bird OSB

Part I
The Beatitudes

Chapter One

The Beatitudes and the Eucharist

When the revised liturgy of the Mass came out after the Second Vatican Council there was much optimism and it was generally hoped and expected that it would be instrumental in the renewal of Christian life throughout the Church. It had gone back to basics and was so constructed as to give maximum opportunity for participation by all in a rite in which the true meaning of the Eucharist was made as clear as possible. Unnecessary symbols had been stripped away to reveal those that are essential to the celebration and, at the same time, the texts were enriched from many traditional sources and by new compositions. The optimism that accompanied the publication of the new liturgy proved to be true in many parts of the Church, and large numbers of people have had their Christian lives transformed and deepened by the greater participation that it made possible. Nevertheless, the desired renewal has not taken place everywhere or in everyone, and there is much pessimism and even defeatism forty years after the council.

This is due to various factors. Firstly, those of us who enthusiastically promoted the changes were, because of our backgrounds, inclined to be rather cerebral in our approach to religion and we failed to notice that many people, especially among the poor and uneducated, were much more instinctive. In fact, by abolishing the devotions which meant so much to them, we robbed them of their religious language. They no longer felt at home, so they left. Thank God that the poor were too numerous in Latin America for that to happen in spite of the efforts of some missionaries. Secondly, by abandoning our ghetto mentality and launching the Church into a largely unbelieving secular world, many who were weak in their faith became immersed in secularism. This was a consequence we had not adequately foreseen. Thirdly, when we abandoned the penny catechism in favour of more modern ways of teaching, it took some time before any really effective method was found to take its place. We religious teachers were all at sixes and sevens and the result is that there is at least a generation of Catholics who are ignorant of the basic tenets of our faith. Solving the problems of young people often became a substitute for teaching doctrine. In other words, Vatican II had indicated to us the way the Church must go, but we were not very good at pursuing the goals that it had placed before us. I hope that all these limitations are ancient history, but there is one failure that remains with us, a failure that was also present in ancient Israel and which we will probably be fighting against until the end of the world.

Liturgy expresses Christ's activity in the Church and also expresses the Church's response. Hence a new liturgy that goes back to basics, that concentrates on what is most authentic and is stripped of all that obscures its deepest meaning, requires a spirituality that does the same. Without this spirituality a change in liturgy could only be superficial. When the new Mass came out, the novelty of it excited some and disturbed others, but for many it was just a new way of celebrating Mass which they accepted without ever allowing it to change them. However, where the new liturgy was matched with a restored spirituality, it became a tremendous force for good in the modern Church.

If we go back to basic essentials in the liturgy we must go back to basics in our spirituality. This is why we are combining here a commentary on the Beatitudes with a commentary on the Mass. Of course, the two commentaries will be different, each with its own emphasis, and they would normally be in separate books; but they belong together because both are about sharing in Christ's death and resurrection to attain intimate communion with God. It is impossible to participate authentically in the Mass without living according to the Beatitudes. They form one single royal road to joy. We must remember the witness of the Old Testament prophets that ritual, however holy and divinely sanctioned it may be, is good only for those whose humble and contrite hearts are in accordance with what is being celebrated. Living according to the Beatitudes guarantees that our hearts are in tune with the Eucharist. What God has united, let us try to keep together.

Repent, for the kingdom of heaven has come near
(Matt. 4.17)
This text implicitly unites the Beatitudes with the Eucharist. 'Repent' means much more than sorrow for sin. It requires a complete change of attitude, of values, of ways of thinking. It implies that there was something in Judaism which was on the wrong track, looked in the wrong direction, had taken the wrong road, and gave importance to things that are unimportant while neglecting things of the utmost importance. Jesus was requiring them to take a complete U-turn and to walk down a completely different road. Why? Because 'the kingdom of heaven has come near'. This is the Good News, information that God was about to do something among them that would transform his relationship with them, with the whole human race and with the cosmos. If they were to take advantage of this event, they had to change their whole mindset, their normal ways of thinking and making value judgements. They were to change their way of looking at themselves and at their neighbour so that they could enjoy a wholly new relationship with God, a relationship that God was about to establish. St Matthew spells out this process of change for

those who have accepted Christ's challenge in the Beatitudes. The day before he died, Jesus instituted the Eucharist by which his followers could celebrate and participate in the kingdom which was about to be brought into being by his death and resurrection. Hence, to participate fruitfully in the Mass we must accept the same challenge, take part personally in the same mental and spiritual revolution, allow the same transformation in us that Jesus required of the Jews. In order to take part in the Eucharist we must follow the way of the Beatitudes.

This book is about coming close to God. We begin by examining the profound process of Christian conversion in which our basic attitudes are radically changed towards ourselves, towards what happens to us, towards other people and, finally, towards God. This 'road to joy' we find in the Beatitudes. They describe our journey through death to resurrection, allowing the Spirit to strip us of all that is not God-centred, layer by layer, until we become pure in heart. Then we love God with our whole being and love our neighbour as Christ loves him, and we become utterly impregnated with God. We become for others what baptism destines us to be: not people who merely talk about God, but people who manifest God's presence in the world. In Christ's own vocabulary and that of apocalyptic Judaism, we come to be called children of God. This process of conversion changes us from egotistic individuals into full Christians. It enables us to participate ever more authentically as members of Christ's body in the eucharistic community which is the Church.

'Coming close' is also the root meaning of *korban*, the Hebrew word for sacrifice. Christ became perfect by his loving obedience unto death and does not need to die again. From his point of view, he was perfectly united to the Father and became the source of our salvation. Nevertheless, the Church on earth is still on its way to perfection and still needs to come ever closer to the Father, which it can only do through Christ. He is the means by which the Father and ourselves approach each other. No one can go to the Father except by him, and so he is our sacrifice. In the Eucharist we present the memorial of his death and resurrection to the Father so that the Father may send the Spirit on bread and wine to make them Christ's body and blood. By receiving Christ in communion we enter into his relationship with the Father as members of his body. Just as the Jews ate the paschal meal in order to share in the covenant relationship that God established with Israel after their flight from Egypt, so we enjoy the covenant relationship with God which was established in Christ through death and resurrection. As the means by which the Church is continually transformed into Christ, the Eucharist is the Church's sacrifice.

The Mass and the Beatitudes are about the same road to joy. In the Mass Christ speaks to us through his word and then leads us to the Father, first by pleading his obedience unto death on our behalf and then uniting us to himself in the Father's presence by holy communion. By practising the Beatitudes we become poor in spirit, accepting Christ as our true riches and our holiness, so that we become living sacrifices and thus form a community of givers rather than consumers, and we can move together towards purity in heart which makes a deep relationship with Christ possible. We participate in the Mass and live by the Beatitudes because we hunger and thirst for God. 'Blessed are the peacemakers' is the result of both taking part in the Mass and practising the Beatitudes. The Beatitudes are about living the Mass; and the Mass integrates our living the Beatitudes into the death and resurrection of Christ by making us one body with him. Without the Beatitudes we would never penetrate through the outward sign into the inner reality of the Eucharist and it would become for us an empty ritual. Without the Mass, without communicating with Christ present in the Church, the Beatitudes would be a road to nowhere. In fact, our eucharistic celebration and the process of conversion that St Matthew describes in the

Beatitudes are simply two dimensions of the same Christian Mystery, of what it means to be the Church, and it is impossible to separate them.

In the apocalyptic thought of Christ's time, whether we visualize our journey as going up into the Cloud of Unknowing or entering into the Holy of Holies or simply allowing ourselves to be united to Christ, we are transformed by grace in a union with God that is nothing less than a sharing in his own life. God crosses the distance between Creator and creature, pierces the darkness that is the result of sin and draws us into intimate union with himself. Heaven and earth become one and we become the means by which others can touch Eternity. In Old Testament times, this was the privilege of a few individuals, of people such as Moses, Isaiah and Enoch. In the New Covenant, Christ's resurrection and ascension have made it possible for all Christians because we are members of his body. All of us can become theophanies, manifestations of Christ in the world, in the measure and in the manner given to each of us by the Spirit; but only to the extent that we are members of his body, only to the extent that we allow Christ to fill and direct our lives. Eucharistic communion only goes as deep as our purity in heart.

In any Christian community there must be a balance between the one-to-one relationship of each member with Christ and the communal sharing of all members in the life of Christ. In the words of the Cistercian Fathers, there must be both solitude with Christ and togetherness in Christ. The same Christ is in the very depths of each soul even as he binds the community together as one body. The Beatitudes map out our interior life as it spills out into the community; while the Eucharist is the community celebration which penetrates into the inner recesses of our souls. If we are to have an authentic Christian community, there must be a reciprocal relationship between our spirituality as individual persons and our outward celebrations of the Mass as members of the

Church. The authentic Christian community manifests Christ's presence through the quality of its love, its special kind of unity: 'As you, Father, are in me and I am in you, may they also be in us, so that the world may believe that you have sent me'. The more we love one another in Christ, the more Christ's presence is tangible in the world.

We now live in a secular society without many of the props and helps we had in the past. Christendom is no more, and our beliefs and values are under attack. The Pope and the bishops have urged on us the need for a new evangelization. We need to remember that, within the context of the 'kingdom of God', where God's grace is the paramount reality, where God is the chief player, the secret of the effectiveness of our evangelization is not the quality of our programmes or communication skills or ability to organize. These are important, but what is absolutely essential is the degree to which we are truly God's instruments; and this depends on our openness to him, on our sanctity, on the way we live the Beatitudes and on the depth of our communion with Christ at Mass. In a word, we need to form authentic Christian communities that the world may know that Christ has been sent by the Father.

The world suffers from a surfeit of information, and we are not going to convert it by adding more and more words. We need to manifest God's presence to those with eyes to see and ears to hear: the world needs actual contact with God. Then it will know what words make sense. The Church has received the Spirit that it may bear witness to the Truth and its function is to be Christ's body on earth. Our community life must manifest Christ's presence in the world. In the words of Charles de Foucauld, we must 'cry out the Gospel with our lives'. Hence the first and most basic task of any 'new evangelization' is to concentrate on having an authentic Christian community. To achieve this we need to concentrate on spirituality and liturgy which are essential components of such a community.

Many new forms of Christian living have started up since the Second World War and especially since Vatican II. Brazil and Peru introduced the Basic Christian Communities in which people collaborate in prayer, in the reading of Scripture, in the apostolate and in fraternal charity. Mutual help in extreme need and the struggle for social justice receive their impetus from the Word of God and prayer. Cardinal Cormac Murphy O'Connor has urged on us the need to turn large and anonymous parishes into a network of communities small enough for people to interact and participate. In my old parish of Negritos in northern Peru there are many groups; and towards the end of the two-year confirmation course, young people discuss what kind of group they would join after receiving confirmation. It is taken for granted by many that, to live a dedicated Catholic life as full members of the parish, membership of a group is normal. In the diocese of Chulucanas, the Plan NIP, designed by the Movement for a Better World, divided the towns into groups of a hundred families; all the caring for old people, youth work, preparation for the sacraments and communal prayer, are done within the context of the hundred families. I once asked a parish priest in Chulucanas how many young people he had participating actively in his parish. He answered that he was not sure because they all belonged to different communities but there must be several thousand. Fr Eugene Kirke, a priest from Drogheda, together with some Little Brothers of Jesus, shared the life of the poorest of the poor in a large anonymous slum with a bad reputation on the outskirts of Lima. Family groups were formed in every block of buildings. These groups not only became the basis for a thriving Church but they also transformed the slum into a model town which received an international prize for the way all its organizations work for the good of the whole. People now say with pride that they come from Villa Salvador, where previously it had been a cause for shame.

Some international movements require a commitment

among their members which leads to various degrees of community living. The Charismatic Renewal has resulted in the spontaneous formation of communities. Opus Dei and the Focolare and the Neo-Catechumenate bring about community by the very dedication they require from their members. There are many more.

The Focolare began in a bomb shelter. A group of students were cowering for protection in a shelter in Milan while Allied bombers were systematically destroying much of the city above them. Chiara Lubich and her friends began to talk of their faith, and they decided that they had never really put it into practice. They did not love one another, let alone other people, as Jesus had taught. Were they ready to die for each other? Were they ready to die for people they did not know? Their answer was negative, even though they believed that Christ had died for them. On the spot they decided to live the Gospel to the full. To the astonishment of other people in the shelter, they went out into the city while the bombs were still dropping and began to help people trapped in the rubble. Focolare was born. Their decision to live by the law of radical love attracted others, and the movement spread like wild fire. They were first called *focolare* or 'people of the hearth' by others who were impressed by the warmth of their love. They and their movement developed and matured, and they are now an international movement. In movements like this which have flourished since the Second World War there are all the signs of growth, and there is no lack of vocations.

Some movements and communities are local. Sant' Egidio was a disused church in Rome until a number of university students in the 1960s decided to dedicate their lives to putting the teaching of Vatican II into practice. They petitioned the town council that owned the church to allow them to use it. The community meets on Saturday evening for the Eucharist which, at least when I attended over twenty years ago, they sang with Russian chants. It was a very good example of what can be done in a contemporary setting. There is a strong emphasis on prayer with engagement in the modern world. They began by instructing the illiterate peasants who crowded into Rome in search of work, and their apostolate has grown so that they have been involved in peace negotiations between countries. A BBC commentator said that governments trust them because they have no self-interest, doing what they do for Christ. The Manquehue Apostolic Movement in Santiago de Chile is made up of lay people, some celibate, some single and many married, who run a number of schools and do other good works while following the Rule of St Benedict in different ways and degrees. There are many similar locally-based communities.

It is not my intention to urge parish priests to join one of the movements or to adopt a pastoral strategy which was formed under very different circumstances and in very different cultures from the situation in England or America. Even the examples I have given differ greatly from one another. What they have in common is their dedication to the Gospel. However, I am certain that authentic Christian community in some form or other is the necessary basic tool for any new evangelization and that authentic spirituality and liturgy are necessary elements in any Christian community. Liturgical renewal and spiritual renewal are interdependent, and each should reflect the other. Whatever pastoral plan or policy a parish adopts, it will work only on a superficial level if it is not accompanied by a deepening conversion of its members.

For a renewed Church we need an authentic spirituality, an authentic liturgy, and authentic Christian community. The Beatitudes provide the first, the Church provides the second, and we must find or form the third. Whether we use existing models as our guide or not, an authentic Christian community will have the following characteristics. Firstly, its members will be aware that they are called by God to be Christians and members of each other. It is a New Testament theme that we are chosen by

God. St Paul tells us that we were chosen before the creation of the world. It is our privilege to enjoy and deepen this relationship. This sense of vocation is growing among Christians as they find themselves in a minority. The second characteristic is that we are called to a life of conversion, the life that is described in the Beatitudes. It is likened by Jesus to ploughing a field, and by St Paul to running a race. The third characteristic is the community's liturgical life, which is centred on the Eucharist because it is not merely a natural community: it is the body of Christ. A rich liturgical life is normal among communities with a strong sense of vocation and an emphasis on personal conversion. However, we do not live this community life just for ourselves. We are the salt of the earth and the light of the world. The fourth characteristic of an authentic Christian community is outreach. Unlike Cain, we are our brother's keeper. 'Blessed are the merciful' summarizes this characteristic. We forgive our neighbour the wrongs he has inflicted on us; we try to fulfil his human needs and we proclaim the Good News to him. The fifth characteristic is the most important of all, without which the other characteristics will be distorted in their message. It must be a community that considers union with God as the supreme good: this is its contemplative dimension. It must be striving to love God with everything it has and does. God is both the source and the goal of any Christian community and his grace gives value to all its activities. The Christian community is primarily a community of faith, and its most important function is to reveal to the world Christ's presence within it. This it will do only if it is truly centred on God.

We shall now look closely at the Beatitudes and see how they bring us to perfection in Christ.

Chapter Two

Introducing the Beatitudes

In the Sermon on the Mount, the author of St Matthew's Gospel collects together many different sayings and teachings of Jesus to give us the New Law of the New Covenant. He places the sermon on a mount to remind us of God's revelation of the Old Law to Moses; and just as this is summarized in the Ten Commandments, so the New Law is summarized in the Beatitudes. In place of *YHWH* there is Jesus and in place of Moses there are the disciples.

These disciples are us; rather, they are ourselves in so far as we are pure in heart: the purer in heart we are, the more capable of listening to Jesus and understanding him. The same point is illustrated in the Gospel of St John by means of the disciple whom Jesus loved. He is both an historical figure, perhaps the origin of the Johannine Christian family with its special vocabulary and spirituality, and a symbolic figure representing the ideal disciple, even the ideal of discipleship. At the Last Supper, it is on him that Peter relies to find out the meaning of Jesus' words. At the tomb on Easter morning, this disciple is the first to believe in the resurrection, even before he sees the risen Christ. On Lake Tiberias, when Jesus appeared on the shore, he is the first to recognize him. For St John, understanding of the things of God arises out of a loving relationship with Jesus and this is very close to St Matthew's purity of heart.

In St John's theology, the whole of the Christian life is directed towards knowing the Father by knowing Jesus.

To know God is to enter into a relationship with God; and this has been made possible by his revelation of himself through the Word made flesh which reached its highest point of clarity on the cross. This knowledge of God or relationship with him, so that he who sees Jesus sees the Father, is what the Christian life is about in the Gospel of St John, just as the purity of heart which allows us to see God is the ultimate goal of the Beatitudes. Thus we become sons and daughters of God, born, not of the flesh or of the will of men, but of God, the means by which other people are brought into the same relationship. In St Matthew's phrase, we become 'peacemakers'.

The point is made in chapter 12 of the Letter to the Hebrews, that, in contrast to the old dispensation, where only Moses was allowed to approach God and everybody else was forbidden under pain of death to ascend the mountain, in the new covenant we are all invited to ascend Mount Zion into the Father's presence, together with Jesus with his blood, the angels and the saints. In the Sermon on the Mount, the disciples are separated from the crowd and, like Moses, come to Jesus to hear the new teaching. We ascend the mountain by means of the Beatitudes.

In this sermon, Jesus improves on the teaching of the Old Testament by his own authority. He does not say, 'God says this', or 'Oracle of the Lord'. He says, 'You have heard that it was said to those of ancient times, "You shall not murder"; ... but I say to you that if you are angry with a brother or sister, you will be liable to judgement'. The Ten Commandments were revealed directly to Moses by God; and Jesus is implying that his authority is no less divine.

It is probable that St Luke's version of the Beatitudes is closer to the actual words of Jesus. St Matthew has to amplify them in order to make them a summary of Christ's teaching. In this he shows a genius for condensing a whole theology into a few words that are easy to remember. He does the same thing with the Our Father. It is not surprising, therefore, that it is his version of these two texts that we use in our daily prayer.

I believe that, in both St Matthew's Beatitudes and the Our Father, the texts are so designed that a straight reading, from beginning to end, will give us one lot of information, while a 'chiastic' reading will complete the theme. A chiastic reading is one where the first beatitude or petition is read with the last, the second with the second from the last, and so on, until we are left with a central one which cannot be paired off with anything and this beatitude or petition has a special importance. There are seven petitions in the Our Father, and there is good reason to believe that there were originally only seven beatitudes.

'Blessed are the meek' is a direct quotation from Psalm 37; and the fact that it is put in second place in some sources and is in third place in others, indicates a strong possibility that it is not original. It probably began life, not as a separate beatitude, but as an expansion of the first. The reason why it is sometimes in third place, it seems to me, is that meekness is better seen as a consequence of mourning where poverty in spirit is interiorized.

'Blessed are those who are persecuted for righteousness' sake' is linked with the first beatitude by a repetition of 'for theirs is the kingdom of heaven'. This is what scholars call an *inclusio*, by which the last statement in a series is an explanation of the first and indicates that the whole series is an expansion of one theme: thus, all the other beatitudes are about being poor in spirit. If this is true, then 'Blessed are you when people revile you . . .' is simply an expansion of 'Blessed are those who are persecuted' and has no independent existence. This leaves us with seven beatitudes.

The number seven has a special significance in the Bible. To give but a few examples: the world was created in seven days; the main Jewish feasts were in the seventh month; and the word for an oath is based on the same number. In St Matthew, there are seven petitions in the Our Father, seven parables in chapter 13 and seven woes in chapter 23. Peter asks Jesus if he should forgive his neighbour seven times, and the Sadducees present to him the hypothetical case of seven brothers who marry the same woman. In the Book of Revelation the Lamb had seven horns and seven eyes.

The number seven, according to the context, means fullness, perfection, completion, or it means a limited, perfect number. The seven days of creation imply the fullness of time, so that there was no time left for an evil demi-god to create anything else. This contradicted the teaching of the Babylonians, in whose country the creation myth took on its final form. The seventh month was the perfect month for festivals. An oath lays down a particular obligation, after which, it is completed. The seven petitions of the Our Father imply that this is the complete and perfect prayer; the seven parables of the kingdom inplies that the teaching is perfect and complete; and the seven woes are a complete condemnation of the Pharisees. When Peter asks if he should forgive seven times, he is asking if there is any particular number of times he should forgive, after which the obligation would be completed; and the Sadducees use the number 'seven' for any particular number when they say there were seven brothers who married the same woman. In the Book of Revelation the Lamb has seven horns, which means that he is all-powerful, and he has seven eyes which stand for the seven spirits of God: and this implies that he is all-seeing and that he is all-spiritual, the source of God's creative act by which God looks after the world.

Here we shall be exploring the Beatitudes as a series of steps along the road to sanctity, as the royal road to joy, as an analysis of Christian conversion which is a continuous process. It is a process through death to resurrection; so I ask you to bear with me if the first steps seem to be singularly uninviting. In our practice of the Beatitudes, the Holy Spirit gradually forms us in the image of the Son. We begin by stripping off the old man of sin, alienated from God, and gradually ascend to purity in heart where we shall 'see God'. Then our relationship with the world will have been transformed because we shall be 'children of God' and peacemakers. This does not imply that we leave the other steps behind: they are all integral ingredients of Christian holiness.

The Beatitudes map out for us the process by which the Christian moves from being egocentric or at least world-centric, so that he or she may become centred on God who invites each disciple to enter into his kingdom. In this kingdom, the will of God is done on earth as in heaven. The paradox is that the more our lives are centred on God rather than on this world, the more we will love the world. For the pure in heart, their love is unconditional and universal because it has become a vehicle on earth for God's love in heaven. Put in other words, the Beatitudes describe the path of conversion from the isolation which is the result of sin, and from the values we have formed in our isolation from God, to a life of full membership of Christ's body. This body was cruci-fied on Calvary and, to the extent that we become 'living sacrifices' by sharing in Christ's life of perfect love for his Father and for mankind, to that extent we are being formed by the Spirit in Christian perfection. The Beati-tudes describe the transformation in us brought about by our sharing in the interior life of God in Christ. The connection between this process and our participation in the sacrifice of the Mass is obvious.

All this is particularly illustrated in the lives of the saints, so we shall end the first part of the book with the lives of two saints. St Seraphim of Sarov and St John Mary Vianney. They are near contemporaries; but they lived far away from each other and were separated by schism and by different spiritualities. St Seraphim was Orthodox and the Curé d'Ars Catholic. Nevertheless, we see them journeying on the same road to joy, and participating in the same fundamental reality. We shall compare them, using the chiastic reading of the Beatitudes; because, while a straight reading shows us our way to God, the chiastic reading gives us the essential, permanent ingre-dients of Christian holiness which manifests itself to others in the practice of mercy in Christian community.

I shall be using concrete examples of poor people, mostly taken from encounters I have had in Peru during the last twenty years. These examples are not exterior to my theology but are incidents that have helped to form it. To live among people so poor that their main attention is on the basic necessities of life, in a society not too different from the one that Jesus knew, is itself a privilege and a joy which has helped me to understand the Gospel.

Saint Luke

Blessed are you who are poor, for yours is the kingdom of God.

Blessed are you who are hungry now, for you will be filled.

Blessed are you who weep now, for you will laugh.

Blessed are you when people hate you, and when they exclude you, revile you, and defame you on account of the Son of Man. Rejoice in that day and leap for joy, for surely your reward is great in heaven; for that is what their ancestors did to the prophets.

Saint Matthew

Blessed are the poor in spirit, for theirs is the kingdom of heaven.

Blessed are those who mourn, for they will be comforted.

Blessed are the meek, for they will inherit the earth.

Blessed are those who hunger and thirst for righteousness, for they will be filled.

Blessed are the merciful, for they will receive mercy.

Blessed are the pure in heart, for they will see God.

Blessed are the peacemakers, for they will be called children of God.

Blessed are those who are persecuted for righteousness' sake, for theirs is the kingdom of heaven.

Blessed are you when people revile you and persecute you, and utter all kinds of evil against you falsely on my account. Rejoice and be glad, for your reward is great in heaven, for in the same way they persecuted the prophets who were before you.

Chapter Three

Blessed are the poor in spirit, for theirs is the kingdom of heaven

Jesus began his public ministry by proclaiming the Good News of the kingdom of heaven. This was not a new programme requiring organizers, nor a new project needing planners. He was telling people that God was about to burst into their world; that God was about to establish his reign in which his will was going to be done on earth as in heaven. The accent was not on what we should be doing, but on what God was about to independently of us. For this reason it is primarily news, rather than an announcement of new obligations.

Obligations arise for those who accept the news; but they are not its content. That people should be converted and obey was a consequence of the coming of the kingdom. God required people who would put themselves completely at his disposal, trusting him absolutely. In effect, he was asking us to do voluntarily what no man has the right to ask of another, to become God's slave. In ancient times, a slave had no rights, no agenda of his own, and his master owned him as he owned his farm animals and furniture. Even a slave's life was at his master's disposal. In St Luke's Gospel, the Blessed Virgin Mary says, 'Here am I, the servant (slave) of the Lord; let it be with me according to your word'. This is the attitude of the poor in spirit. Jesus promises that anyone who accepts this degree of dependence on God will be happy because the kingdom of heaven is already his.

There is a subtle difference between St Matthew's version of this beatitude and that of St Luke, which fits the different function that the Beatitudes have in St Matthew's scheme. St Luke is saying that the poor are blessed because they have nothing to lose, so that they will find it easier to make the necessary sacrifice that the Christian life imposes. The rich are attached to what they have; so, like the rich young man, they are more likely to respond negatively to Christ's invitation. In St Matthew, Jesus is giving a rule of life to people who are already disciples.

Nevertheless, although 'poor in spirit' is synonymous with 'disciple' in St Matthew, we must be careful not to spiritualize real poverty out of existence. To become a Christian involved becoming physically poor in St Matthew's time. Even if a disciple was from a rich background, his brother Christians were mostly poor, no strangers to hunger, to oppression, to being losers or despised; he was required to give when asked, and to suffer with the rest.

It must be remembered that the majority of people lived on or below the poverty line. It has been estimated that Jesus in Nazareth probably only ate one meal a day. Even though there are many exhortations in the Old Testament to help the poor, and it was even suggested that, among the *anawim*, the word they used for the poor, you were likely to find the purest form of religion, if the rich did not obey God in this, there was nothing the poor could do about it; they had no influence over their own fate. There is also a contrary tradition in the Old Testament that God rewards the righteous with health, good fortune and wealth, and punishes the wicked with poverty and bad health. The Book of Job was written to combat this idea, but it was still largely held.

There has always been plenty of evidence to support those who despise the poor. Where there is no hope of change, where there is little self-respect and a feeling of inferiority, where there are few legitimate means of enjoyment, then different forms of vice flourish. The Evangelicals in nineteenth-century England discovered this when they went to work in the slums of the big cities. It is clearly the case in the towns and cities of Latin America. There is irresponsibility, where a woman will leave her twelve-year-old daughter to fend for herself in an empty house for four months while she goes to visit relatives; there is thievery, where the victims are those who can least afford it; there is marriage infidelity, where a man will leave his family without any means of support while he satisfies himself with another woman; there is cruelty, as when a ten-year-old boy I met in Bolivia ran away to live on the streets because his stepfather used to punish him by burning the soles of his feet with a lighted candle; there is prostitution, where a respectable mother will sell herself to men as the only way to feed her children. You also find genuine sanctity and heroism, and so many people go on living ordinary lives under extreme conditions, which is also a kind of heroism; but it is the nature of prejudice to generalize, and to overlook what is good.

Things were not all that different in Christ's day, and many of the prostitutes and sinners with whom he ate and drank were probably his neighbours. The struggle to survive meant that people would be unable or unwilling to observe all the precepts of the law which, with all the details insisted on by the Pharisees, required a certain amount of leisure to obey them. Consequently, the poor were despised by many Pharisees, and the Essenes regarded them as 'sons of darkness'. The significance of the shepherds who welcomed the new-born Messiah is that they worked seven days a week: there was no sabbath for shepherds. All this adds some colour to St Paul's phrase about Jesus, 'He became sin for us'.

Jesus once said, perhaps a little bitterly, that he had not come to bring peace but to create family discord. There must have been many cases where the new convert was thrown out of his house and disinherited. They would then go and live with their fellow-Christians in a poor area of the town, with all the hardships this involved, which included persecution and people speaking ill of them. After the destruction of the Temple in AD 70, the Christians were excluded from the synagogues. This meant that they came under the Roman law that all citizens had to offer incense before the statue of the emperor, and that those who refused were liable to be put to death. Jewish Christians were regarded by the Jews as apostates, and the Romans disapproved because Christianity came under no known category of religion. Moreover, by the time this gospel was written, Rome had been burnt to the ground by Nero, who blamed it on the Christians. 'Blessed are those who are persecuted for righteousness' sake' is included in the meaning of 'Blessed are the poor in spirit'. It is clear that, to become a Christian, a person had to be prepared to give up everything.

Much water has flowed under the bridge since then; and, although there have always been areas of the world where the Church has been marginalized, has suffered poverty, or has been persecuted for its faith, this has not been the experience of the majority of Christians since the conversion of Constantine. We must ask ourselves what this beatitude means for those of us who live in the modern, secular and prosperous First World.

The story of Adam and Eve implies that there is something radically wrong with our desire to possess. God made them in his image and likeness, so it was their nature to want to be more like God. However, they wanted to attain this greater likeness by their own efforts, to grasp this likeness for themselves, even in disobedience to God. Tragically, this made them very unlike God. If we want to be like God, we must receive this likeness as a gift.

God the Father is Father because he pours out the fullness of the Godhead on his Son. In his turn, the Son does not consider his equality with God a thing to be tightly held on to (Phil 2.6), but pours himself into the incarnation. This 'pouring out' of divine Power is the Holy Spirit. The Adam and Eve story is saying in mythical terms that we distort our God-given urge to be like God by trying to attain it by our own efforts. As the Sonship of the Word is an eternal 'gift' of the Father, so we too can only become adopted sons of God by gift. Moreover, this gift is not to be grasped by us egoistically, but must be poured out on others through intercession, evangelization and works of mercy: as the Prayer of St Francis says, 'In giving we receive'. This is the law in heaven and on earth.

With this distorted urge to possess, riches can be a substitute for God, and acquiring them a substitute for religion. Like all idols, wealth can give us a false sense of security and superiority, and its absence a false sense of insecurity and inferiority, dividing society into 'us' and 'them'. Guarding our wealth can make us deaf to what God wants us to do, and blind to the needs of the poor.

In Peru, the richer a person is, the more securely guarded is his home. In wealthy parts of Lima, it is possible to live one's whole life without ever being conscious of the quiet desperation of those who supply the essential services, and the even greater desperation of those without a job.

How terrible it would be if, when we arrive at the judgement seat, after a life dedicated to the acquisition of wealth, we hear the words, 'You have had your reward'!

In St Luke's version of this beatitude, he is saying that anything that will encourage us to give up control of our lives and turn it over to God is a good thing. Although health, wealth, or having a particularly satisfying and successful job are good in themselves, if their loss leads us to accept Christ's invitation to follow him, then this loss is a blessing and, eventually, a joy.

St Matthew's version of the beatitude is saying all disciples must put nothing before the love of God, and must account as rubbish all that stands in the way of our serving God. Our wealth and even our physical security have value for us only if they serve God's purposes, and should be easily sacrificed if they do not. We must be ready to embrace poverty if that is God's will.

There seems to be a direct connection between the spirit of poverty and the insight that the world is sacred. Among primitive peoples who have not developed a strong sense of property, this is noticeable. The American Indians could not understand the white man's passion to own land. 'You cannot own the wind, nor the hawk that flies overhead. How can you own land?' they asked. The Australian Aborigines also walk the land without owning it. Both groups consider themselves part of the world in which they live and both value its holiness. This sense of holiness disappears when we see the earth only as something to be exploited.

Within the Church, those saints whose quest for God led them to embrace extreme poverty have been blessed by their capacity to see God in nature. The most famous of these is St Francis of Assisi. When he and Brother Masseo sat down on a flat stone to eat the bread they had begged, Francis said:

> That is just why I regard this as so great a treasure, because man has had no hand in it. Everything has been arranged for us by God's providence, plain to see in this fountain so clear, this beautiful stone table, and this bread of charity. So, do let us beg God to help us love the treasure of holy poverty with all our heart.[1a]

He thanks God for Brothers Sun and Fire:

> In the morning when the sun rises, everybody ought to praise God who created the sun for our benefit; through it our eyes get the light in daytime. At night, when darkness falls, everybody ought to praise God because of brother fire through whom our eyes get the light at night time. For all of us are as it were blind, and the Lord with these two brothers of ours gives light to our eyes. Because of them in particular, and all the creatures we make use of day by day, we ought to praise the Creator.[1b]

Those who follow a life of poverty, living by radical faith, can often be led by God who uses their own need to show them what he wants them to do. A few years ago, two Peruvian girls belonging to the Neo-Catechumenate were sent to Madrid, with only the means of getting there, in order to evangelize. They arrived on the streets of the city without plans or a peseta in their pockets and it was teeming with rain. They sought shelter in a shop doorway with no idea what to do next, without friends or contacts, and one of them was running a temperature: they had been thrown in at the deep end. It grew dark, and they saw the prostitutes touting for business on the pavement. One prostitute passed them many times. Eventually, she came over to them and asked them what was the matter. They explained their plight. She delved into her pocket and handed them a wad of notes, and told them to look for an hotel. This was their first contact with the people who would be the object of their apostolate.

This beatitude is a call to radical faith. The poor in spirit will find security in discovering that God provides for their needs. It requires great faith because Christ does not promise to provide for what they think they need. He promises that whatever he may give us is what we really do need. If we have to do without what we think we do need, our confidence in him must be stronger than our thought.

'Blessed are the poor in spirit' points towards putting up cheerfully with a lack of means, but that is not enough. We can be very proud of being satisfied with little, and we can compare ourselves favourably with the rest of mankind in its hot pursuit of consumerism. Indeed, we automatically do this when we are left to ourselves. Conversion involves making the very difficult transition from judging ourselves by our relationship with other human beings, to judging ourselves in relationship to God. We cannot do this without a rigorous discipline which prohibits all forms of judging others, and of comparing ourselves favourably with them. When we criticize the bad guys and, by doing this, put ourselves among the good guys, even if we don't say so explicitly, we are blocking our way to God. We have to be poor in spirit in the very core of our being. This is dealt with in the next beatitude.

Notes

1a and 1b. *The Words of St Francis*, by James Meyer OFM (Franciscan Herald Press, Chicago, Illinois, 1966).

Chapter Four

Blessed are those who mourn, for they shall be comforted

The sacrifice acceptable to God is a broken spirit, a broken and contrite heart, O God, you will not despise. (Ps. 51 [50])

Return to me with all your heart, with fasting, with weeping, and with mourning; rend your hearts and not your clothing. Return to the Lord, your God, for he is gracious and merciful, slow to anger, and abounding in steadfast love. (Joel 2. 12–13)

One of the things that surprised and shocked the Pharisees was Jesus' attitude towards sinners and the way he treated them. He ate and drank with them, accepted their hospitality and even allowed them to touch him. He would not condemn the woman taken in adultery and he was very free with his 'Your sins are forgiven you', sometimes not waiting for the sinner to ask. He even asked his Father to forgive those who had crucified him before any had shown the slightest sign of repentance, while they were still in the act of crucifying him. From all this we know that to seek forgiveness from God is easy and a positive result assured.

However, if receiving pardon from God is easy, dying to sin is not. The early Fathers knew that the sins we commit are only the tip of an iceberg, a manifestation on the surface of our lives of the spiritual distortion within of our refusal to allow God to be God in our lives. Moreover, as Origen pointed out, every time we sin, we contribute to this distortion; and the weakness or scar of sin remains, even after the sin has been forgiven. If I have the tendency to sin in a particular direction, then every time I sin, it makes it easier to commit the same sin again and the tendency is strengthened. True conversion involves not only receiving pardon for sins committed, but allowing God into our inner life so that he may burn away what is bad and heal us. The present beatitude is concerned with this process.

It is natural for human beings to take refuge in diversions, because there is an emptiness, a loneliness within, from which we wish to escape. God may have forgiven our sins and we may be very active members of the Church but how many of us are willing to face this emptiness, enter into it, and cry out to God in our weakness as we discover how egoistic, how proud we are? It is so much easier to concentrate on our known abilities, on our usefulness, and busy ourselves with what we are good at. If there is no opportunity to do this, we can always switch on the television. The Desert Fathers were people with the courage to look within, and what they saw there moved them to tears. This anguish at their own sinfulness they called 'compunction'.

They considered tears as a gift from God, a sign that the Holy Spirit is at work, melting the hardness of hearts. The gift of tears was often called 'Baptism in the Spirit'. St Isaac the Syrian tells us that the beginning of the process is a crying out in darkness, a longing for healing and for union with God. As the person's Christian life progresses, the tears of sorrow become transformed into tears of joy as we experience the divine mercy.

This sorrow should always be accompanied by thanksgiving because we know by faith that God is answering us. Sorrow without thanksgiving is despair, which has nothing to do with Christianity: while thanksgiving without sorrow for sin is presumption, which isn't very Christian either. The more we practise compunction, the more genuine is our thanksgiving, which is why the Eucharist is our prayer only in so far as we have a humble and contrite heart.

If we compare ourselves with our neighbours we will probably have very little motivation to practise compunction, especially if our faults differ very little from those of the people around us. The world condemns harshly only those sins it is not tempted to commit. We do very little harm to anyone, pay our taxes and fulfil our duties as well as anyone else, and we actively promote good causes of which we and our neighbours approve. We are rather decent people really: so this beatitude is for other people, for bank robbers, adulterers, wife-beaters and paedophiles. We are the good guys.

Jesus told a parable to some people who believed themselves righteous and regarded others with contempt. A Pharisee and a tax-collector went to the temple to pray. The Pharisee thanked God that he was not like other people. He had been brought up properly and lived a strict religious life and he was very good to the poor: he wasn't like the tax-collector who enriched himself by collaborating with the Romans at his own people's expense. In contrast, the tax-collector stood at the entrance and, beating his breast, said, 'God, be merciful to me a sinner'. Jesus is saying that those who place themselves among the good guys cannot come close to God. As coming close to God is what the Beatitudes are about, the practice of this beatitude is essential for everyone. It would be a mistake to think that the Pharisees are in the Gospel so that we may condemn them. If we do that, we miss the point. They are a warning because there is a Pharisee in all of us.

Jesus said that he came into the world to convince the world of sin. The most important thing about sin is not that it does harm to our neighbour but that it is completely incompatible with the holiness of God. Our criterion for judging our sinfulness is not how we compare with our neighbour but whether we love God with our whole mind, heart and being, and whether we love our neighbour as Christ loved him by dying for him. Repentance is not something that belongs to the initial stages of conversion, the need for which is done away with once we have been forgiven: it grows with our awareness of God. The nearer we get to God, the more we are aware of our sinfulness and the deeper our repentance. People who have no sense of sin have no sense of God, and no saint has ever existed who did not consider himself a sinner.

The Fathers have two rigid rules by which we attain true compunction: firstly, never to judge our neighbour or compare ourselves favourably to him; and, secondly, to have our sins constantly before our eyes.

St Antony the Great was once asked if he believed in hell. He said, 'Yes, but only for me'. In the Eastern Church, there is a prayer which people use constantly: 'Lord Jesus Christ, Son of the living God, have mercy on me a sinner'. When it is recited in common, they miss out 'a sinner', because sin is individual. For the same reason, in the Sacrament of Reconciliation a person normally only confesses individually. Of course, there is a real sense in which we share the condition of being sinners and there is such a thing as social sin; but the Church wishes to avoid any circumstance in which we begin to judge our neighbour and thus fall into the sin of the Pharisee. As far as I am concerned, I am the only sinner on the planet.

Once there was a gathering of monks in Egypt which cast out a monk for his sin. As the man left the assembly, one of the most revered members of the group got up and left with him. As he neared the door, he turned to the rest and explained, 'I too am a sinner'. There are many stories among the Desert Fathers with the same moral.

There is the story of the old monk who went with a novice who was under his charge to an all-night vigil. One by one, the other monks fell asleep until only the old man and his novice remained awake. The novice remarked on the lack of Christian fervour among the other monks. The old man replied, 'It would have been better for you if you had fallen asleep too. They have only given into human weakness but you have judged them and have thus gone against Christ's command.'

People were instructed that, if they came upon someone in the very act of sinning, they were to make an act of humility and cast out of the mind any urge to judge him. If they did judge him, they were told they were as bad as he, because they too had broken a commandment of God. In the world's habit of making judgements by comparison with others, there is always 'us' and 'them', always good guys and bad guys, always winners and losers, always groups of people who are despised by the rest or feel themselves despised. In the Christian community there are only 'us' who are sinners whom God loves. It is within this context that we must understand St Augustine's remark, when he and a group of his friends came upon a notorious sinner in the street: 'There, but for the grace of God, go I'.

Many monks avoided like the plague any position of authority which involved them correcting others. They did this because they knew that there was inside them a little Pharisee trying to get out. They could not trust themselves to remain humble enough to avoid feeling superior to the person they were correcting.

The second rule among the ancients was to keep their sins constantly before their eyes. They were tolerant of others because they did not judge them but they were not tolerant of their own sins. God does not forgive those who forgive themselves. We remember that only our sins are completely our own: everything else emanates from God. St Benedict tells us that we should 'daily in one's prayer, with tears and sighs, confess one's past sins to God'. However, we should 'never despair of God's mercy'. One Desert Father says that we should be prepared to go to hell, but without even a trace of despair. We must remem-

ber our sins, but from the standpoint of redeemed
sinners: the deeper our repentance, the deeper our
'eucharist' (thanksgiving). St Thérèse of Lisieux said that
she was glad that she was so imperfect because it gave God
the opportunity to show his steadfast love. As we delve
into our imperfection, our weakness and our sin, so we
experience the joy of forgiveness. Fr George Maloney SJ
writes: 'Compunction was the dying process and joy the
resurrection of all one's powers into a new life that
produced a hundredfold in peace and happiness'.

Progress in the Christian life is progress in humility. St
Antony was asked what is the greatest Christian virtue. He
answered that, just as Satan was cast down from heaven
because of pride, so humility is the most important virtue
to attain. This was not meant to dethrone charity. St
Antony is speaking practically, like most monastic teachers. True humility is easier to discern than charity,
because our love for others can rise from so many different motives. Humility is the guarantee that our love is
Christian. Indeed, without it, no virtue is Christian.

St Benedict says we must ascend the ladder of humility.
The first rung is fear of the Lord. Of course, this may
involve fear of punishment, but it is much greater than
this. It arises from our appreciation of the tremendous
holiness of God in whose presence nothing defiled may
enter. The Christian must keep in mind the commandments, especially love of God and neighbour, and remember that non-observance leads to hell and obedience leads
to heaven. We should be constantly aware of God's presence and that he sees us everywhere and knows our most
secret thoughts. We should seek God's will rather than
our own in everything, and accept whatever is negative in
our circumstances as a sharing in Christ's Passion. We
should practise compunction and constantly say in our
heart, 'Lord, I a sinner am not worthy to raise my eyes to
heaven'. If we follow this way, we will come to live an
integral Christian life, naturally and by habit, and God
will show in his workman the power of the Spirit.

It is important to note that all this concentrating on our sins and imperfections and this insistence on humility bear no relationship to fostering an inferiority complex. A neurotic feeling of inferiority to one's peers springs from the same basic error as a Pharisee complex of superiority which is more common. Our worth as persons does not come from the people around us but from God's love manifested on the cross. This accent on repentance and humility is positive only within the context of our relationship and dialogue with God. Indeed, our very existence as persons with a divine vocation comes from our relationship with God.

Compunction is not wallowing in our own guilt, because a guilt complex is incompatible with thanksgiving. We saw how St Francis's practice of extreme poverty led him and his companions to enjoy only what they received from God's hands; and this caused them to be thankful for everything that God gave them. In this beatitude, we are denying ourselves pleasure in our own achievement and frustration at our own failure in comparison with others. We concentrate on our own sins and failures rather than those of other people, but only within the context of God's redeeming love; and this causes us to accept our true worth as children of God and to thank God for his steadfast love in which we find our fulfilment as persons. Poverty and compunction restore in us our eucharistic relationship to God that we lost through original sin. Guilt complexes belong to humankind in its alienation from God.

Another important point is that this teaching should be given only to people who have made the adult decision to enter into this dialogue with God. I have heard of it being used in the old days by nuns with adolescents who had a very shaky self-confidence and the need to find their place in the world; within that context, it amounted to mental bullying. It isn't a guide on how to find our place in the world; and kids need as much encouragement as they can get to develop their talents with confidence.

Telling them all the time that they are sinners and attempting to humble them doesn't help, and will give them a very distorted picture of God. Compunction is a gift from God which he gives us when we are ready for it. Building up their self-confidence in relationship to others is necessary and can only be safely replaced by confidence in God when God is sufficiently real to them. For those who are going to travel the path of the Gospel, confidence in competition with others is like water wings when we begin to learn to swim: very necessary at the beginning, but laid aside when we are ready to hand over our confidence to God.

There is no point in trying to cry. God does not want us to conform our emotions to other people. 'Tears' is a gift. If God decides to give it to us, glory be to him; if he does not, then glory be to him again: he knows what is best for us. The essential is, of set purpose, to remember daily our sins and our lost opportunities and to ask God earnestly and honestly for healing, and to do so again whenever we are tempted to criticize others and, whenever we remind ourselves of God's presence and whenever we pray, to do so as redeemed sinners confident in the love of God, rather than in our own goodness.

The gift of tears was often called 'Baptism in the Spirit', the water that came from their eyes bringing to mind the waters of baptism. Olivier Clement writes:

> Thus life in the Spirit means gradually becoming aware of 'baptismal grace', and this awareness transforms the whole person. The baptismal sequence of death and resurrection is repeated throughout our pilgrimage, enlightening its 'initiatory' moments. When everything seems lost, baptismal grace, if we pay heed to it, can convert a situation of death into one of resurrection, an apparent deadlock into a necessary breakthrough. We have to learn – and this is the whole meaning of ascesis – to get round obstacles, to tear away dead sin, to let the very life of Christ arise in us by the power of his resur-

rection. Each present moment has to become baptismal: a moment of anguish and death if we seek to cling to it and so experience its non-existence, but a moment of resurrection if I accept it as 'present' in both senses of the word, almost like the gift of manna – but here we pass from the mystery of baptism to that of the Eucharist. We come finally to the moment of agony when we are overwhelmed by the waters of death. Through our baptism, according to the measure of our faith, they will be transformed into the womb of eternity.[1]

If each moment can become baptismal, then some can be more baptismal than others, moments which initiate the Christian into a new level of Christian existence. It is not surprising then that movements so far apart as Oriental monasticism and the Charismatic Renewal can identify a particular moment and call it 'Baptism in the Spirit'. Here is a testimony, taken from *Catholic Pentecostals*, edited by Kevin Ranaghan:

> Before I knew it was I walking into the chapel. I stood before the altar and the next thing I knew I was lying prostrate on the floor crying and feeling such ecstasy as I may never feel again. I cried harder than I ever cried in my life, but I did not shed one tear. All of a sudden Jesus Christ was so real and so present that I could feel him all around. I was overcome by a feeling of love that I cannot begin to describe.
>
> (Testimony of David Mangan)[2]

The monastic Fathers would have seen special significance in the crying, as a sign that the Spirit was melting the person's heart. Many charismatics would give special importance to speaking in tongues. Catholics would say that no particular sign is universally necessary. This is up to the Spirit, using the particular environment and culture of the people concerned. Nevertheless, there is testimony in the Charismatic Renewal of both tears of mourning and tears of joy.

When a person mourns over his sins, he is implicitly making himself one with all other sinners of the world. This is the whole thrust of the incarnation and, in doing so, he is making himself one with Christ. As his love expands, he will eventually come to mourn for all sinners as Jesus wept over Jerusalem. However, he will not be weeping for 'them' but for 'us'. We have talked of tears of mourning and tears of joy. We can also talk of tears of solidarity.

This is illustrated very well in *The Cross and the Switchblade* by David Wilkerson. One night, he was sitting at home, unable to relax. He had been praying for some time, and yet could not throw off the feeling of great sadness. Eventually, he picked up a copy of *Life* magazine, opened it and saw a pen drawing of seven teenage boys who had been convicted of murder in New York, and he began to cry his eyes out for these kids. This was the start of his great adventure and apostolate among the gangs of Harlem.

Christian conversion does not separate us from the common run of men but unites us to them, even to the worst, because we know that we are of the same weak flesh and blood. As love transforms our tears, we come to love all and this is our sharing in the love of God for the world. St Isaac of Nineveh wrote:

> What is a compassionate heart? [He tells us] It is a heart that burns for all creation, for birds, for the beasts, for the devils, for every creature. When he thinks about them, when he looks at them, his eyes fill with tears. So strong and violent is his compassion ... that his heart breaks when he sees the pain and the suffering of the humblest creature. That is why he prays with tears every moment ... for all the enemies of truth and for all who cause harm, that they may be protected and forgiven. He prays even for serpents in the boundless

compassion that wells up in his heart after God's likeness.

I was parish priest of Negritos in northern Peru for almost seven years. It is a Charismatic parish. I have known people there of deep spirituality, and I have no doubt that the Charismatic Renewal is a genuine movement of the Spirit. However, not all that glitters is gold, and not all things charismatic are authentic, even among people of goodwill.

There is a kind of spirituality which puts emphasis on what is agreeable and exciting: emotional devotions, spectacular healings, interesting charisms. Christian singsongs and hand-clapping, and self-satisfaction that all is well. The resurrection is separated from the cross, Christian exaltation from humility, and joy from repentance. There is no room for fasting because the Bridegroom is with them, and no room for silence among the cacophony of prayers. That they have allowed personal prayer in private to lapse is not noticed because of their attendance at many prayer meetings. This is not a description of the Charismatic community in Negritos, but something we all had to guard against and which some had to leave behind. It was these external things which attracted some people to the movement at first.

I want to tell you the story of Peter, as he would tell it himself. He had helped me in my house in my first years in Negritos before he married. The marriage didn't work out very well, largely due to the girl's family who couldn't accept it. From the age of eleven to the age of eighteen, when he returned to Negritos and met me, Peter had lived on the street in Tumbes. Unlike most street children, he had put himself through secondary school and had become an altar boy in the local parish. Nevertheless, he had been a street child, and street children are the lowest of the low. I had already left the parish when the significant part of my tale happened.

He had been a catechist in the parish for a long time,

and, in 1998, he signed on for the 'Sword of the Spirit' seminars in preparation for 'Baptism in the Spirit'. It wasn't the initiatory experience that it has been for many. Nevertheless, he took part in the assemblies of the Charismatic Renewal and identified himself with it. Meanwhile, his wife's brothers kept accusing him of adultery and tried to persuade his wife to leave him. She believed them and attacked him physically in the street, throwing stones at him and clawing his neck with her fingernails. Eventually, she would not let him in the house, a poor shack made by him out of bits of wood.

He went to pieces and became an alcoholic tramp, begging in the streets for money to buy booze and to spend on women; because, yes, he began to do exactly what she had accused him of earlier without justification. He even contemplated suicide, because life had lost its meaning for him. However, he sought help from Jorge, a converted alcoholic who had been a catechist with him in the parish. Jorge told him that there was to be a retreat the next weekend, organized by the John XXIII movement, and he advised him to go on it.

John XXIII retreats are extremely gruelling. They last from Friday night to Sunday evening and they use a very well-thought-out technique which forces people to face themselves and invites them to accept the Gospel in its fullness. From Puerto Rico, where it began, to Peru and Ecuador, people who have been on these retreats form the backbone of many of the parishes where they live.

Peter faced himself and broke down in tears. To face oneself honestly in an atmosphere where the love of God is almost palpable does no one any harm, and tears heal. He gave up drink and resumed his work as a catechist. He began to say the rosary while walking in the street. About half a year later, someone in the John XXIII movement offered him a job as a cook. This had been one of the problems. Around 85% of the people in Negritos are unemployed. Imagine the reaction of a mother when her husband cannot buy milk or much-needed medicine for her children, especially a mother who is being fuelled with false rumours by her brothers. Many a home breaks up because of poverty. Peter is now back with his wife and children; and, although his job disappeared when his employer lost his contract, the marriage is now going strong. I hope it remains so, in spite of the grinding poverty.

What is interesting from a charismatic point of view, is that, while the 'laying on of hands' had had no observable effect on him, once he came back from the retreat, people began to approach him to pray for their sick. He was puzzled and intrigued by this, and asked my advice during one of my visits to Negritos. He now belongs to the team that prays over people for healing. It seems that he needed true compunction for the 'Baptism in the Spirit' to work.

All this may seem very gloomy, but, in reality, Christianity is about the kingdom which means 'righteousness and peace and joy in the Holy Spirit'. (Rom. 14.17). However, the righteousness, peace and joy are not *any* righteousness, peace and joy. They are not attained by singing happy songs about the resurrection or by a party atmosphere. 'Humility is the road to joy', is the only way to Christian joy, and there are no short cuts. Here we are face to face with the paradox of the cross which is the only way to resurrection. The deeper our humility, the nearer we will be to God who is far from the proud and close to the humble. The nearer we are to God, the more we shall realize our own imperfection in relation to him. Too often we give great importance to relatively superficial emotions of happiness and satisfaction brought about by our participation in a well-run prayer meeting or well-performed liturgy. These emotions are not to be despised; but we would be leading ourselves and others astray if we gave the impression that they are identical to the peace and joy promised in the Gospel.

St Bernard teaches us that grace reconciles us with ourselves, with our neighbour, and with God. This beatitude concerns our reconciliation with ourselves, our true selves and not the selves we invent for ourselves. We recognize ourselves as sinners who are loved by God. In the light of his love, we can acknowledge, not only our good side, but also our bad side. We can admit how little we have allowed God to be God in our lives, how much we have wasted valuable time on things that don't matter. We can freely accept our past sins, our present egoism, and how much we need to change in order to become saints.

All this will become very real to us and will cause us much sorrow; but, at the same time, we will know that God loves us; and this knowledge will allow us to love ourselves, not the edited version of ourselves that we loved before, nor at the cost of pretending that our faults don't really matter, but as God loves us, just as we are. In this we find our consolation. Before this conversion, we valued ourselves in terms of our achievements and our reputation: after conversion, we value ourselves because God loves us.

In order to attain the consolation promised in this beatitude, we must declare holy war on our tendency to judge others and to compare ourselves favourably to them; we must meditate constantly on our sins, even those that have been absolved, because we still bear the scars and the weaknesses that they have left behind. Above all, we must maintain our confidence in God.

There is one other way in which mourning is inseparable from the Christian vocation. When Adam and Eve lived in Paradise, they sinned against God because they valued his gifts more than his will. This is a tendency in all of us. The greater the gift, the greater the danger that it will replace God as the most important factor in our lives. Often it can be a work of the apostolate that suits us, or a friendship that benefits us, or a situation in which we are very happy. When we lose it we can look back on it with nostalgia, with satisfaction at something well done and with gratitude to God. We can also be very bitter because of the circumstances in which we lost it, at the injustice of it all. However, God does not want us to commit Adam's sin while we are fulfilling our Christian vocation and, whatever the means he may use, whether in direct fulfilment of his will or by allowing injustice to happen, God shows his love for us by withdrawing his gift. As St Bernadette said, we must allow ourselves to become mere instruments in God's hands, to be used when he wills and to be cast aside when he wills. Until our wills are in complete synchrony with God's, we will experience sometimes in our lives the sadness that comes from moving on, of doing without what is so evidently good. When we look at the lives of St Seraphim and St John Mary Vianney, we shall see how they lost contact with those works that gave them the greatest satisfaction. God earnestly wants our sanctity and will not allow a certain amount of sadness on our part to get in his way.

Of course, our chief source of mourning is death. All our acts of dying are but preparations for the great day when we will die physically for real, and our union with the risen Christ will be equally real to us. Faith will make way for vision and we shall know even as we are known. Looking at the lives of the saints, we notice that a certain 'dark night of the spirit' is a necessary part of letting go. All that is familiar to them in their relationship with God becomes inadequate, and they are left only with their weakness and their trust in God. Saint Thérèse of Lisieux, talking of this time of desolation, said that her faith had become a wall between herself and God. Saints Martin de Porres and Bernadette suffered from feelings of despair and of demonic attacks. Saint Thérèse and Mother Teresa of Calcutta felt that their whole lives had been useless and their religious lives were empty. Their prayer may well have been, 'My God, my God, why have you forsaken me?' Their fidelity in spite of all these feelings pulled them through. God's love for us takes many forms, some only recognized by faith. Perhaps we lesser mortals have this waiting for us in purgatory.

Notes
1. *The Roots of Christian Mysticism* by Olivier Clement.
2. *Catholic Pentecostals*, ed. Kevin Ranaghan.

Chapter Five

Blessed are the meek, for they will inherit the earth

> Yet a little while, and the wicked will be no more;
> though you look diligently for their place, they will
>   not be there.
> But the meek shall inherit the land,
> and delight themselves in abundant prosperity.
>   (Ps. 37.10–11)

> The Lord has laid on him the iniquity of us all. He was
> oppressed, and he was afflicted, yet he did not open his
> mouth; like a lamb that is led to the slaughter, and like
> a sheep that before its shearers is silent, so he did not
> open his mouth. (Isa. 53.7)

> 'Do not weep. See, the Lion of the tribe of Judah, the
> Root of David, has conquered ...' Then I saw between
> the throne and the four living creatures and among the
> elders a Lamb standing as if it had been slaughtered ...
> (Rev. 5.5,6)

This beatitude is a direct quotation from Psalm 37 and is
probably a gloss on the first beatitude, though it is often
placed after 'Blessed are those who mourn'. In the
Hebrew text of the psalm, the word we translate as 'meek'
is *anawim*, which means the poor, the marginalized, those
without influence, money or power.

Koki was sixteen when he came to live in my house. I

accepted him because the parish secretary, who was a friend of his, asked me so earnestly. He told me that Koki was in moral danger because he belonged to a gang which took drugs, drank and was given to violence. Koki was rather like a boat without a rudder and I had a number of problems with him, though he was fiercely loyal to me. Now he is twenty-two, and is married with a baby daughter. Being father of a family has given him a purpose in life. He does not drink or smoke, and he lives with his family in a small house made of plywood, with boxes for chairs. As he dropped out of school he cannot find employment, so he has followed in his father's footsteps, earning what he can from fishing. He goes into the sea at low tide as far out as he can and drives two stakes into the sea bed, with something like a tennis net between them. When the sea comes in, fish are caught in the net. His family eats some, and he sells the rest to buy sugar, rice, and milk for his baby. However, if the sea is too turbulent or its temperature is not right for the fish, then he gets nothing and the family is without the means to support itself. His wife returns with the baby to her parents; but he is too proud to eat off them so he goes without, eating from time to time with his friends. This can last months.

During these hard times, he can go for days without eating. He tells me, 'Don't worry about it. It is not your problem. What do I do? Well, as thinking about food won't fill my stomach, I dismiss it from my mind and go out and play football.' Sometimes he earns a bit on the football field when a local club takes him on and has enough money to pay him. Yet he and his wife are happy, even when they are without the basics. When I asked him how he can stand it, he tells me, 'The only thing a man can't do is bear children'.

I have found the same quiet and happy acceptance of life among many poor people. During the catastrophic rains of 1983, we would meet peasants carrying heavy sacks who almost certainly hadn't eaten that day. 'Hello,

Father,' they would call cheerily, as though everything was right with the world. No wonder Jesus used these people as a model of what he wants from his disciples.

In this beatitude, Jesus is talking about the Christian who is on the royal road to salvation, not those who are only materially poor and are merely making the best of a bad situation. He says to his disciples:

> Therefore, I tell you, do not worry about your life, what you will eat, or about your body, what you will wear. For life is more than food, and the body more than clothing. Consider the ravens: they neither sow nor reap, they have neither storehouse nor barn, and yet God feeds them. Of how much more value are you than the birds. And can any of you by worrying add a single hour to your span of life? If then you are not able to do so small a thing as that, why do you worry about the rest? Consider the lilies, how they grow; they neither toil nor spin, yet I tell you, even Solomon in all his glory was not clothed like one of these. But if God so clothes the grass of the field, which is alive today and tomorrow is thrown into the oven, how much more will he clothe you – you of little faith. And do not keep striving for what you are to eat and what you are to drink, and do not keep worrying. For it is the nations of the world that strive after all these things, and your Father knows that you need them. Instead, strive for his kingdom, and these things will be given to you as well.

We have no control over our lives because we have handed everything over to God. We know that, in fact, we have given him very little because everybody, whether they want to or not, lives within his providence, and the only thing that is really our own is sin. Christian conversion moves a person from a false self-sufficiency to an utter trust in God. The Christian remembers Christ's words, 'Without me you can do nothing,' and realizes that his capacity to live in relationship with God comes from

outside himself. In his relationship with God, he is poorer
than the poorest person. At least Koki can fish when the
sea is right, but we can do nothing apart from God, and
the Christian life is all gift.

Once the Christian realizes that everything is in God's
hands except for sin, he accepts the condition in which
he finds himself and all that life throws at him, the good
and the bad, the pleasant and the unpleasant. When he
does that, everything works for his good except sin.
When his needs are met, he glorifies God; when he has
to go without, he glorifies God. When he sins and
repents, the memory of the sin helps him to understand
his true relationship with God and inhibits him from
judging his neighbour, and he sings God's praises. Moreover, he realizes that his utter poverty in relation to God
is also the source of his strength; he can do whatever God
wants him to do, and so he is able to accept any challenge
that God's providence presents to him. If without Christ
he can do nothing, with Christ he can do anything. 'The
only thing a man can't do is bear children' takes on a new
meaning.

This meek acceptance of Christ's presence in every situation in which he finds himself, in every person he meets,
in every work he has to undertake, as well as in the depth
of his own heart, together with a consciousness of his own
poverty in relation to Christ, allows the Christian to
extend his communion with Christ beyond the Eucharist
to every moment in the day.

Putting oneself completely at God's disposal does not
come naturally, even to people with the best of intentions.
We are too prone to interpret God's will as identical to
our own wishes, ideals and prejudices, and to accept too
uncritically the values of our culture. As a 'gringo' living
in Peru, I can too often assume the superiority of my own
Anglo-Saxon ways of thinking and doing things. This can
make me blind and deaf to what God wants to teach me
through the poor with whom I live. To come to the point
where I actually live 'Not my will but yours be done', I

have to go through a conversion process which never finishes in this life.

For this reason, as a monk, I have to practise obedience as an ascetic exercise, to get into the habit of seeking God's will rather than my own. The Benedictine Rule is a 'school of the Lord's service', and is geared to teach those who follow it to be completely at God's disposal and hence able to hear and obey God's word, which is the condition of all faithful discipleship, whether monastic or not. The monastic life is a 'labour of obedience', and a monk is one who 'desires to have an abbot over him'. He eagerly obeys the abbot because 'he that hears you hears me'. He obeys in such a way that 'almost at the same time that the master's order is given, is the disciple's work completed.' We can change a text from St John, 'How can we obey God whom we cannot see, if we are unwilling to obey our neighbour whom we can see.' The monks even obey each other. The abbot too has to practise obedience; in fact, in an ideal situation, he has been chosen precisely because he has been shown to be adept at obedience. One of the Cistercian fathers said that it is unsafe to elect an abbot who was not noted for his obedience when he was an ordinary monk. This is because he has to obey, listen and be ready to act, even against his own interests, without anyone to control him. On him lies the responsibility of listening to the brethren, even to the very youngest, because God can let his will be known through any one of them. The whole purpose of monastic obedience is to enable the monk to discern and obey God's will, in whatever way it presents itself, by attacking the egotism which makes us blind and deaf to God.

Listening to Christ is 'the one thing necessary' in the Gospel, and we can only hear him if we are ready to obey him. In the Christian family, individual members should listen to one another: the father to the mother, the mother to the father, and both should listen to their children who must also listen to their parents. If they listen with the motive of finding out God's will for them, then, when God wills, the other person will be used by God to instruct them. Many problems arise in families because there is an unwillingness to listen to each other.

Many religious congregations have given up obedience to a superior in favour of communal discernment by the community to which the individual member is obedient. As with any Christian community, the quality of their obedience will depend on how much they have made their own the practice of the Beatitudes. Unlike a secular community, the source of unity within a Christian community or family is the risen Christ who is present among them through his Spirit. To be on Christ's wave-length, it requires humility among the people who make up the community, whether they are those who give orders, those who make decisions communally, or those who simply obey. These congregations that have chosen communal discernment are dedicated to the apostolate, and their obedience is about unity of service rather than ascetic training. It is the Lord who trains them in obedi-ence to himself through the concrete experiences of their apostolic lives. An Abbot of Belmont was present at a discernment session of the Sisters of Notre Dame of Namur; he was so impressed that he introduced the prac-tice in his monastery, of course within the monastic framework.

There are different patterns of obedience in different Christian communities but the basic principles are the same. All are trying to live, 'Not my will, but yours be done'.

In Psalm 37, the situation of the meek (the marginalized poor without power) is contrasted with that of those who do not obey God's will and who are well off. The natural reaction towards bad people, towards those who harm us or who harm the innocent and the weak, is anger. The psalm says that we should 'refrain from anger and forsake wrath', because it only leads to evil. It is the wicked who 'gnash their teeth', who 'draw their swords and bend their bows'. There is no need to be like them. The meek, those who 'wait for the Lord' are on the winning side, even when it doesn't look that way, because God will neutralize what is evil, will break the bow, and the sword of the wicked will enter into their own heart. The meek should concentrate on doing good without fear, not waste their energies on anger.

Evil is the opposite of good, but it has no separate existence. God is the only Creator, and all he has created is good; therefore evil can be only the distortion of good. Straighten out what is distorted, or place it in a new situation in which it is no longer a distortion, and evil disappears like a bad dream. Of course, some viruses and parasites have been formed in situations where they are intrinsically bad for others and they can only be eliminated; but there is nothing bad in the material from which they are made, only in their relationship to others which is intrinsic to their continued existence.

The greatest sin in human history was the crucifixion of Jesus. Malice, cowardice, sadism, cruelty, injustice and direct enmity against God were all involved. Yet, even as the nails were being driven into Christ's hands and feet, the human race was being saved, and creation was being given a new relationship with its Maker. The evil of the crucifixion is over, it is past history, but Jesus' fidelity unto death and the Father's love in accepting him transcend history, and are the source of salvation for people of all times and places.

As Christians remembered the role of the chief priests, the crowds, and the Sadducees and Pharisees, there grew up anti-Semitism; but this is evidence that the full significance of the cross was not appreciated by Christians. The malice of the Jewish authorities, the cowardice of Pilate and of the apostles, were neutralized and the evil of their actions simply disappeared in the glory of the resurrection. God turns evil into good, and anger is inappropriate because evil has no substance.

The prophet of meekness in the twentieth century was Mahatma Gandhi who resisted evil non-violently. He knew that India's self-respect could only be achieved through independence from the British, but said that it was not worth the death of one single British soldier. His 'We are all children of God' was the most revolutionary statement of the century, and the world has still to catch up with it.

Anger is a denial of the truth taught by faith. It ignores the fact that everything is in God's hands, and that God uses even sinful actions and bad people to serve his purposes; and that he straightens out what is distorted and abolishes evil by putting it into a new context by his providence. It also separates the angry person from the object of his anger in a way that is contrary to Christian faith. It forgets that there is good in the worst of us and bad in the best of us, and that we are all in need of the mercy of God. It divides the world into good guys and bad guys, and the angry man places himself by implication among the good; and this goes against Christ's command not to judge. Moreover, continued anger is unrealistic, because it freezes the person who is resented forever in the moment when he offended, whereas life goes on and situations and people change. In the imagination of the angry person his enemy is two-dimensional and is seen only in his relationship with the person who hates him. In St Matthew's Gospel, Jesus says that he who is angry with his brother shall answer for it before the court; and St James tells us that God's righteousness is never served by man's anger.

The opposite of anger is gentleness. 'Gentle' is another word used to translate the Greek word *praus* which is translated here as 'meek'. We can afford to be gentle because God's reign has already begun. We have faith in God's power, and we know that we have no need of human force to bring about God's will. (Eph. 4.1–6) St Paul's attitude towards the erring Church of Corinth is one of gentleness, which some mistake for weakness. He warns them that the muscles he is using are not those of the flesh but are strong enough to destroy fortresses. The reason for his confidence is that he is fighting in God's cause. As the Russian proverb says, 'God plus one is a majority'. Gentleness in the face of opposition is a radical act of faith in God.

This beatitude reflects the covenant made by God with Abraham: 'Raise your eyes now, and look from the place where you are, northwards and southwards and eastwards and westwards; for all the land that you see I will give to you and to your offspring for ever.' Abraham is the model of those who are meek before the Lord. He put himself completely at God's disposal, obeying him at every turn and accepting from him both good and bad, even being ready to sacrifice his son if God demanded it. Just as the poor were completely in the power of the rich in ancient times, so Abraham obeyed God's every wish because he trusted him.

The land which the lowly inherit is the kingdom of heaven where God's will is done on earth as in heaven. 'They will inherit the earth' can be interpreted in the light of Christ's claim to kingship in John 18.36–7: 'My kingdom is not from this world. If my kingdom were from this world, my followers would be fighting to keep me from being handed over to the Jews ... You say that I am a king. For this I was born, and for this I came into the world, to testify to the truth.' If Jesus is king, he is not a king in the way that Caesar was king. His kingship is related to God's dominion over the world rather than man's dominion over man. In fact, Caesar's power was minute in comparison with Christ's kingship by whom the whole universe was created and is held in being, and by whose kingly and priestly act, 'in Christ all men are brought to life'. Jesus exercised his kingly power by testifying to this truth; and the meek inherit the earth in the same paradoxical way, by testifying by their lives to the same truth. Nowhere is the contrast between the kingdom of heaven and the kingdoms of this world, between God's power and the power exercised among human beings, so clear. Nowhere is the challenge and test of faith so stark as in the Christian exercise of meekness. It is where God's word goes against common sense; and how often in history has the Church itself followed the wisdom of the world rather than the wisdom of the cross!

'They shall inherit the earth' can be interpreted in the light of Christ's parable of the pounds. (Luke 19.11–27). The man who gained ten pounds from the one that the king had given him receives the rule of ten cities, while the one who gained five pounds was given five cities. The fact that they were slaves meant that they had no natural right to any reward at all. St Thérèse of Lisieux said, as she was dying, that she had spent her life interceding for people; but, after her death, she would be able to intercede much more effectively in heaven. The saints are those whose love of God and their neighbour has been perfected and so are able to be instruments of God's love for us by their intercession, and there is joy in heaven over the conversion of a single sinner. The canonized saints have the added joy that the example of their lives and of their teaching bring people to Christ long after their death.

While 'Blessed are those who mourn' refers to a growing awareness of what it means to be a redeemed sinner, 'Blessed are the meek' refers to the appropriate attitude of the redeemed sinner towards divine providence manifested in the concrete conditions of his life. The truly meek person is Christ-like in that he is 'lamb-like'. At the beginning of this chapter, I quote a text from Isaiah about the meekness of the Suffering Servant, and another text from the Book of Revelation about the Lamb, standing as if it had been slaughtered. In Aramaic, the native language of the author of the Apocalypse, the words 'servant' and 'lamb' are the same word. In his own mind, the author could see the Lamb and the Suffering Servant as one. Christians follow their Master in humbly accepting the tasks they are given, and the conditions in which they live, without egotism and with complete confidence in the Father's love.

In a scene which reminds us of a Walt Disney cartoon, the Lion of Judah is heralded, but a Lamb appears. The author is saying that, in the kingdom, the meekness of the Lamb is as strong as the strength of a lion. The meek are the only ones strong enough to inherit the earth because they use God's own strength. We have seen in the last twenty years the meekness of the Church outlive its communist oppressors; and we have seen the Papacy grow as it has steadily lost power. St Paul says 'When we are weak, then we are strong'. As the consumer society tries to do without God and sees the Church get steadily weaker, it should beware of the meek, for they are stronger than any earthly power.

When the Book of Revelation taught this to a Church being persecuted by the greatest and most stable power of the ancient world, it looked very unlikely indeed; but Rome passed away, and the Gospel triumphed. We do not know what God has in store for the Church, nor do we know its future role in society as a whole; but one thing we can be sure of, that God's will shall be done. If we wish to be instruments in the accomplishment of his will, then we must become meek, rather than seek the illusion of being in the mainstream by adopting the world's agenda and calling it 'modern Catholicism'. Of course, we need to become engaged with modern problems, looking at them from the point of view of the Gospel, but it is more important to be meek. St John Chrysostom says that we can choose either to be meek lambs or fierce wolves. The world admires the fierce wolves. However, if we choose that road, we will fail because we will have left the flock over which Christ is the Good Shepherd. If we choose to be meek lambs, then nothing can withstand us because our power comes from Christ.

Chapter Six

Blessed are those who hunger and thirst for righteousness for they will be filled

One does not live by bread alone, but by every word that comes from the mouth of God. (Matt. 4.4)

My food is to do the will of him who sent me and to complete his work. (John 4.34)

No one in his right mind would voluntarily embrace poverty, accept insults and persecution with joy, meditate on his sins and failings, and remain meek in all situations, however adverse, unless he had a strong motive for doing so. This beatitude is concerned with this motivation.

The whole Bible is very concerned with righteousness. God is righteous when he judges justly, and especially when he rescues his people from their oppressors. Kings and judges are righteous when they administer justice fairly, and do not favour the rich at the expense of the poor. The Jews are righteous when they obey the law or when they are innocent of any offences against the law.

In St Matthew, Joseph is righteous because he does not want to impose the full rigour of the law against Mary when he discovers she is pregnant: he is right with God who always tempers justice with mercy (Matt. 1.19). Here 'righteousness' means 'in tune with God's mind'. When Jesus says, 'Unless your righteousness exceeds that of the scribes and Pharisees, you will never enter the kingdom of heaven,' (Matt. 5.20), he means that being in tune with God's mind is achieved not merely by a slavish following of legal norms but by being open to God himself. When John the Baptist protests at having to baptize Jesus, Jesus says, 'Let it be so now; for it is proper for us in this way to fulfil all righteousness'. (Matt. 3.15) 'Righteousness' here means 'God's will', which was his plan of salvation.

Hunger and thirst bring to mind the first temptation of Jesus. After forty days and nights of fasting, Jesus was hungry; and the devil tempted him to put his hunger and thirst before his Father's will and, probably, to see his messianic role as fulfilled in giving food to the hungry. We have already quoted Christ's reply. One reason why the Jews looked forward to messianic times was that the prophets had foretold that they would be times of feasting, and, in a population that was no stranger to hunger, this was a very inviting prospect. Isaiah had written, 'On this holy mountain the Lord of hosts will make for all peoples a feast of rich food, a feast of well-matured wines, of rich food filled with marrow, of well-matured wines strained clear.' (Isa. 25.6). Jesus would have had no trouble finding disciples if he had dedicated himself to filling their stomachs. If he had used his powers permanently to abolish hunger, even the most secular would have praised him. However, he was concerned with doing God's will, even before feeding the hungry.

He certainly wanted the hungry to be fed, the naked clothed, the sick healed, and the prisoners set free, or, at least, visited; but he was primarily concerned with something more important. He wished to stir up in people a hunger and a thirst for God, and for what God wanted, and then to satisfy them. His task was to bring about the kingdom of God; and this required people who would be ready completely to change their way of thinking and their value system, so that they would become instruments of his power in the world. Instead of aiming directly at their natural needs, he wanted to awake in them their need for God. As Pope John Paul said in

Brazil, 'Hunger for bread, No: hunger for God, Yes.'

With our great desire to catch the attention of the secular world, it is very tempting to try and find out what it most wants, or what the most enlightened part of it wants, and then to mould the Christian message around that, pretending that these needs are central to the Gospel. This is giving in to the first of the three temptations in the desert. It gives us the comforting illusion that we are still in the mainstream of western civilized thought; it gains us friends and collaborators, it earns us approving smiles; but it converts no one. Psychological wholeness, social justice, communist society, feminism, race relations, even capitalist secularism, have all received the treatment. Put 'Christian' in front of any one of them, and then say, 'This is what the Gospel means in the modern world. If we achieve this, we achieve what Christ died for.'

Thus, it is often said that we construct the kingdom of God on earth by our own activity. But there is ecumenical agreement among Scripture scholars that the kingdom is God's own work, not something we can achieve by our own effort, even though we may admit that we need God's help. We can no more construct the kingdom of God than we can create the universe out of nothing. In the New Testament, the kingdom is a New Creation. Liberation theologians have answered this objection by saying that Catholic biblical scholars have become Lutherans in that they deny that something can be both God's work and man's, at the same time. God forgives sin in and through the Church's forgiveness in Confession, so why cannot he construct the kingdom through our efforts? However, the Church Fathers identify the kingdom with the Holy Spirit or with the divine energy which makes all things new. How is it possible to construct the Holy Spirit? We can enter the kingdom, and the kingdom can be present among us, but we cannot construct it; at least, we cannot do so if we are talking about the kingdom as it is in the New Testament.

Thus, Jesus had to awaken in people a hunger and

thirst for God and for what God is doing through him. That is also our task today. 'Justice' in the Bible is God's rights. Human beings have rights because they are made in God's image and share in his dignity. For Christians, human rights only exist in so far as they reflect and respect God's rights. Anything less is falling into the temptation that Jesus resisted. He promises that, if we seek God's reign and its righteousness, everything else will simply fall into place. We do not have to know how, any more than Abraham had to know how God's will would be done. Christian conversion involves a radical faith that God reigns through his providence, even in the secular world. If we don't live that faith, who else will believe it?

When we start out on our religious quest, it is usually because we believe that God will solve our problems and satisfy our needs. He keeps us safe and healthy, helps us over hurdles, and allows us to live our lives with the minimum of pain or inconvenience. In return, we obey his rules, but live our own lives and fulfil our own ambitions. We live within the parameters he has set except when it is too inconvenient. We follow our own ambitions and are only motivated to pray when these ambitions are threatened, or when we are stimulated by some outside factor like a sermon, a pilgrimage, or by a religious film. Our hunger and thirst for God in himself and for what he wants to do in the world is merely theoretical, without substance in reality.

As our Christian conversion deepens, so our picture of God itself gains depth, and we begin to desire him for himself. It can be truly said that progress in our spiritual life can be measured by the intensity of our hunger and thirst for God. When our personal ambitions give way to the kingdom of God, which becomes our primary concern, then we shall begin to move forward along the road to God.

To say that until we put God first we are still near the starting line may be rather discouraging. There are two ways of avoiding the challenge of the Gospel: we can simply ignore it and carry on as usual; and we can pretend that we have already arrived. The first leaves us open to many kinds of sin and to the danger of gradually slipping into a completely non-Christian frame of mind; while the second underestimates God in what he wants to give us and ourselves, in what we are capable of receiving.

The main problem is that, as St Augustine says, we were made for God, and our hearts are restless until we are united with him. Animals eat when they are hungry and drink when they are thirsty; but we still have an emptiness after our basic needs are met which can only be filled by God. Nature hates a vacuum, so we try to fill our emptiness with anything at hand. Some try to fill it with food and drink, some with sexual activity, some watch television or hide behind a computer. If we are lucky, we will look for something which is capable of opening us up to God, like the pursuit of beauty, true love or truth. Idols are the worst substitutes for God: the Nazis worshipped the fatherland, the Communists the future of mankind, and some worship Science with a capital S. Just about anything other than God can become an idol if we want to make it so, even our mental image of God, even Catholicism as an institution, an ideology, or as a tribal loyalty. When something other than God demands our absolute attention, it becomes demonic to those who worship it, and hateful to those who are its victims.

When the emptiness is not filled by God, all our desires are thrown out of true and take on a life of their own, and we become subject to them. For the Christian who is starting out on the path to holiness, there is a need to practise asceticism to rectify what remains disordered after conversion. We have already seen that being poor in spirit, moving from self-estimation based on our comparison with others to esteeming ourselves as loved by God, and being meek, are not easy and require self-discipline. If rightly motivated, penitential practices will help us to reorientate our hunger and thirst towards God. Fasting, and doing without what we want but do not need, are ways of rectifying our disordered appetites. In order to allow God into our emptiness, we have to face that emptiness. Resurrection only comes through the cross.

It is extremely important that we make no comparison between ourselves and those around us, even when they show no notice or interest in anything remotely penitential, or when they try and fail in their attempts. 'Do not judge,' is an absolute prohibition like 'Do not commit adultery,' when it puts us among the good and other people among the bad. We simply do not know what God is doing in their souls, nor do we know how he plans to counteract their sins, errors or weaknesses. Criticizing others in this way is a covert way of expressing satisfaction with ourselves, and self-satisfaction in things of the Spirit renders a Christian life inauthentic.

Fasting and other penitential practices have no value in themselves, and are only useful as a faith response to God's love. If they lead to criticizing others or self-satisfaction, then it is better not to practise them. Then we are left with humbly accepting what God sends to us in life, whether good or bad, considering each moment as God's gift to us, and fulfilling our duties which include living the Beatitudes according to circumstances. This is enough. Each of us has his special gifts from God: God is leading each of us according to the divine plan to which we are not privy, and hence comparisons are odious.

Another way of escaping from hungering and thirsting is to pretend that we have already arrived, and that the call to conversion is meant for others, not ourselves, because we are converted. 'I am a good Catholic, Father. I love God and my neighbour, and I go to Mass and communion every Sunday.' Some Evangelicals go around asking people if they have been saved; which is strange because no one in the New Testament ever asks anybody that question. When satisfaction at having arrived or having been saved dominates a person's attitude, then the pharisaical prayer, 'God, I thank you that I am not like other people,' is not very far off. Another mistake can arise from the very richness of a person's conversion experience, and he can think that progress in the Christian life depends on recapturing that experience instead of moving on. Master Eckhart, the mediaeval Dominican mystic, writes:

> God gives no gift, God has never given any gift, in order that anyone should have the gift and rest content with it. Rather, all the gifts he has ever given, in heaven and on earth, were given in view of his single purpose, to give one gift which is himself ... In this life, there is no settling down for us in any way, and there never was for any man, however far he may have progressed.[1]

If we underestimate what God wants to give us, believing that his gift of himself which he gives through the other gifts we have already received is sufficient, then we also underestimate our own capacity to receive him. Our souls, being spiritual, are as large as we allow God to make them. They can be as small as 'little me', or they can be large enough to receive God, and thus larger than the universe. God has created us to be *capax Dei*, capable of union with God. Our capacity grows as we get nearer to God, grows with our hunger and thirst; and hence we can never have enough of him. St Gregory the Great tells us in his *Dialogues* how St Benedict saw the whole world in a ray of sunlight. He asks how this is possible, and says that the light of interior contemplation expands the soul. When someone sees the Creator, the soul of the seer is large enough for the world to seem very small and limited.

'Father, I simply cannot pray by myself. Prayer meetings are not a problem; Mass is not a problem; my problem begins when I try to pray alone', said a leading member of the Charismatic Renewal in Negritos. St Gregory the Great tells us that there are three stages of prayer, the beginning, the middle and the perfection.

The first stage is when prayer is sweet. We have enthusiasm and we are experiencing novelty, and all seems well. The second begins when the novelty wears off and we have to battle against the temptation not to pray. It is surprising how many duties, how many good deeds, how many distractions, present themselves to our mind in order to entice us away from prayer. Prayer later rather than praying now becomes very attractive for good Christian reasons. If we wish really to love God with our whole being we must resist these temptations. We can spend our time for prayer in fighting off distractions about our job, our household chores or anything; and we can come to the end of it, discouraged and thinking how we have wasted our time. However, if we persevere, trusting in God's steadfast love rather than in our own feelings and efforts, it is not a waste of time.

St Paul tells us that we don't know how to pray; but that the Spirit is praying within us, calling 'Abba, Father'. This middle period of prayer is very important, and much better than our prayer at the beginning, however much more agreeable and religiously satisfying that had been. In this prayer of duty we experience our weakness and we have the opportunity to make an act of faith in the Spirit's presence, even when we feel our prayer to be a waste of time. If the Spirit is present within, our prayer cannot be a waste of time, however boring it may be, however devoid of a devotional feeling of accomplishment. We are doing battle, not trusting in our own capacity, which is obviously nil, but in the Spirit who prays in us. In the most religious moment in history, Jesus felt no satisfaction, but cried out, 'My God, my God, why have you forsaken me?' and, 'I thirst!' We are sharing in his Passion. We are hungering and thirsting for righteousness, knowing that, in God's good time, we will be filled.

Just as it is necessary to clean our teeth and wash our bodies if we are to remain healthy, so we must pray with regularity if we are to remain spiritually healthy. Apart from our participation in the sacraments, especially the

Eucharist, and any other group prayers, there are two kinds of prayer we may practise by ourselves: a regular extended time of prayer, and short, sharp intense prayers during the day.

If we are not used to praying for a period each day, we should plan it, not leaving it to chance when we are going to pray. Our position in prayer is important, but must be something we decide for ourselves; perhaps sitting in a chair which is not too comfortable, so that we will not go to sleep, but not uncomfortable either. Set yourself a fixed time, not so long as to be impossible, nor too short to be useful: perhaps a quarter or half an hour, according to your circumstances. Calm yourself down: imagine yourself surrounded and impregnated with God's love, which is true, and then put yourself in his hands and respond. Afterwards, you can say the rosary, or read a pre-selected passage of Scripture and respond to it by turning it into prayer, or repeat a short invocation, or simply talk to God: do what is best for you. If you find it difficult, talk to someone. The most important thing is to be determined to pray, no matter what, and to accept the prayer that God gives you. You will discover for yourself that it is worth it.

The other kind of prayer can be done anywhere, in any posture, while you are living your ordinary life. Here, intensity is better than length. This kind of prayer costs nothing but commitment. 'Jesus, I love you'; 'Forgive me, Lord'; 'Help me'; 'Look after him/her, Lord'; 'I don't like this, Lord'. The list is endless and easily invented on the spot. In Christ's time, the Jews would thank God for everything they did: 'Thank you, Lord, for giving me a new day'; 'Thank you, Lord, for water and soap'; 'Thank you, Lord, for giving me clothes to wear'; 'Thank you, Lord, for my wife'; and so on throughout the day. If you pray in this way, the time you use for extended prayer won't be an interruption of your day, but rather, a climax.

If you pray regularly, God will transform your relationships with himself and with your neighbour, and you will 'hunger and thirst' for what is right and according to God's will in all aspects of Christian life. The Cistercian Fathers have said that any Christian group, whether family, religious community, or parish, has to retain a balance between two poles, community and solitude. Community is only as good as the one-to-one relationship between each member and God; while the one-to-one relationship is only Christian if it provides the motivation for binding the community together.

I once worked in a parish where the parish priest was keen on Liberation Theology. For him, evangelization was principally directed at transforming society from a crowd of people, each looking after his own interests, into a community of sharers. Pastoral activity consisted in providing people with the opportunity and encouragement to share. Prayer and liturgy were seen within this context. Although this priest had a personal prayer life, no effort was made towards fostering a one-to-one relationship with Christ among the people who lacked it. The pastoral policy didn't work. Only those with a strong personal devotional life really cooperated while the majority of the townspeople took part when they wanted to and were chiefly concerned with preserving the religious customs of the town. Meetings to organize the parish were ill-attended, enthusiasms were short-lived, and the main work of the parish always fell on the same few shoulders. There was no growth. All the parish priest and his team could say was that the people of that town were particularly hard. It never occurred to them that their evangelization programme was putting second things first.

Ideology prevented him and his team from seeing that, for many parishioners, the 'one thing necessary' was missing; and that, if they wanted improvement, then pastoral effort had to be directed towards personal conversion to Christ. In Cistercian language, it was an attempt to build community without solitude. Christian community is made up of persons, each with his unique relationship with God, because God is the source of his personhood and of his Christian vocation in the community. Whatever type of Christian community a person may belong to, he has to develop his hunger and thirst for God, enough to live the life of the Beatitudes, so that genuine Christian community can be formed. This is the subject of the next beatitude.

Notes
1. *Beatitudes* by Simon Tugwell OP (Templegate).

Chapter Seven

Blessed are the merciful, for they will receive mercy

Like other key words in the Bible, what we normally translate as 'mercy' (*hesed* in Hebrew, *eleos* in Greek) has a number of interrelated meanings which make our English translation inadequate. The previous beatitudes recommended attitudes which are associated in the profane world with slaves, the poor and the powerless. In contrast, this beatitude recommends us to practise a virtue associated with God and with kings.

It can be translated 'steadfast love' or the 'benevolent will to save'. It is an attribute of God which motivated him to create the universe and the human race, to rescue the Israelites from Egypt, to set up his covenant with Moses, to deliver Israel from its enemies, and to restore the covenant after they had been unfaithful. Jewish kings were expected to practise *hesed* in their judgements because they ruled in God's name. It also describes a feeling, a sentiment, of good will to those in need by a person with the capacity to help; and this gives people confidence that they will be helped. The person who has *hesed* is dependable.

Jesus shows his *eleos* by eating and drinking with sinners. *Eleos* is the basic principle that Jesus uses to interpret the law of Moses and takes the place of the customs and traditions of the scribes and Pharisees. His favourite quotation is from Hosea 6.6, 'I desire steadfast love and not sacrifice'. God allows the sun to shine and the rain to fall on good and bad alike, and this is evidence that God wants to help even his declared enemies. Thus, we must love our enemies and pray for those who persecute us. (Matt. 5.43–8). We must be ready to do good to those in need and forgive those who offend us. This is an absolute condition for entering the kingdom. We cannot receive forgiveness ourselves if we do not forgive others (Matt. 6.12, 14–15); and this is reinforced later by the parable of the unforgiving debtor (Matt. 18.23–35). Helping those in need is the outstanding characteristic of the sheep that are saved, and not doing so is the characteristic of the goats that are condemned, in the parable on the judgement (Matt. 25.31–46). Thus this beatitude means, 'Blessed are those who forgive those who offend them and who help the needy, for they will be forgiven and helped in their need.'

Why is our practice of mercy an absolute condition for receiving mercy? Christ's answer is simply: because God is merciful. If we ask God to forgive us without forgiving others, we haven't really left the world of our own creation in which we are the centre, and entered the world in which God is the centre, because he wills all sins forgiven and all needs met. In our own little self-centred world, God's forgiveness has no meaning and God has no place because we are its god. Moreover, to be Christian our prayer is offered in Christ's name; it is a sharing in Jesus' own prayer, and he prays not only for me but for all. By refusing to help those in need and by refusing to forgive, we are cutting ourselves off from Christ's prayer.

Although we are exercising the virtue of kings, we are not doing so from a position of power but from weakness. This allows God's power to work through us. A Russian bishop was a prisoner in a Nazi concentration camp. Before he died, he wrote a prayer in which he thanked God for allowing him the privilege to suffer at the hands of his Nazi guards. This gave him the opportunity and the power to forgive them, so that when they all appeared at the judgement seat, he could say to God that he had forgiven them, and God would have nothing against them: they would be saved.

We shall not practise this beatitude properly if we have not practised the preceding ones, if we are not poor in spirit, in mourning, and meek, with the dedication of those who hunger and thirst for righteousness. In so far as we are proud, our ego keeps getting in the way. True mercy springs from a humble heart. Dietrich Bonhoeffer wrote:

> Anybody who lives beneath the cross and who has discerned the utter wickedness of all men and of his own heart will find that there is no sin that can ever be alien to him. Anybody who has once been horrified by the dreadfulness of his own sin that nailed Jesus Christ to the cross will no longer be horrified by even the rankest sins of a brother. Looking at the cross of Jesus, he knows the human heart. He knows how utterly lost it is in sin and weakness, how it goes astray in the ways of sin, and he also knows that it is accepted in grace and mercy. Only the brother under the cross can accept the sinner. In the presence of a psychiatrist I can only be a sick man; in the presence of a Christian, I can dare to be a sinner.[1]

We have noted that Christian holiness differs from that of the Pharisee in the parable, in that, the deeper our repentance, the closer we feel to all sinners. The more we know how much we need the mercy of God, the more we realize that we are brothers and sisters to the worst sinners in the world. Even if we must separate ourselves from a sinner, it is not because we feel superior to him, but because we know we are like him and can too easily fall into his sin, and so be much worse than he is because we have received so much grace from God.

There are many similarities between the Jewish community of Qumran and the early monks; but there is also a glaring difference: the Qumran monks regarded all outside their sect as unclean and degenerate, while the Desert Fathers knew they were monks because they were unclean and degenerate and could not resist the temptations of the world by remaining in it, and they recognized that there were people in the world who were holier than they. When they mourned for the sins of the world, they mourned for their own sins first.

When we set ourselves up to judge or criticize people, we do harm to them and to ourselves. When we refuse to forgive, we forget our own solidarity with them as sinners.

Once in Negritos I went against my own principles. A boy in my house stole my camera, and two others furnished me with strong evidence which identified one of the group as the thief. I had been repeatedly told that I should be tough with the boys and, in this case, I decided to follow this advice. I called a meeting of all seven boys and the two outlined their evidence against him. The accused boy said quietly to them, 'You are taking from me the only thing I have'. My heart bled for him at that moment. All the boys were there because they needed to be. However, I steeled my heart and expelled him from the house. I let him back later because he had nowhere else to go. He was one of the boys who saw me off when I left, but it was never the same. He now sells drugs and forged banknotes in the street, and hides when I visit Negritos.

Can I say that his present sins have nothing to do with me? If I had given him a better Christian example when he was with me, if I had followed my heart instead of my head during the 'trial', perhaps things would have been different. I have special reason to blame myself because I later came to suspect that the evidence was fabricated. Our bad example, and even our lack of good example, have a knock-on effect, and our own sins add to the general sin of the world.

Another reason why we cannot look at other people's sins completely from the outside, as though they have nothing to do with us, is found in the unity of the human race. This unity is basic to Christianity, and ought to be glaringly obvious to all Christians. It is told in mythical language in the story of Adam and Eve, our first parents. There is a unity which comes from the fact that each one of us was created by the same Word, so that we are all united in him by whom we exist. This same Word became flesh in order to heal this unity which has been partly disrupted by sin, and to transform it into unity with God. Thus, in the divine dimension of things, there is a unity in which the holiness of one person enriches the whole, and the sin of one impoverishes the whole.

This conviction is found in the Jewish teaching on the *zaddik*, a just man who may appear to others to be a failure who is being punished by God, but whose righteousness is preserving the world. It is found in Jesus' teaching that we are the salt of the earth and the light of the world. It is the context in which Christ's 'obedience unto death' has brought about an amnesty for all the sins of the world, and his resurrection is our source of eternal life. It makes understandable the invitations of our Lady in Fatima and Medjugorje that we should pray and do penance for peace in the world.

This being the case, we cannot discount a connection between our own sins and lack of love and the murderous wars in Africa, the conflict between Israelis and Palestinians, and the sins of those who offend us. We are all in need of forgiveness, so we had better start forgiving others.

At the end of the film *Titanic*, we see people crammed into a lifeboat. They are of different social classes, have different characters, good and bad, and all are menaced by the same sea and protected by the same boat. Some are wetter than others, some are more responsible and helpful than others, and there is general concern for those still in the water. This is a good image of the human race: all are menaced by sin and death, all are in need of God's mercy, and we clutch at anything that will keep us afloat. In such a scenario, forgiving our neighbour should be easy, and helping one another should be natural.

How far should we help those in need, whether by direct action or by donations? Mother Teresa's answer is, 'Until it hurts'. Unless we learn to sacrifice ourselves in forgiving and giving to our neighbour, we shall never really appreciate what Christ has done for us, nor come to love our neighbour as he has loved us.

According to Ecclesiasticus, almsgiving is a sacrifice of thanksgiving (Ecclus. 35.4); and in Tobit (Ecclus. 12.11–15) the memorial of his good deeds in helping the poor is carried up by the archangel Raphael into God's presence. The angels are the priests of the heavenly sanctuary, so it follows that the memorial of these deeds has a sacrificial character. St Paul says, about the collection he was making for Jerusalem, 'The one who sows sparingly will reap sparingly, and the one who sows bountifully will also reap bountifully' (2 Cor. 9.6), and that the Corinthians' generosity 'will produce thanksgivings to God through us', and 'overflows with many thanksgivings to God' (2 Cor. 9.11–12). In Philippians he calls the gifts he had received from them 'a fragrant offering, a sacrifice acceptable and pleasing to God' (Phil. 4.18).

What we do for those in need, either directly or by proxy with money, has a sacrificial character and is directed as a sacrifice of thanksgiving to God. Like all sacrifice, it is not the simple giving of gifts that is sacrificial: it must be an expression of our self-giving, as Jesus taught when he compared the gifts of the rich with the widow's mite.

The word *eleos*, when applied to God, usually means his will to save. 'God, who is rich in mercy, out of the great love with which he loved us even when we were dead through our trespasses, made us alive together with Christ.' (Eph. 2.4–5). It is not human merit but *eleos* which motivates God to save us (Tit. 3.5). God entrusted the apostolic vocation to Paul by an act of *eleos* (2 Cor. 4.1).

Just as preaching the Good News had priority over all other activities of Jesus in his public ministry, so evangelization has precedence over all other works of mercy. There is nothing better than bringing people into a relationship with God in Christ. This too is a priestly ministry, because those we bring to Christ are an acceptable offering, sanctified by the Holy Spirit (Rom. 15.15–16). In fact, we must not make too clear a distinction between evangelization and other works of mercy, because our whole Christian life is a witness to the Good News; and for that we have received the Holy Spirit. No one can deny that Mother Teresa's life evangelized people, and photos of her embracing a child or nursing a leper are good evangelistic tools.

St Bernard tells us that, while the first three beatitudes are about reconciling ourselves to ourselves in relation to God, this beatitude reconciles us to our neighbour. The poor in spirit who refuse to judge their neighbour and are only too willing to forgive him, who recognize that God, and not themselves, is the centre of their world, and are at least as concerned with the good of their neighbour as they are with their own, and who see Christ in every encounter and are ready to evangelize and be evangelized, when they get together, form a community with special characteristics.

Christian community life is the cause of another dimension of joy. St Aelred wrote:

> Each of you, my brethren, before coming here, had a soul which belonged to him alone. You have been converted to God, and behold, the Holy Spirit, the fire from heaven that Our Lord has cast upon earth and would see kindled, has reached your souls and out of all your hearts has made one heart and soul. This soul, our community, has all the virtues of the angels, and above all, that unity and concord thanks to which, although there are superiors and inferiors, what belongs to each individually belongs to all and what belongs to all belongs to each.[2]

This unity among brethren turns the community into a paradise: 'I think this paradise is preferable, by its beauty and spiritual fecundity, to the paradise from which the first man was cast out' (St Aelred).

St Luke remembers that the Jewish people expected fortunes to be reversed when the Messiah came; 'He has brought down the powerful from their thrones, and lifted up the lowly; he has filled the hungry with good things and sent the rich away empty'. He underlines this by contrasting beatitudes and woes: 'Blessed are you who are poor, for yours is the kingdom of heaven ... Woe to you who are rich, for you have received your consolation'. Although he knew this process would be made perfect only at the Parousia or end of the world, he tells us how the poor will be rewarded even now in this life.

> Now the whole group of those who believed were of one heart and soul, and no one claimed private owner-ship of any possessions, but everything they owned was held in common. With great power the apostles gave their testimony to the resurrection of the Lord Jesus, and great grace was upon them all. There was not a needy person among them, for as many as owned land or houses sold them and brought the proceeds of what was sold. They laid it at the apostles' feet, and it was distributed to each as any had need. (Acts 4.32–5)

Not too long ago, I met a boy in Cajamarca who had been in my house in Negritos. Another boy from my house called Jose had recently joined our monastery. The following conversation took place:

'How is Jose getting on?'
'He seems very happy. He talked enthusiastically about his vocation the last time I saw him.'
'How much is his salary?'
'He doesn't have a salary. No one does in the monastery.'

'Then how does he eat?'

'Everything is owned in common, and people receive what they need from the prior. If anything needs to be bought, the money comes from the common fund.'

'He is not poor: in fact, he is rich. Being poor means not knowing if you are going to eat tomorrow. If you have work, it means not knowing if you will be employed next week. Poverty is insecurity.'

This boy was an expert because, except for the year he spent in my house, he had been poor all his life. He came to me after conditions at home caused him to go up on to the cliffs to throw himself off. Not having the courage to go through with it, he knocked on my door and asked me to take him in. I didn't know about the suicide bit until he told me in my meeting with him in Cajamarca.

The Church in Jerusalem, Jose's monastery, and any Christian family that is living by the Gospel, may be menaced from outside by persecution or by the injustices of society, but they are rich within, because they are communities of givers, not consumers, and 'in giving we receive'.

One day, a man asked God to show him heaven and hell; so God sent an angel to accompany him. The angel took the man to a great hall, richly adorned with gold. On a table was every kind of tasty food. 'Is this heaven?' he asked the angel. 'No, it is hell', the angel replied. 'Wait and see'. A bell rang, and many people entered the hall. They looked as though they were starving. They sat down and began the meal. Each person had been given a very long spoon; and they tried to put food into their mouths with it but could not. The more they tried to shovel food in, the more it fell on their laps, on the table and on the floor. After a time, the bell rang again, and they rose from the table and went out. No one had managed to eat anything.

The angel said, 'Now we shall visit heaven'. He took the man to an identical hall, all richly decorated in gold. On the table there was the same rich food and the long spoons. 'But this is the same as hell', protested the man. 'Wait and see', instructed the angel. The bell rang, and a crowd of well-fed, happy people entered. They all sat down and began to eat. Each took his spoon and was intent on feeding the people around him; and all rose from the table satisfied. The spoons had not been designed for people to feed themselves, but they were perfect instruments for feeding other people. Such is Christian community, based as it is on the life of the Blessed Trinity, and such will be heaven.

Jose is no longer in the monastery. He went home for three months' leave, and found his mother in bed, gasping for breath and surrounded by squalor. He has elder brothers who had promised to look after her, but obviously they had not done so. She was in bed with bad asthma. 'I don't understand my brothers. It is clear that I can't just leave her. I must go to work because she needs medicine. It looks as though God doesn't want me to be a monk.' I hope he comes back because he is a man of deep prayer and is popular with the others; but it won't be for a while.

St Luke's picture of the Jerusalem Church has been an ideal down the ages, and clearly is behind St Aelred's own description of the monastic community at Rievaulx. The practice of complete sharing of goods was not obligatory throughout the apostolic Church. Nevertheless Tertullian, when asked why Christians did not tithe, said that all their property and they themselves were completely at God's disposal; and, for the first few centuries, Christians were extremely generous to the Church and to the poor.

St Ignatius Loyola, St Francis de Sales and de Caussade, among others, opened up Catholic spirituality, and made their teaching available to all, stressing that Christian perfection can be reached in any walk of life. Thus we can apply to any Christian community what St Bernard and St Aelred said to monks, especially to the family.

Now that we do not have the support of civil society to

keep the family together, we must rely on the riches of Catholic spirituality. Too often we are content to teach the rules themselves, without giving couples the spirituality which makes sense of the rules and can give them the motivation and strength to keep them. Christian conversion brings about a deep change of basic attitude towards ourselves, towards others, and towards God; and it is within this context that Christ made marriage indissoluble. If there is no such change, then it is little wonder that there is so much divorce among Catholics.

As we said in the last chapter, there are two poles in any Christian community, whether it is a religious community, a parish, a prayer group or a family. These are the personal relationship which each one has with God, and togetherness. They interact with each other and contribute to each other, and neither can do without the other. To give little importance to one of them, or to leave one of them out completely, is a recipe for disaster. Without a personal relationship with Christ, the community deteriorates into a crowd, having become an impossible ideal. Without unity in Christ, religious practice becomes an egoistic form of unchristian isolationism.

Without personal conversion, as outlined in the first three beatitudes, with the best will in the world, Christian community becomes an ideal divorced from charity. I quote D. Bonhoeffer:

> He who loves his dream of a community more than the Christian community itself becomes a destroyer of the latter, even though his personal intentions may be ever so honest and earnest and sacrificial.[3]

Christian conversion requires a fundamental reappraisal of oneself as a sinner, and hence an acceptance of others, even in their weakness; and this is the basis of true Christian community. When this reappraisal has not happened, the Christian community becomes an idea, separate from the members who make it up; and they are rejected as stupid, confused, ignorant or sinful, if they do not share the same ideal as oneself. This leads to divisions and bitterness. It happens in sects all the time; but it can happen anywhere, even in the Catholic Church.

Without a deep relationship with Christ being a priority of each member, a community can become a kind of club in which each member guards his space; while the superior's job is to protect the space round each member while trying to keep the community functioning. It is a comfortable way of life, but it is far removed from the ideal of St Luke and St Aelred, and is not likely to bring down the blessing promised in this beatitude.

Without a relationship with Christ, the links between husband and wife will last only as long as it is in the interest of each of them to keep the family going. As with the community mentioned above, Christ is simply not involved in the commitment or lack of it which binds these human beings together. Again, the special quality of joy which should characterize a Christian family is missing. It cannot be obtained without sacrifice.

On the other hand, an individual can use his religion to escape from his real life commitments to his community or to the people at large. He can cut himself off from his family in order to take part in religious devotions, and prefer the company of priests to his own wife or children. We must remember that 'Blessed are the merciful' enjoins us to seek the well-being of all with whom we have contact and who need our help. Whether in the context of a religious community, or a Catholic family, or in the Church's relationship with the wider world, our personal devotion to Christ should propel us to a constant love and care of the neighbour God has given us.

Christian communities in general, and the Church in particular, are a participation in the life of the Blessed Trinity, in which the Father is Father because he has given all he is to the Son, as the Son gives all he is to the Father, and this Gift of Self is the Holy Spirit. God is the perfect unity in love of Father, Son and Holy Spirit.

Christian community is an imperfect but real copy and manifestation of the Blessed Trinity on earth, in which human persons relate to one another and to the Trinity, united in the one body of Christ. Thus Jesus prays, 'that they all may be one. As you, Father, are in me and I am in you, may they also be one in us, so that the world may believe that you have sent me.' Not content with this, we must show God's steadfast love to all by forgiving those who offend us and by helping those in need. In this way, and in any other possible way, we will evangelize the world, and experience the joy of Christian community.

Imagine a eucharistic community composed of the poor in spirit. Their most characteristic attitude would be one of thanksgiving towards God because they would realize how much he has given them. Without egoistically grasping this world's goods for themselves they would see the whole world as God's gift. As they realize the great contrast between their present state and the holiness of God, they would acknowledge God's tremendous love for them which is revealed in Christ. As they see all the circumstances of their lives, good and bad, and all the tasks they perform, enjoyable or painful, as means that Christ uses for their sanctification, they are ever conscious of his attentive love. It would be a community whose members do not judge each other and are anxious to forgive each other without anger. It would be a community in which its members help each other out. It would also be a community that strives to deepen its own relationship with God and to share that relationship with others. In the same spirit, St Paul tells the Philippians that their communal life of faith is a 'sacrifice and offering', and that his life of witness and his approaching death are part and parcel of that sacrifice, and he talks of his and their joy. (Phil. 2.17). The insights that the Christian community has gained by practising these beatitudes would lead its members to offer all they have, all they do and all they are at the Presentation of Gifts. The bread and wine would symbolize in God's presence their self-offering, and would await the prayer of consecration when they would become the expression of Christ's self-offering. In offering themselves with hunger and thirst for God's will, they will be brought to purity of heart and thus be open to receive Christ in holy communion.

Notes

1. Dietrich Bonhoeffer in *Life Together*, quoted from 'The Theology of Contemplative Community' by Tarsicius Connor OCSO in *Contemplative Community*, edited by Basil Pennington OCSO, Cistercian Studies Series, Cistercian Publications, Consortium Press, Washington DC, 1972.
2. Charles Dumont OCSO; 'Seeking God in Community According to St Aelred', in the same book.
3. Tarsicius Connor OCSO; op. cit.

Chapter Eight

Blessed are the pure in heart, for they will see God

Moses took the blood and dashed it on the people, and said, 'See the blood of the covenant that the Lord has made with you in accordance with all these words.' Then Moses and Aaron, Nadab, and Abihu, and seventy of the elders of Israel went up, and they saw the God of Israel. (Exod. 24.8–10)

'You approached and stood at the foot of the mountain while the mountain was blazing up to the very heavens, shrouded in dark clouds. Then the Lord spoke to you out of the fire. You heard the sound of words but saw no form ... Since you saw no form when the Lord spoke to you at Horeb out of the fire, take care and watch yourselves closely, so that you do not act corruptly by making an idol for yourselves.' (Deut. 4.11–16)

Up till now we have been dealing with what the Fathers of the Church call the active life, what we have to do to attain eternal life. It is a process of cleaning out and reorientating the soul, removing the distortions caused by sin, reforging its relationship with the self and with other people so that, together with them, the Christian may enter into God's presence. According to John Cassian who wrote about the teaching and lives of the fourth-century Egyptian monastic fathers, the whole purpose of

Christian asceticism is to become pure in heart. It is our destiny to see God, in a glass darkly in this life, and face to face in heaven. This is what the Syrian bishop of Lyons in the second century, St Irenaeus, meant when he wrote that 'the glory of God is man fully alive'. Every circumstance of our lives, in so far as it is willed or permitted by God, is designed to help us attain that object. Unfortunately, we are inclined to turn means into ends, so putting ourselves on the path to God and facing in his direction is inevitably painful.

Purity of heart is total surrender to God, so that the means by which we attain it are no longer at the forefront of our minds, which become centred on God whom we desire with our whole being. We do not leave behind the word and sacraments, or the created world, in order to concentrate on Ultimate Reality, as do Buddhists and some kinds of Hindu holy men: rather, we see them and love them because they are illumined with his presence; and we begin to see them from his point of view. We come to love God for God's sake. Words and sacraments are celebrated with the greatest possible devotion, if only because God works through them to raise our attention to him who is beyond all words and sacraments. This is the contemplative life, the end result, the ultimate joy of all Christian activity in this life.

St Seraphim of Sarov speaks for both East and West:

> Two stages are to be noted in the spiritual life: the active life and the contemplative life. The first consists in renunciation and ascetic effort; the second is the goal. The active life consists in fastings, abstinence, vigils, prostrations and other exercises which help us to progress in the narrow way that leads to eternal life ... Man's activity enables him to purify his passions and, when he was freed himself from all stain, he can draw near, very humbly, to the contemplative life. This consists in raising the mind towards the Lord God in 'pure prayer', as St Isaac the Syrian calls it, in

watchfulness of heart, in spiritual recollection. The
practice of the active life is not to be laid aside when one
has attained to the lofty heights of the contemplative
life; on the contrary, it has to be strengthened. Everyone wishing to progress in the spiritual life has to
ascend the ladder of perfection, rung by rung, occupy-
ing himself in the practical labours of the active life and
gradually ascending towards the heights of contemplation.[1]

In the patristic tradition, any Christian life which is fully
lived will lead to contemplation, and Martha will eventually become like Mary. From this point of view, there is no
difference in kind between active and contemplative
orders. When Blessed Ptolemy and his fellow monks left
their hermitages to tend the cholera victims in Siena, they
did not believe they were abandoning their contemplative
vocations to become active. Contemplation involves listening to God, and listening to God involves obeying him in
the concrete circumstances in which we find ourselves.

Of course, some people are called by grace to separate
themselves more radically from the world to concentrate
on prayer, and thus bear witness to the contemplative
dimension of all Christian life; while others are called to
work for the good of those in need, and thus bear witness
to that aspect of Christian living. However, those who live
an active life in the apostolate or by doing works of
charity, if they do so in a balanced way, should also arrive
at contemplation. Many of the active saints had very
contemplative relations with God because they were pure
in heart; and many contemplatives are married and fully
engaged in secular occupations.

It must be borne in mind that St Seraphim was an
Orthodox hermit; and the ascetic practices he advocates
are those of an Orthodox hermit. In this connection we
should remember the words of de Caussade: 'The
doctrine of pure love can only be learned through the
action of God, and not as a result of our own activity of

mind. God instructs the heart by sufferings and contradictions, not by ideas'. 'In order to reach the highest stage
of perfection, the crosses sent by Providence, which are
provided by their state at every moment, open to them a
surer and far quicker road than extraordinary states and
works.' Thus, those of us who are not called to be Orthodox hermits will find all necessary penance within our
own way of life.

Pure love is the principal activity of the pure in heart. It
cannot be practised unless we ascend through the previous beatitudes, unless we are poor in spirit in the deepest
recesses of our soul. De Caussade writes:

> To possess this science, it is necessary to be disengaged
> from all particular goods; and to arrive at this detach-
> ment, it is necessary to be really deprived of these
> goods. Thus, it is only by mortification of all sorts, by
> trials and deprivations of all kinds, that we can be estab-
> lished in pure love. We must reach the point at which
> the whole creation is nothing and God is everything ...
> first reduced to nothing and then be given the value it
> has in God's Order.

We make this journey, whether we are priests, religious,
married or single, by making the Beatitudes our rule of
life, according to the concrete circumstances of our vocation. We have been reconciled to ourselves in our true
relationship to God, through poverty of spirit and
mourning, and this has made us meek, ready to accept
whatever God sends us and to do whatever God wants us
to do. Moved on by our hunger and thirst for God's will,
we forgive those who have offended us and spend
ourselves for the good of others. This gives our community life its Christian characteristics: the Church is a
community of people who are reconciled to each other
because they have been reconciled to God. This is the
work of the Holy Spirit from beginning to end, and it is
our job to cooperate by practising these beatitudes. Then

he will lead us, using trials and contradictions, dark nights or what some Greek Fathers call educative desolations, to purity of heart and pure love, either in this world or in the next. Then, as St Benedict says:

> Then, when all these degrees of humility have been climbed, the monk (or ordinary Christian) will presently come to that perfect love of God which casts out all fear; whereby he will begin to observe without labour, as though naturally and by habit, all those precepts which formerly he did not observe without fear, no longer for fear of hell, but for love of Christ and through good habit and delight in virtue. And all this will the Lord deign to show forth by the power of his Spirit in his workman how cleansed from vice and from sin. (*Rule of St Benedict*, ch. 7)

St Bernard uses the imagery of the Three Kisses to describe progress in the Christian life. The first is the kiss of Christ's feet, which corresponds to conversion and the first part of the Beatitudes. The second is the kiss of Christ's hands, which is the practice of the virtues in the community, corresponding to 'Blessed are the merciful'. These two stages belong to the active life. The third stage is the kiss of the mouth. The kiss between the Father and the Son is the Holy Spirit; and contemplation is nothing less than the highest form of participation in the mutual love of Father and Son, a participation in the Holy Spirit, above words, in the divine silence. St Bernard attaches a book from the Old Testament to each of the three stages: the Book of Ecclesiastes, which treats of the vanity of worldly glory, to the first three beatitudes; the Book of Proverbs for acquiring those virtues necessary for community living, corresponding to 'Blessed are the merciful'; and the Song of Songs he offers to contemplatives, for those who are pure in heart.

Jesus promises that the pure in heart will see God. The question whether human beings are capable of seeing

God was a contentious issue among the Jews, and this debate is reflected in the Old Testament. At the beginning of this chapter, we quoted two accounts of God's appearance to Israel. In Exodus, it is said that they saw him; while in Deuteronomy it is specially emphasized that they did not see him. According to Margaret Barker, who has made a special study of this problem in scriptural times, there were two basic types of Judaism after the return from Babylon: that represented by the quotation from Exodus was centred on Temple worship, where God manifested his covenant presence to the Jews who approached him in their sacrificial worship; while the other type, represented by the quotation from Deuteronomy, stressed the transcendence of God who could be heard but not seen; they saw the Torah as the main manifestation of God to his people, and the observance of the law as the way to respond to it.

In the time of Jesus, these were not distinct parties, because both accepted that Temple and Torah were important. However, with the destruction of the Temple by the Romans in AD 70, the 'deuteronomist' rabbis gained the upper hand and formed a Jewish orthodoxy at Jamnia which did not depend on the Temple, thus ensuring the survival of the Jews down the ages. They excluded from the synagogues the Christians whose theology was apocalyptic and therefore in the Temple tradition. Perhaps Jews whose religion was Temple-centred had a tendency to become Christians in those traumatic decades after the Temple's destruction. The Letter to the Hebrews was probably written by such a person. This would have added to the Jews' resolve to root out this kind of religion from their midst.

Nevertheless, both traditions are in the Bible; and we must try to find the key to resolve the dispute and discover the truth behind the differences. As the experience of the Church of living the Gospel down the ages is also the fruit of the Holy Spirit, it is sensible to look for the answer in Tradition.

Theophilus of Antioch wrote in the second century:

> The form of God is ineffable: in glory he is uncontainable, in greatness incomprehensible, in height inconceivable, in might incomparable, in wisdom without peer, in goodness inimitable, in well-being indescribable ... He is without beginning because he is uncreated, and he is unchangeable because he is immortal.

We belong to a totally different order of being: God is our Creator and we are his creatures; he is infinite, and we are extremely finite; he is omniscient, and we do not even know very much about how our own universe works. If Conan Doyle had God's power and Sherlock Holmes had some kind of dependent but real existence, no amount of detective work by the latter would enable him to build up a picture of what Conan Doyle was like, even though they are both men, because Conan Doyle did not belong to Sherlock Holmes's world. Even more so is the case with God who is infinite. As St Thomas Aquinas wrote, 'We can know THAT God is: we cannot know WHAT God is.' What reason tells us is confirmed by the mystics. St John of the Cross wrote, 'One of the greatest favours bestowed on the soul transiently in this life is to see distinctly and to feel so profoundly that it cannot comprehend God at all.' This incomprehension is not agnosticism but a gradual or overwhelming experience of God's greatness.

Nevertheless, God has chosen to reveal himself and to form a covenant relationship, first with the Jews and then with the Christians; and these are particular and privileged expressions of a universal covenant with the whole of creation and of the whole of humankind.

This has produced points of contact between God in his infinite existence and human beings in our earthly existence. The luminous cloud, the *shekinath Yahweh*, both manifested God's presence and hid him at the same time. In the Temple, the veil of the Holy of Holies was such a point of contact. It revealed God's presence for the Jews without denying that God is everywhere; while at the same time, it showed them that God is a hidden God. On the Day of the Atonement, when the High Priest entered through the veil, he filled the sanctuary with the smoke of incense, partly as a gesture of adoration, but also as a protection, so that, if God chose to manifest himself to the High Priest, there was the hope that the smoke would lessen the impact. There was a substitute High Priest standing by in case the real High Priest died; and there was a cord attached to his foot so that, if he died, the priests could pull him out without entering themselves. The High Priest and his attendants approached the Holy of Holies as we would approach a nuclear reactor that could explode at any minute.

Jesus in his human nature was seen as the veil between God and ourselves (Heb. 10.19–20). After Peter had drawn a large catch of fish, he realized that God was in Christ, and he said, 'Depart from me, for I am a sinful man'; and after Jesus had exorcized a man and had sent the devils into a herd of swine, the people asked him to leave their coast. The presence of God was regarded as dangerous. When it is said in the gospels that the veil of the Temple was split from the bottom to the top, this expresses a theological meaning of Christ's death. If the Temple was a shadow of the reality which was Christ, then their killing of Christ was the destruction of the true veil between God and the Jews; and this required an entirely new order of things.

As Moses passed into the cloud, as the High Priest entered the Holy of Holies on the Day of the Atonement, Temple theology accepted the possibility that human beings could pass through the veil into God's presence, from time into Eternity. In the sixth chapter of Isaiah, there is a short 'theophany' or manifestation of God to the prophet in which he is sent as messenger to the people. Ezekiel was a priest in exile: he too experiences a theophany and is sent on a mission. Stories of such 'visions' became common. At least two books of Enoch were well known to Christians in the first centuries. They graphically describe Enoch's transformation by fire in the heavenly Temple, of which the Temple in Jerusalem was a copy, so that he may enter God's presence. Just as the face of Moses was illumined, and the people could not look on him when he came down from the mountain, so those who were taken up into heaven were transformed, and were enabled to see God without them, because the initiative came from God.

This forms the background to this beatitude, 'Blessed are the pure in heart, for they will see God'. They will ascend through the seven heavens and be brought into God's presence. As there have been many 'pure in heart' in the course of history, it does no harm to describe what is said by those who have entered into the joys of contemplation. 'Contemplation' means 'joining the two temples, the earthly and the heavenly'. However, as details about Temple worship became somewhat vague, Christian mystics such as St John of the Cross and poets such as John Donne have preferred to use the imagery from the Bible they understand, like entering the 'Cloud of Unknowing', and the human erotic language of the Song of Songs.

They all agree that the knowledge thus obtained is not like ordinary knowledge, the experience is not like ordinary experience, that they do not see, or hear or are spoken to, as in ordinary life; yet the experience is so immediate, so obviously and profoundly real that such verbs have to be used. God is revealed as incomprehensible, but they are raised above discursive thinking, concepts and words, and come to know and love God at a completely new level. Something of the reality of this is found in the simplest act of faith. However, the pure in heart enjoy a habitual, non-discursive awareness of God's presence in everything and in every situation, and this intensifies as the Spirit deepens their faith and causes their souls to grow.

In our commentary on the Eucharist, we shall find that

communion in Christ's body and blood is the ultimate priestly ritual act of God's people, in which we are taken into the inner sanctuary of heaven before the throne of God the Father, by being united in his Son. In this beatitude, we are reminded that our communion with Christ in the Eucharist will take place, not only by receiving his body and blood but by being pure in heart; because communion requires not only Christ's self-giving but ours as well. While his self-giving is absolutely perfect every time, because he was made perfect by his sufferings, ours is continually being refined and transformed by the Holy Spirit, until we become perfect images of him who is uniting himself to us. By our extraliturgical prayer life we extend our communion into the everyday, while preparing ourselves for our next communion; and the level of our prayer life is the level at which we receive our Lord in holy communion. Finally, the level of our prayer life depends on the extent we put into practice the Beatitudes so as to become pure in our heart.

Notes
1. *Saint Seraphim of Sarov* by Valentine Zander (St Vladimir Press, 1985).

Chapter Nine

Blessed are the peacemakers, for they will be called children of God

Do not think that I have come to bring peace to the earth; I have not come to bring peace, but a sword. For I have come to set a man against his father, and a daughter against her mother, and a daughter-in-law against her mother-in-law; and one's foes will be members of one's own household. (Matt. 10.34–6)

And the peace of God, which surpasses all understanding, will guard your hearts and your minds in Christ Jesus. (Phil. 4.7)

Peace I leave with you; my peace I give to you. I do not give to you as the world gives. (John 14.27)

Beloved, we are God's children now; what we will be has not yet been revealed. What we do know is this: when he is revealed, we will be like him, for we will see him as he is. And all who have this hope in him purify themselves, just as he is pure. (1 John 3.2–3)

Shalom in Hebrew and *irene* in Greek, which we translate as 'peace', is so full of meaning that it can scarcely be translated by one English word. As well as harmony and tranquillity, it contains the idea of perfection, a situation in which nothing is missing: it is synonymous with all that is contained in salvation. This peace is a gift from God in both Old and New Testaments, and involves perfect harmony with him. It was the normal Christian greeting and, as such, it was more than a mere wish: it was a word which received its power from God and actually bestowed what it signified. If it was rejected, the peace returned to the person who gave the greeting (Matt. 10.13). As peace is communion with God, it is given by preaching the Gospel of peace (Eph. 6.15), and reigns in the hearts of Christians who are joined in the peace of the body of Christ (Col. 3.15).

The peace that this world knows is a balance of opposing forces so that people can live in tranquillity. The third temptation of Christ was to make some arrangement between the contrary claims of God and the devil so that the world could live in peace and prosperity. This is a temptation of human beings at their man-made best. Another way of acquiring a kind of peace is by escapism, by pretending that problems do not exist, by burying our heads in the sand, by living in a fantasy world. Hence, there are many examples in the Old Testament of false prophets proclaiming peace when there was no peace: anything for a comfortable life (Jer. 6.16; 8.11; 28.9).

Those of us who are religiously inclined can seek peace in a comfortable religion in which God's claims are reduced to make room for our own. We strive to get rid of those vices that cannot live in harmony with our self-image but leave in place those with which we are comfortable. We can even misuse the sacrament of Confession so that our sins won't accumulate and thus dent our self-image, rather than making a serious attempt at conversion. The Gospel directly attacks all those versions of peace which become an obstacle to acquiring the real thing, the peace which is a gift from God. Hence our Lord's words that he brings the sword rather than peace.

St Paul talks about the peace of the body of Christ, which is a gift from God and a consequence of our faith in Christ. The problem is, quite often, that this peace can degenerate into a mere balancing of egos, easily disturbed when one ego becomes dominant and other egos are aggrieved. Faith is forgotten, or egoistic urges are mistaken for Christian zeal. In this case, the only solution is Christ, and the only peacemaker is someone who can act as an instrument of Christ. There are two kinds of people who can function in this way: there is a figure of authority whom all accept as representing Christ to them and whom they obey; and there is the 'peacemaker' who can draw people into the harmony brought about by the grace of God. The second kind is someone who has ascended through the Beatitudes to become pure in heart. He may use techniques learned as a counsellor, or he may not. What is essential is that his presence will wake up the faith of the members of the community which has become dormant or has been partly smothered by anger, so that they will respond to Christ and come to love each other in Christ once again. If someone tries to act as a 'guru', relying on a mixture of techniques and common sense, then his own ego can become involved, and he fails to tackle the chief problem, which is a lack of openness to Christ. The peace which should be a Christian community's most attractive feature is a gift from Christ who is its invisible member. Hence, we cannot become peacemakers on the cheap.

In Margaret Barker's reconstruction of Temple theology, someone who enters into God's presence in the Holy of Holies is transformed. There is a dramatic picture of Enoch's whole body being turned into a living flame, and he becomes an angel. Isaiah's lips are touched by a coal. Associated with fire is the theme of light. After entering the cloud, the face of Moses is so bright that no one can look upon him. Jesus is transformed in the Transfiguration, though the implication is that the apostles had their eyes opened and saw Christ as he really is. When those who had been transformed by being brought into the divine presence descended once more among men, they became manifestations on earth of this same presence. They are called 'sons of God', though modern translations say 'children of God' in deference to women. This is the background of the present beatitude.[1]

Of course, all this was abhorrent to the Deuteronomists, as it is to classical Protestantism, and for the same reason: it seemed to dilute the utter uniqueness and transcendence of God. To have human beings who are themselves theophanies or manifestations of God seemed to be letting in minor gods through the back door; just as the Protestants believe our saints threaten the unique mediatorship of Christ, and our devotion to them is considered a disguised form of polytheism. This preoccupation may have even influenced the choice of books for the Hebrew scriptural canon. However, it was common currency in the time of Jesus, and its acceptance is implicit and sometimes explicit throughout the New Testament. For Christians, Jesus is the definitive and only-begotten Son of God; but this did not imply that there had not been and were not to be other sons of God. On the contrary, we are all made children of God at baptism. As St John puts it, we are born, not by the will of the flesh, but from God (John 1.12–13). Anyone who loves is born of God and knows God (1 John 4.7). God lives in us and we in him because he has given us his Spirit. What was the privilege of a few has become the common possession of the many. While Christ is Son by nature, we are by adoption; but our function as peacemakers is to manifest Christ. In our modern world this is of paramount importance, because there are few reminders of God's presence in our secular society, and it is through the peacemakers that our neighbour meets Christ.

We have noted that 'contemplation' originally meant uniting the heavenly and earthly temples through prayer. This points to a paradox, one among many, in Christianity: that the more we are centred on God and make room for him in our lives, the more God becomes present on earth. Mother Teresa is world-famous not because she helped the poor in India – there are many people who do that – but because of her holiness. As one Hindu lady who knew her said, when she was near Mother Teresa, she was aware of the presence of God. Padre Pio is still bringing people back to the faith, mainly Italians, long after his death. St Thérèse of Lisieux has had an immense influence on Catholics, and she never left her convent. Charles de Foucauld had the right idea: if we want to make the Gospel relevant to the modern world, we must live it; we must 'cry out the Gospel with our lives'. We must hunger and thirst for God who is reigning in Christ, and the rest will follow. The world needs evidence, and the saints are evidence. Hence, we must concentrate on God; and in concentrating on him discover what he wants us to do, and then we must do it. The rest will follow. There is no authentic alternative.

The pure in heart have ascended the ladder of humility and consider themselves, quite naturally, as in no way above the worst. They have no difficulty in having a fellow-feeling with sinners, even if they have not personally committed the sins they see in others. They can identify themselves with everyone, not just in theory, but in fact. This wisdom is not arrived at by book learning but by 'sufferings and contradictions': they are truly Catholic men and women. We are members of the Catholic Church, but, until our love expands to include all those to whom the Gospel is addressed, we remain sub-Catholic, and our participation in Catholic communion is less than that to which we are entitled as members of the Church. For the pure in heart, their shadow side, that part of their character which leads them to sin, has been integrated into a Catholic whole in which the evil simply disappears. If they love everybody, they are on everybody's side and they can sympathize with all. This makes them admirable peacemakers.

The pure in heart once had minds which were like a market-place, full of good things and bad. Through practising the other beatitudes they have allowed Christ to unify these minds through his Spirit and they concentrate on 'the one thing necessary'. Martha has become like

Mary and they have achieved the peace or harmony which comes from a right relationship with God. They now become the salt of the earth and light of the world, the means by which Christ establishes his peace among the people that surround them. Before we become pure in heart we are more full of ourselves than we are of Christ, even when we are doing Christian things. People naturally say, 'How good is Father So-and-so', 'What wonderful work the sisters are doing' or 'That family is very kind'. When the pure in heart become peacemakers, the goodness of Father So-and-so, the work of the sisters and the kindness of the Christian family make people aware of the goodness, the work and the kindness of God. As Jesus said, 'Let your light shine before men that people may glorify your Father in heaven.' Their love for people make those who witness it aware of the love of God. Their presence among people make others aware of the presence of God. We were all baptized and the presence of the Holy Spirit within us has made us children of God, but the salt can only give its savour to others, and the light is only uncovered, to the extent that we live the Beatitudes.

There are two ways of being all things to all men: one is by hypocrisy, by saying one thing to one person and another thing to the other; and there is the way of the pure in heart. These love each side with an equal love; and this helps the opposing factions to find a solution at a deeper level. Even when one side is wrong, the love which the pure in heart has for him gives him the human space to change; he does not have to be on the defensive and knows that the other is not pressing for some kind of victory for himself, but only for Christ. For Christ, the Mediator between God and the human race, had to be made perfect through suffering (Heb. 2.10). His disciples are not above their Master, and the path to becoming a peacemaker is the same.

All this is in accordance with our Lady's message at Medjugorje. The world needs peace, and it is for us to pray for it; but only the prayer of those who have achieved peace through conversion expressed in prayer and penance will have any value. There must be peace within us before we can become peacemakers, even through prayer. We cannot give what we have not got. However, the fruit of a Christian life fully lived is to be a source of peace, in the Christian sense of the word: a full and perfect communion between God and humankind.

There have always been people who, by living the Beatitudes, have become peacemakers, sometimes to an extraordinary degree. Nelson Mandela is a good example from South Africa. After a very long time in prison he forgave his captors and strove to make peace. When someone exclaimed that he must be a saint, he replied, in the spirit of the Beatitudes, 'A saint is only a sinner who keeps trying'. If any evidence is needed that God's grace can be found outside the Christian fold, there is the case of Mahatma Gandhi in India, who left the world a wonderful legacy on how to fight injustice without ceasing to be a man of peace. Mother Teresa brought people together in harmony who would not normally have met each other, as they strove together to alleviate suffering.

However, we must not make the mistake of thinking that the basis of our role as peacemakers is our selfless service of others, even though this is demanded of us if we wish to live an integral Christian life. This is true despite the fact that Jesus relieved suffering, taught the poor and showed kindness to the outcasts of society. Nor is the basis of our role as peacemakers found in miraculous happenings, even though Jesus worked many miracles and was transformed by light in the Transfiguration, and there have been disciples of his throughout the ages who have gained fame by the miracles they have worked. If Jesus manifested God's presence on earth by service to others and by miracles, the climax of his role as supreme revelation of God was his death on the cross. Humanly speaking, Jesus was not serving others nor working miracles on the cross. He was being obedient unto death to his heavenly Father. It was the extreme extent of his humble and loving obedience that allowed the Father to show us his true nature as Self-giving Love. From Jesus' point of view, the cross was a move Fatherward first and a move manward only second, and it was this that made his death the supreme theophany and the supreme act of peace-making, which it is his disciples' vocation to reflect in their own lives as they take up their crosses and follow him. Moreover, when he did serve others and work miracles, it was his orientation towards his Father in humble obedience that made these activities revelations of the Father. This is the true interpretation of St Paul's opposition of a religion of faith with a religion of works, in his Letter to the Romans. Faith is open and trustful obedience to the Father who is revealed in Jesus so that we can become his instruments, because it is Christ who saves. The source of all value in our religion is Christ himself. It is his free love and presence in us through the Spirit that gives value to our lives as children of God and therefore value to our works. It is radically mistaken to estimate our value by looking at the works themselves. That is why being a peacemaker is dependent on purity of heart, and not on our efficiency as workers in his vineyard.

The Russian tradition has the institution of the *starets* which has become known in the West through Dostoyevsky's novel, *The Brothers Karamazov*. Dostoyevsky uses the fictional character of Starets Zossima to inform us about this tradition. The *startsy* are monks who have become instruments of Christ's peace in the tradition of the Beatitudes. For our purposes, it is useful to quote a few of Father Zossima's words:

> Brothers, do not be afraid of men's sins. Love man even in his sin, for that already bears a semblance of divine love and is the highest love on earth ... At some ideas you stand perplexed, especially at the sight of men's sins, asking yourself whether to combat it by force or by humble love. Always decide: 'I will combat it with humble love.' If you make up your mind about that

once and for all, you may be able to conquer the world. Loving humility is a terrible force, the strongest of all, and there is nothing like it.[2]

If individual peacemakers are few and far between because of the price one has to pay to become one, Christian communities are more frequently available to fulfil that role because the limitations of individual members are complemented by the gifts of the rest, and because a Christian community is greater than the sum of its parts and manifests Christ by its very nature. St Paul, writing about the Christian community, says:

> I therefore, the prisoner in the Lord, beg you to lead a life worthy of the calling to which you have been called, with all humility and gentleness, with patience, bearing with one another in love, making every effort to maintain the unity of the Spirit in the bond of peace. (Eph. 4.1–3)

Where this is done, then the community becomes a source of peace. For St Paul, peace is synonymous with salvation, which is manifested in the communal life of the Church. Salvation is experienced as deep interior peace among those who practise fraternal charity. This is clearly so in the contemporary Church. Religious communities and monastic guest houses are attracting a growing number of people, Catholics, members of other churches, and even non-believers; and what they find there is peace. For most communities, being a source of peace is a by-product of their Christian life and is hardly noticed; but some communities have a positive charism for peacemaking.

Taizé was founded after the Second World War in Burgundy, only six kilometres from the ruins of Cluny, by Roger Schutz. It was the first Protestant monastery in continental Europe; but it rose above the restrictions of its Protestant roots without renouncing them and has become a centre of unity and peace for thousands of people,

Catholics, Protestants and Orthodox, who have flocked there for half a century. We have already mentioned the lay community of Sant' Egidio which began in Rome when a number of students answered the challenge of Vatican II and decided to live the Christian life full-time. Its Saturday night Eucharist became a focal point for young people from all over Rome; and they dedicated themselves to helping the poor. Far from being a flash in the pan, it has striven to deepen its spirituality and widen its scope. It has even brokered peace between warring factions in Africa. L'Arche, founded by Jean Vanier, unites healthy people and those suffering mental illness in single Christian communities which strive to live the Gospel. Then there is the example of the Benedictine community in the United States which is of mixed race and was founded as a witness to Christian values in a state which practised racial segregation. There are many other examples.

We can pray to God that we may become peacekeepers. The prayer attributed to St Francis says it all:

Lord, make me an instrument of your peace.
Where there is hatred, let me sow love;
where there is injury, let me sow pardon;
where there is doubt, let me sow faith;
where there is despair, let me sow hope;
where there is darkness, let me give light;
where there is sadness, let me sow joy.
O Divine Master, grant that I may not so much seek
to be consoled as to console,
to be understood as to understand,
to be loved as to love.
For it is in giving that we receive;
it is in pardoning that we are pardoned;
and it is in dying that we are born to eternal life.

By living the Beatitudes, we become pure gift to God and to our neighbour and thus become instruments of God's peace. We can truly be called 'sons of God' because the

Spirit has formed us into the likeness of God's Son, and
God lives in us. St Bernard describes the peacemaker:

> With how much affection ought we to embrace that
> brother who lives among the brethren without quarrel,
> who is most solicitous that there is nothing in his
> conduct that others will have to bear with and at the
> same time most patiently bears with what is onerous in
> others; who considers the scandals of each to be his own
> ... indeed he is a son of peace, and worthy to be called
> a son of God.[3]

Nothing is perfect in this life; and there is an inevitable
conflict between two kinds of peace: the peace which
appeals to our sinfulness, and is a balance between our
best and as many of our worst inclinations as possible; and
the peace which Christ offers us, which depends on our
complete selflessness as we become one with Christ. We
tend to gravitate naturally to the easier second-best; so
that the conflict is within each of us as well as socially in
the world outside ourselves. The saints have usually had
opponents from their own household who resented their
holiness because it threatened the balance they had found
for themselves. Not being prepared to pay the price
themselves, the saints threatened their peace. We tend to
build up barriers to defend our space, and this threatens
true peace because it sets limits on our self-giving. God
uses 'sufferings and contradictions' to break down these
barriers. This leads us to the next beatitude.

Notes
1. Margaret Baker: *The Gate of Heaven*, SPCK, 1991.
   On Earth As It Is In Heaven, T & T Clark, Edinburgh, 1991.
2. Fyodor Dostoyevsky: *The Brothers Karamazov*, translated by
   David Magarshack, Penguin Books; Book Six, *The Russian
   Monk*.
3. 'A Way to Holiness' from *The Last of the Fathers*, by Basil
   Pennington OCSO, St Bede's Publications, Still River, Mass-
   achusetts, USA.

Chapter Ten

Blessed are those who are persecuted for righteousness' sake, for theirs is the kingdom of heaven

Blessed are you when people revile you and
persecute you and utter all kinds of evil against
you falsely on my account.

Rejoice and be glad, for your reward is great in
heaven, for in the same way they
persecuted the prophets who were before you.

We are now back where we started, although we never really left the first beatitude because all the others explore different degrees and ways of being 'poor in spirit'. This beatitude describes the conditions that Christians experienced in the time of St Matthew up till the peace of Constantine early in the fourth century.

After Constantine had adopted Christianity, and it became respectable and even materially advantageous to be a Christian, this caused a crisis of faith in the Church which had come to accept marginalization, poverty, bad reputation and martyrdom as part of its identity. Christians, as one early writer put it, were at home in all places but citizens of none. They were citizens of no earthly kingdom because they belonged to a heavenly one. Gospel values turn worldly values on their head. How could they be humble when the world honoured them?

How could they be poor when the Empire showered them with riches? How could they give witness to Christ when they were merged into imperial society?

Many people in the early Church embraced celibacy and many widows refrained from marrying a second time 'for the sake of the kingdom of God'. As baptism involved total commitment, there was no idea of professional and amateur Christians: all were Christians full-time. Hence, it was as natural for a lay person to embrace celibacy as for a priest to do so. The single person could dedicate his life to prayer and to the service of the Church. As part of the local church community they gave themselves whole-heartedly to Christian activity and prayer. After the peace of the Church the number of celibates grew. Thousands went into the desert or deep in the countryside, and others formed communities in the towns in search of 'the one thing necessary'. The monastic movement was a spontaneous response to a new situation. Asceticism replaced martyrdom, and poverty became voluntary rather than being forced on Christians by circumstances. People did not become monks and nuns in order to embrace a superior kind of Christianity. They simply wanted to live a Christian life away from the temptations that the new order of things held out to them. The relationship between this monastic movement and the Christians who lived 'in the world' helped the Church not wholly to identify itself with the new 'Christian' empire.

Nowadays, there is a crisis of faith which comes from exactly the opposite cause. We are accustomed to being in the mainstream, a situation that the early Christians feared. Since the fourth century, the Christian religion has been an essential dimension of European society, but now this is no longer the case. Contemporary society is kept together by modern communications and by market forces within the context of the rule of law. There no longer exists a civil society in Europe that is held together by one single religious faith. Christians, Buddhists, Moslems, atheists and agnostics rub shoulders in the same streets. The only universally-accepted truths are those that come from Science; and while there is an almost universal acceptance of human rights, at least in western democratic countries, there is no universal agreement on what these rights are based. It is said that we live in a global village.

There is no logical connection between these facts and the rise of secularism, but there is a psychological one. Public morality is no longer automatically Christian, and those who are content to receive their values from the society in which they live receive too many conflicting indications to give them a firm basis for action. Therefore there is a tendency to seek the easiest solution, and no one can accuse Christianity of being easy. We see Mass attendance going down and we hear the faith belittled on the radio and television as something from a past age. It is lumped together with superstition and magic by people we look up to and admire. How should we evaluate this situation and what form should our evangelization take? Should we rewrite the Christian message, underemphasizing the differences that a belief in the resurrection necessarily involves, and moulding the message around those truths we hold in common with enlightened public opinion? There have been many attempts at this in the last forty years. Should we resist the modern pluralist world and strive to bring back Christendom, in which the civil and the religious were seen as dimensions of the same society? There are Catholics in France who have had that dream, and the Greek and Russian Orthodox are fighting a rearguard action to preserve or restore the historic identity of their nationalities with the national Orthodox Church. Outside Christianity, many in Islam strive to keep or bring into being civil societies which are purely Moslem in faith. In a world of great mobility and constant communications these attempts, Christian, Jewish and Moslem, lead to great injustice and suppression, to wars and ethnic cleansing. Do we adapt our religious faith to suit the values and prejudices of the secular

city, or do we form our own ghettos, waiting the time
when it is feasible to restore some form of Christendom?
I believe meditation on the Beatitudes will show us a third
way: by changing our basic attitudes through conversion
and hence by crying out the Gospel with our lives, we bear
witness to Christ and leave the results in his hands. Once
we are instruments in his hands, nothing else matters.

The present beatitude can be put in other terms:
Blessed are those who accept reversals as gifts of God;
Blessed are those who are content to be different from
decent people who are not Christians; Blessed are those
who are prepared to be a rejected minority for Christ's
sake: theirs is the kingdom of heaven. Christendom, with
its great public influence, is a thing of the past: but Christianity is very much alive. Nowadays, for the first time
since the peace of Constantine, we can really be ourselves
as a Church without worrying about what is politically
possible or publicly acceptable. Since the papacy has been
stripped of its political power, there is no longer the
temptation to dabble in war, and no death penalty has
been carried out in the pope's name for a long time. The
popes have grown in stature. St Paul said, 'When I am
weak, then I am strong'. That is the Christian paradox.
When, like Christ, our only authority is to bear witness to
the truth even if it is rejected, then there is power because
the Spirit is at work. Let us rejoice in our weakness and
serve the modern world by living the Gospel. The rest is
up to God.

When we receive communion, each of us receives, not a
little bit of Christ, but Christ in his fullness. We are therefore united to all who are united to him. One day, when
our souls are big enough, those who are united to Christ
will all be in us as we are in them, and as all of us are in
Christ. Our souls are as deep and wide as our love. As St
Aelred said, what belongs to all belongs to each and what
belongs to each belongs to all. It follows that, to the extent
that we make the life of the Church our own by living
according to the Beatitudes, each of us becomes a mani-

festation of the life of the whole Church; we become truly
Catholic men and women. Some saints, because of the
sheer wealth of charisms that the Lord has given them,
and by the enormous depth and extent of their love even
in this life, bear witness to the truth by showing us something of the fullness of Christian life. I have chosen for the
next two chapters two such saints, one Orthodox and one
Catholic, to illustrate to us how the Beatitudes can be
lived. Even though the Orthodox are separated from us
by schism, they enjoy the full sacramental life. The schism
happened a long time ago and is not St Seraphim's fault.
These two lives prove that the walls of schism do not reach
heaven, whatever the tragic effect they have on earth. St
John Mary Vianney is patron saint of the secular clergy
but could be a model for monks! Important for our
purpose, they show that the Beatitudes are not abstract
principles, but transforming grace.

Chapter Eleven

St Seraphim of Sarov

Prokhor was born on July 19th, probably in 1759, the third child of Isidor and Agatha Moshnin, in the town of Kursk. Isidor was a master builder and was hard-working, of moderate but sufficient means. The family was deeply Christian. At the time of Prokhor's birth, his father was constructing a new church, dedicated to St Sergius, which was the pride of his life; but he was unable to finish it, because he died while Prokhor was still a baby. The business was taken over by Agatha, his wife.

When Prokhor was about four, the family was visiting Isidor's grave when they were caught in a thunderstorm. Agatha scooped up little Prokhor in her arms and ran for shelter. From behind some trees stepped out Grisha the Fool, a ragged beggar whose eccentric life style and odd ravings caused him to be feared by many people. He crops up constantly in St Seraphim's story. He shouted out to Prokhor's mother, 'Put it down, let it be, woman! Once it was yours to hold and tend, but it is yours no longer. Let it be. The flame shall rise as it must, rise to its Creator, One in Three and Three in One. The flaming prayer shall rise, and grace will rain down on the world of sin.' That night, Prokhor fell ill, and he tossed and turned for a week, but gradually recovered.

The first extraordinary happening took place when Prokhor was seven. The church of St Sergius was nearing completion. As a special treat for his birthday, Agatha took him up to the top of the belfry to have a look. Up there, she fell into conversation with the foreman. She suddenly realized that Prokhor was not at her side. She looked wildly round in sudden fear, just in time to see him fall over the edge. She rushed down the steps and out into the open, and found her son standing in the road, examining a pile of rubble. 'I fell; but the Queen of the Skies collected me in her cloak and we floated down. Where is the cloak? It was here, a wonderful blue colour. Why isn't it here?'

When he was ten, Prokhor fell ill, and nobody knew what was wrong. He grew weaker, and the family feared for his life as he gradually faded away. Much of the time he slept. One day he opened his eyes and said to his mother who was hovering round his bed, 'I am going to get well. I dreamt a whole jumble of things, but they gradually sorted themselves out; and the Queen of the Skies came to me and told me not to worry as I was going to get better. Soon she will come and visit me, and I will get better.' He remained sick in bed until, during the annual procession of our Lady, he was blessed with the icon of the Mother of God. From that moment, he began to get better. When his health was restored, he resolved to become an architect and to dedicate his life to building churches all over the world. Meanwhile, he dedicated himself to his studies.

He had an insatiable thirst for knowledge; and it has been suggested that his illness was due to overworking and over-thinking. As he wanted to be an architect, he concentrated especially on mathematics. At the same time, he was very pious, and he loved the sessions with his mother when he used to read to her stories from the Desert Fathers. Since his dream when the 'Queen of the Skies' came to him, his inward life continued to develop. The years rolled on.

One day he went into the cemetery where he met Grisha the Fool. Grisha muttered, as though to himself, 'The mind must humble itself to the heart. It leads the

weak heart astray so that humility is lost'. Prokhor understood that Grisha had something important to say. 'I must
know these things because they are important for my
vocation. I must build churches'. 'No, not churches,
Church!' exclaimed Grisha. Prokhor was puzzled, 'Does
that mean I must build only one church?' but Grisha
moved off, muttering.

Some time later, Prokhor visited his father's grave again
and met Grisha. 'I go abroad; to build our Russian
churches there; to show foreigners what our Church is.'
(From now on, I will quote *Flame in the Snow* because
Grisha's answer is so important to our theme.)

> 'What Russian Church?' asked Grisha in a bitter,
> raucous voice. ... 'Torn, bleeding, a house divided
> against itself ... I've wandered far and wide in the land,
> I've measured, inch by inch, the depths of the chasm ...
> Yes, go abroad,' he hissed, his dark eyes flashing, 'show
> it to the foreigners, show it to the Lutherans, show it to
> the Papists. Let them gloat on the trembling, naked,
> bleeding body of your Mother Church.'
>
> Prokhor, grown pale, moved his lips silently a few
> times. Then, 'Tell me what to do, you must!'
>
> 'Heal the wound; heal it. Make the body of Christ
> whole. Have pity. Don't show off its plight. There was
> enough of that on Calvary.'
>
> 'How can I heal?'
>
> 'Pray.'[1]

This encounter with Grisha made a great impression on
Prokhor and he discussed it much with his friends. Even-
tually, he had a group of five boys who were prepared to
combine with him to solve the problems of the Church.
On his next meeting with Grisha, he told him the news.
He then asked Grisha what his next step should be.

'Curb your pride'; which was not the answer he
expected. Grisha continued (*Flame in the Snow* again):

'Only he may touch the sacred body, who has overcome the devil's sin (men's sins don't count). Pride brought the dark angels tumbling out of heaven. And it is there, at your feet; making a fool of you. Oh, I'm sorry, it's Grisha, the fool.'

(On the next occasion) 'Pride blocks man's way. Let him grind his way through the block with the tool of obedience.'

Grisha then began to mumble on about the monastery of Sarov as though he was talking about something completely different.

Prokhor had now decided that his vocation was to be one of obedience; but how? He was advised to go to Kiev where there was an old hermit, Dosifie, who was known for his spiritual insight. So, on 4 July 1776, he set off with his five companions to walk the two hundred and fifty miles to Kiev. On arrival at the monastic guesthouse, his five friends settled down while he continued seven miles further to meet Dosifie. He told the hermit the story of his whole life and asked him what he had to do next. Dosifie somewhat startled him by telling him to return home and submit to his family. He added that, after two years at home, Prokhor would be ready to join the monastery of Sarov as a novice.

Thus, at the age of nineteen, Prokhor entered the monastery and was never to leave it. The abbot, Pakhomius, was from Kursk and had been a boyhood friend of his father, Isidor. He made him very welcome and put him under the direction of Fr Joseph, the Cellarer. At that time, Prokhor was tall, handsome, with fair hair and blue eyes, an obvious leader who had enjoyed great popularity among his friends.

Fr Joseph gave him many tasks: he worked in the sacristy, in the bakery, in the carpenter's shop, and in other jobs. The main work of the monastery was lumbering, cutting down trees in the forest and placing the logs on top of the ice so that they would be carried downstream when the spring thaw set in.

While they were out in the forest, the monks and novices were allowed to chat; and much of the banter was not what Prokhor expected from people dedicated to the monastic life. Moreover, the chatting interfered with his interior prayer. Ever since his meeting with Dosifie, he had followed the hermit's advice to pray the 'Jesus Prayer' constantly; and he discovered that conversation interrupted him in this practice. He refused to join in the banter, and this earned him the disapproval of his companions. Even one of the boys who had accompanied him to the monastery spoke against him. He found Fr Joseph's advice disconcerting: he was not to worry too much if he could not pray while he was with his fellow monks, but should join in the conversation. He was also feeling terribly homesick for Kursk. The only place where he found comfort was in the church where he would pray for hours. He felt lonely and his prayer became dry and unsatisfying.

Prokhor sought relief in solitude. The abbot gave him permission to build a small hermitage in the forest and he was allowed to stay there as often as his monastic duties allowed. He wanted to practise extra penances by cutting down on food and sleep, but Fr Joseph would not let him. Eventually, he was allowed to leave out the evening meal and to fast on Wednesdays and Fridays.

In 1780, he fell ill with dropsy and was in bed for sometime between one and three years, sometimes unconscious and always in pain. His hair fell out and, when it grew again, it was snow white. Abbot Pakhomius and Fr Joseph nursed him as if they were novices. However, during this time of trial, he grew spiritually. Legend says that he became better after a visit from the Blessed Virgin Mary, accompanied by St Peter and St John. When he was well enough, he was sent back to his family in Kursk to recuperate. Once he recovered, he returned to the monastery and was professed, taking the name Seraphim. In 1786, he was ordained deacon.

Although white-haired, he was twenty-seven years old.

During the six years and ten months he was deacon, he always served when either Abbot Pakhomius or Fr Joseph was celebrating Mass. It was his custom to pass the whole night in prayer in preparation and he often saw angels taking part; sometimes he saw even greater things:

> One Holy Thursday, I celebrated with Fr Pakhomius. Before the Entrance with the Gospel, while the priest in the sanctuary was uttering the words, 'Grant that the holy angels may enter with our entrance to minister with us and to glorify thy goodness', and while I was standing before the Royal Doors, I was suddenly dazzled by a sunbeam, and, as I glanced towards the light, I saw our Lord Jesus Christ in his aspect as Son of Man, appearing in dazzling glory, surrounded by the heavenly host, the seraphim and cherubim! He was walking through the air, coming from the west door towards the middle of the church. He stopped before the sanctuary, raised his arms and blessed the cele-brants and the people. Then, transfigured, he went into his icon by the Royal Door, still surrounded by the angelic escort which continued to illumine the church with its shining light. As for me, who am only dust and ashes, I was given the grace of receiving an individual blessing from the Lord so that my heart overflowed with joy.

Towards the end of his diaconate, famine struck the district. Abbot Pakhomius ordered that all the monastery's store of grain should be at the disposal of the starving population. Many monks became angry at his lack of responsibility as they saw their food disappearing. How could the monastery survive without food? The abbot called a community meeting and asked why the monks wished to live longer than their neighbours. How could they possibly live while their neighbours starved? Many left the meeting full of zeal, but others thought the abbot was being impractical. A little later, Seraphim went and found the grain barn completely full; and neither the monks nor the people starved during that famine.

On 2 September 1793, Seraphim was ordained priest; and in October, Abbot Pakhomius died. He had always resisted Seraphim's requests to take up the solitary life, saying that he needed to deepen his obedience by taking part in the communal exercises; however, on his deathbed, Fr Pakhomius told Seraphim that he was now ready, but that he should be prepared for a bitter fight. He suggested that Fr Isaiah should be made abbot in his place, so that, after he breathed his last, Fr Isaiah became abbot, and Seraphim left the community to become a full-time hermit. It was exactly sixteen years since Seraphim had joined the monastery.

For a time, Seraphim enjoyed the sweetness of silence and solitude; and he wondered what Abbot Pakhomius could have meant when he warned him of the bitter fight ahead. Nothing could be more wonderful than living constantly in the presence of God without distraction; and he had everything he had ever yearned for. He followed the strictest of rules, sharing out his time between prayer, the meditative reading of Scripture, and felling trees. In his heart, he continually prayed, 'Lord Jesus Christ, Son of the living God, have mercy on me, a sinner.' Every weekend, he would go to the monastery, pass Saturday night there, receive communion, and give his counsel to the abbot and to any other monk who wanted it. Grisha heard of a monk who lived in the forest and decided to visit him. He approached and recognized Prokhor, now Seraphim, standing motionless with raised arms, lost in contemplation. He watched for a long time, during which Seraphim never moved. Grisha departed without making himself known. Winter went into Spring, and Spring into Summer.

The blow fell in the summer. The heat was intense and there was much talk of forest fires. One hot night, some-time after midnight, while Seraphim was kneeling in prayer, he smelt smoke and saw flames licking at the window. He rushed out, but there was nothing to be seen. He heard a horrible laugh: the devil had come in person. He dug out a cave for himself with its entrance within his hut. He resumed his nightly vigils and took no further notice of the tricks of the devil. Satan could create illusions of fires or howl like a wild animal or whatever, and Seraphim ignored him. More difficult to ignore was the utter dread, the cold fear, that accompanied these manifestations, the feeling that he was damned and abandoned by God. Later he said, 'He who has chosen the hermit's life must feel himself constantly crucified ... The hermit, tempted by the spirit of darkness, is like dead leaves chased by the winds, like clouds driven by the storm; the demon of the desert bears down on the hermit at about mid-day and sows restless worries in him and distressing desires as well. These temptations can only be overcome by prayer.' Seraphim intensified his prayer. It was only near the end of his life that Seraphim let it be known that he had spent a thousand days and nights kneeling on a granite rock or prostrate in his hut in prayer, fighting off the attacks of the devil. During this time, he barricaded himself off from the outside world. According to written sources, he did this because he found the visits of pious women distracting. According to unwritten legend, he was made to do this by the abbot because certain members of the community had complained that it was unseemly for a monk to receive women into his hermitage when he was living alone. The important thing is that he did it.

This stage in his life was brought to an end by three brigands who were convinced that a hermit of his fame must receive many gifts from the pious faithful. As he was felling trees at the time, he had an axe in his hand. Moreover, he was tall and strong. They demanded that he give them what he had. He dropped the axe and began to pray. They hit him over the head with the shaft and then began to kick and beat him. He was found next day and was carried back to the monastery. For a long time he was in a coma, with a fractured skull, broken ribs and other severe injuries. From that time, he was a hunchback and could only walk with a stick.

When he returned to his beloved hermitage, he took upon himself the ascetic practice of complete silence. This lasted until Abbot Isaiah retired from his post. The community voted Seraphim as abbot, but he refused, saying that his vocation was not that of a superior. Instead, Abbot Isaiah's nephew, Niphont, was elected. He was one of the community who thoroughly disapproved of Seraphim's way of life. He ordered Seraphim back to the monastery.

On his arrival at the monastery, he went to the infirmary to have the sores on his legs attended to. Since his illness as a novice, this had been a recurrent problem. After Mass the next day, he went to the abbot and asked his permission to become a recluse. He then went to his cell and remained there, his only exercise being a solitary walk at midnight. Brother Paul, who was his neighbour, brought him food daily, leaving it outside his door, but many times he had to take it back because it was not touched. Seraphim used to receive communion after the Sunday Mass. That is how he lived for five years; and he refused all visitors, even though many people came to seek his counsel.

Then, one day, a young couple came to seek his blessing. To everybody's astonishment, Seraphim opened the door and blessed them. His time of complete seclusion was over. Visitors streamed to his cell. Very often, he did not answer their questions but continued to pray as though they were not in the room. However, they discovered that, after leaving his cell disappointed, their problems were somehow solved. He had said nothing, but their attitudes had changed and their problems had vanished. Some visitors wanted to become monks in order to dodge recruitment to the army; but he insisted to them that monastic life is not an escape:

A monk is like a cloth that the fuller presses, beats, washes, and rinses to make it white as snow. In bearing humiliations, insults, and afflictions, a monk purifies his soul and becomes shining like silver refined in fire.

It is no good becoming a monk without trying to learn patience. The true mark of a monk is bearing wrongs patiently and meekly. Just as a soldier cannot go to war without bearing arms, no more can a monk begin a life of prayer without arming himself with patience.

External prayer is not enough, and monks who do not unite it with inner prayer are like a puff of smoke. A monk without inner prayer is like a fish out of water.

He did not encourage monks to become hermits, saying that the devil is best resisted in community. In the hermitage, he said, the devil pounces on a monk like a lion devouring its prey. The solitary life is a vocation which can only be lived by those who are called to it.

Seraphim lived in a small, stuffy cell with little windows; and it was only lit by the lamp that burned before the icon of Our Lady of Tenderness. When people came to see him, he would rise and embrace them. If they were superiors of monasteries or priests, he would prostrate before them. His fame spread far and wide. He had become a *starets*, a window for those who came to him through which they could see God's presence. As he became more famous, so a section of the community became more hostile. Like St John Vianney, St Martin de Porres and many other saints, his sanctity showed up their mediocrity and his popularity provoked their jealousy. People came in droves.

He saw into their souls. Like St John Vianney in France and Padre Pio in Italy, he could single out people in a crowd and knew their problem before they opened their mouths. When necessary he cured them or showed them what would happen in the future. Peasants, soldiers, businessmen, court ladies and members of the imperial family came to him; and he was open to all.

There was Michael Manturov who had once had a government job in the Baltic States and had married there. However, his legs became infected, and, as the doctors could do nothing for him, he had to leave his job and return to Russia. Hardly able to walk, he was taken to see Seraphim, who put oil from the lamp before the icon of our Lady on his legs, and gave him holy water to drink. He was cured and, filled with joy, he promised that he would do anything that Seraphim suggested. On another opportunity, Seraphim reminded him of his promise. He told him to sell all he had and to live by faith. With apprehension, but with the full support of his wife, Manturov did as Seraphim had instructed. A little later, he received the offer of a job which paid him enough to keep body and soul together. In time, he too began to have a reputation for holiness.

Then there was the man who wanted to become a monk. Filled with enthusiasm, he came to Seraphim to ask his advice on how to begin. He was astonished and disconcerted when Seraphim told him to go to the monastic guest house where he would find a woman with a young daughter. It was God's will that he should marry the daughter. When he protested, Seraphim told him that he would only be happy if he married the girl. He repeated his instruction that he should go to the guest house and tell the woman and daughter to accompany him to Seraphim's cell. When he arrived at the guest house, a woman and daughter were just alighting from the coach that had brought them. They were surprised that they had been summoned to the cell of the *starets* so soon. When the man arrived with his charges, Seraphim instructed him and the daughter to marry, which they did.

There was Mother Xenia, superior of the convent of Diveyevo, who came to him to complain about her nuns. She was a rigorist who judged her sisters on how they observed the strict rule she had imposed on them. Seraphim told her that we must make our bodies the

friends of our spirits, which long to work through them.
He said that this is not done by copying the external
details of Christ's life, only by dedicating to him our own.
The visible pattern of every single life of God's choosing,
not ours. No two leaves from the same tree are identical,
and neither are two human beings. Then he asked her
why she did not love our Lady's children more. Why did
she insist that they should fear the devil when there is
nothing to be afraid of? Fear of God is felt only by those
who are aware that he is shaping the lives of people
around them. He then told her, 'Work hard, and prepare
to receive child Mary'. Mother Xenia had thought that
Seraphim, who was known for his austerity, would have
been on her side. Somewhat dazed, she departed,
wondering who 'child Mary' could be.

Once, the superior of a neighbouring monastery saw
him gently reproving a man for debauchery, even though
the man had said nothing about it. As the repentant
sinner left in tears, the superior asked Seraphim how he
was able to read the human heart. Seraphim replied:

> No, my joy, the human heart is open to God alone, and
> when one approaches it, one finds oneself on the brink
> of an abyss. ... You see, this man came, like all the
> others, like you for instance, seeing in me a servant of
> God, which in fact I am, a wretched and unworthy
> servant, but a servant all the same. To everyone – as to
> yourself – I give only what God tells me to give. I
> believe the first word that comes to me to be inspired by
> the Holy Spirit, and when I start speaking, I honestly
> do not know what lies in the heart of the man who is
> questioning me. I only know that God directs my words
> for his benefit. But were I to give an answer out of my
> own judgement without having previously brought it to
> God, I would make a mistake. As iron committing itself
> to the smith, I give myself to God completely and make
> no move without his will. I do not say anything save
> what God urges me to say.

St Seraphim saw people all day and every day, except for Wednesdays and Fridays which he spent in solitude in the forest. He became spiritual father to the nuns of Diveyevo; and many of the nuns came to him to complain about Mother Xenia, their superior. Some of them owed their vocation to Seraphim. He used to call the superior the 'holy scourge'. Mother Xenia continued to be a problem.

One day, a mother with her thirteen-year-old daughter came to see him. He informed them that it was our Lady's wish that the daughter should become a nun, and he sent her to Diveyevo. Her humility, her observance and her spirit of prayer were such that even Mother Xenia had nothing but praise for her. She was called 'little Mary'. Using his authority as spiritual father, he separated the young nuns from the rest and formed a new community, using the money that Michael Manturov had given him. Perhaps remembering Fr Joseph's treatment of him as a young monk, he did not allow them to follow the strict rule and made sure that they had adequate rest and food. This community became the apple of his eye.

As he got older, he began to spend more and more time in the forest. One day our Lady visited him, accompanied by St Peter and St John. The Blessed Virgin touched the ground with her staff, and water began to bubble from the spot. 'This water will be the occasion for many miracles,' she said. Seraphim moved his hermitage near to that spot. He began to stay there during the week, returning to the monastery on Sundays and feastdays. Wild animals came to keep him company; and, one day, a visiting nun was alarmed to see him stroking a bear. He made no effort to separate himself from the people, though it was said that there was a greater chance of seeing him to talk to if one was accompanied by children. He loved children. One child remarked, 'He is not really an old man. Inside he is a child like us.'

He remarked one day to a visitor, 'There are two kinds of people: those like you, friend of God, who try and shape their own lives; and those who let the Lord do it for them.'

His trials increased, mostly from fellow clerics and members of his community. He saw his work in his beloved community of nuns partly undone because the monastic choirmaster considered that Seraphim's ways of doing things were old-fashioned and decided to take over the direction of them himself. Monks said that his relationship with the nuns was unhealthy; and they accused him of stealing monastic property to give to them. The offerings left him by visitors normally found their way to these sisters and there were monks who said that the alms he received belonged by right to his own community. His friend, Michael Manturov, left for another part of Russia and his other friends began to die off. All this contributed to his growth in sanctity.

Seraphim died in the monastery just after Christmas in 1833. The day before, he was heard singing Easter hymns in his cell: 'We have seen Christ's resurrection. Let us worship the Lord Jesus!' 'O Passover, great and most holy, O Christ, O Wisdom, Word and Power of God, grant that we may more perfectly partake of you in the day that knows no end, in your kingdom'. At the time of his death, a monk and a novice were walking through the streets of his native Kursk. A light lit up the sky. The monk said to the novice, 'It is the soul of Father Seraphim flying to heaven.'

Notes

All quotations and material are from *Saint Seraphim of Sarov* by Valentine Zander, St Vladimir's Press, 1985; and *Flame in the Snow* by Iulia de Beausobre, Templegate, 1996.

Chapter Twelve

St John Mary Vianney

Jean-Marie Vianney was born in 1786, the fourth of six children in the Vianney household, in the village of Dardilly, not far from Lyons, in France. They were poor peasants and, although he taught himself to read at the age of eight, his own enthusiasm was not enough to compensate for the general lack of cultural background when he began to study.

In his early years, the most important political event was the French Revolution in which true religion was banished from the land. The revolutionaries sent a priest to Dardilly who had sworn an oath to the new government. His sermons were nothing more than justification for the revolution, backed by scriptural quotations and, little by little, the people stayed away. Priests loyal to the Church visited the village secretly and celebrated Mass in kitchens and barns, using tables or boxes for an altar. Everyone knew that, if caught by the police, the priest would go to the guillotine and the people to the galleys. These clandestine Masses, where Christ's sacrifice was joined to that of the people so harmoniously, were the first Masses that John-Mary knew. They taught him that the Mass is worth sacrificing everything for, and that a priest is someone who is ready to die to bring the sacraments to the people.

Everyone worked in a peasant household and, from a very early age, John was sent out to mind the sheep. He was skilful with his hands, and he modelled a small statue of our Lady out of clay and made a shrine with flowers in the fields where he worked. He prayed the rosary there and this attracted other children, many of whom belonged to families that had allowed their religion to lapse since the revolution. He enjoyed teaching them what he had learned from his family or heard during the forbidden Masses. He organized little processions in the fields, carrying his statue behind a cross made from sticks. Older children sometimes scoffed, but he managed to win many over. Thus, at seven and eight years of age, his vocation was already becoming clear. Watching sheep ensured that he spent long periods alone, and he developed a love of solitude which grew with his holiness. In later years, it became a longing for the contemplative life, a longing that was never to be satisfied. 'God seems always to grant me what I ask for others', he one day said ruefully, 'but he never gives me what I want for myself.' At the age of eleven, he asked God to allow him to live a solitary life so that he could dedicate his whole attention to him, but it was not to be.

In 1800, God was allowed to return to France, and the bishops did their best to fill the empty parishes as far as they could with the reduced number of priests. There came to the neighbouring parish of Écully a very saintly and apostolic priest called Fr Bailey who was to have a decisive influence on John's life. John's own desire to study for the priesthood was frustrated by the economic circumstances of his family, because he was needed at the farm. However, he read the Gospels, *The Imitation of Christ*, and the *Lives of the Fathers*, and awaited his opportunity. At nineteen years of age, he presented himself to Fr Bailey, physically toughened by farm work but practically illiterate. Fr Bailey was not impressed at first; but, when he heard John talk of God, he knew that he was in the presence of a very special person.

John moved to his aunt's house in Écully and studied in Fr Bailey's house, where the priest tried to make up for the absence of even a primary education. All seemed set when, in 1809, when John was twenty-three, he was called up into Napoleon's army. He intended to comply at first but, when the soldiers were ready to move up to the front, he slipped into church to say a prayer. He was so long there that, when he came out, the army had already left. He reported to barracks where he received a dressing-down and was then given his papers and told to catch up. He never did. He fell in with a deserter in the hamlet of Les Noes where the mayor was a secret opponent of the imperial regime. The official placed him in the house of his cousin, Claudine Fayot. For two months, while the heat was on, he hid in the barn, but afterwards went to live in the house, taking the name Jerome Vincent and pretending to be a distant cousin of the Fayot family. Two years later, his position was regularized with the government and he was allowed to return to Écully to continue his studies. He was sent to the minor seminary where he was the least able of all the students, who used to laugh at him. However, he became a friend of another student who had difficulties, Marcellin Champagnat, who was to become the founder of the Marists, and is another canonized saint. They continued to be friends in the major seminary in Lyons.

After six months in the seminary, they sent John away because he could not manage the studies. He thought of becoming a lay brother but Fr Bailey would not hear of it. 'Your vocation is that of parish priest', he informed John. Fr Bailey went to see the vicar-general of the diocese who was administrator in the absence of the Archbishop. He impressed on the vicar-general the great piety of John Vianney. 'Good', said the vicar-general, 'The grace of God will do the rest'. John was ordained priest, after receiving very little training, in Grenoble, on 13 August 1815. The only stipulation was that he would not be allowed to hear confessions because he had failed Moral Theology hopelessly.

John Vianney spent three years as curate of Fr Bailey in

Écully. The people already knew him, and he had relations in the village. First the poor, and then the rest made
use of his services. His sermons were no better than
anyone else's, but people flocked to hear them. He wasn't
allowed to hear confessions, but everybody sought his
advice. Within the presbytery, Fr Bailey and he followed
a monastic regime, eating the grossest food, fasting and
praying much, and practising penances so extreme that
they earned the rebuke of the vicar-general. Such was his
success and the clear will of the people that he received
his faculties to hear confessions; and the first confession
he heard was that of his parish priest.

At the end of three years, Fr Bailey died. John Vianney
had been the crowning fruit of his ministry, and his work
was done. On his deathbed, he asked John to hide his
instruments of penance. 'If people find them after my
death, they will believe that I have done something by
way of expiation for my sins; and they will leave me in
purgatory till the end of the world.' A few days later, John
Mary Vianney started off on foot to his first and only
parish in an obscure village called Ars. Because of the
fewness of vocations, there were many large and important parishes without a priest; but it was probably thought
that he would do no harm in Ars.

He walked trundling an old cart in which was his furniture. He was accompanied by an old woman who was to
be his housekeeper. As he neared the village, he met a
small boy. He put his hand on his shoulder and said, 'You
show me the way to Ars, and I will show you the way to
God'. The vicar-general had said to him, 'Ars is a village
where there is very little love of God. You must put some
into it.' This was what he was about to do.

The small village had a church with a wooden spire.
The presbytery was a single-storey building on one side of
the church, and the cemetery was on the other. He
entered the presbytery and found that the countess who
lived in the big house had furnished it very well. He sent
the furniture back with thanks, telling her that he would

use only his own furniture. Soon the mattress on his bed went to a sick person, and his pillow and bolster followed. The fact that he slept on planks was hidden by the coverlet. He began as he meant to continue. He wore a hair shirt. Each morning he ate a crust, while at midday and in the evening he ate one or two cold cooked potatoes which were cooked for the whole week. Occasionally he would accept an egg or a corn cake. In Lent he would go without food for three days at a time. He spent meal times visiting parishioners. He would find them at the table and would chat knowledgeably without sitting down. In that way he got to know them all. They were surprised at his knowledge of farming and came to realize that he was one of themselves. He spent hours preparing his sermons and spent long periods in prayer.

The faith had very much weakened during the years of revolution. There was much drinking to excess; people danced whenever there was the opportunity, and the men swore all the time. When he arrived, most of the women went to church, but very few of the men, who used to use Sundays for looking after their plots of land. Most of us priests would probably be content to say, 'That is how the people are', and accept the situation; but not St John Vianney.

His first sermons are remembered to this day. 'Does God exist?' he bellowed; 'If he does exist, we must honour him as he wishes or be asked why.' 'Jesus wept over Jerusalem ... I weep over you. How can I help weeping, my brethren? Hell exists. I did not invent it. God has told us and you pay no heed!' They could not be offended because he was really weeping in the pulpit. 'You blaspheme the Name of God. You spend your evenings in the cabarets. You give yourselves over to the sinful pleasures of dancing. You steal from your neighbour's field. You do a world of things which are offences against God. Do you think that God does not see you? Do you think that your priest will allow you to be cast into hell to burn there for ever?' This theme of God's judgement seems hard, and

unfortunately old-fashioned. However, he did not stop
there. He went on to treat of the alternative of union with
Christ and of the final end of Christian life in heaven. 'We
shall see God! We shall see him! Have you ever thought of
that? We shall see him, my brethren!' His eyes were
shining, and his whole being seemed transformed.
Through these words and others like them, he recalled a
village from laxity to fervour. More than anything, it
wasn't just the words by themselves. He believed them
and conveyed that belief to his hearers. For St John
Vianney, laxity is a sign of the devil's presence, and the
devil can only be cast out by prayer and fasting; so John
prayed and fasted.

The people saw a contrast between the priest who
visited them at mealtimes and who talked so knowledgeably on rearing sheep and sowing crops, and this prophet
of God who cried over sin and went into ecstasy over the
goodness of God. He seemed to be able to smell out sin
and turn up when it was being committed. One man who
hid from him was asked, 'Do you think you can hide from
God?'

He declared war on the dances in the village. On one
occasion, he stopped a violinist who was going to play at a
dance and asked him how much they were paying him.
He gave the man double the amount and sent him away.
He preached, 'When you go to a dance, you leave your
guardian angel outside the door and a devil takes his
place; so that there are as many devils on the dance floor
as there are dancers.' Little by little, dancing became less
and less common until it disappeared altogether. The fact
was that they liked him and were rather proud of him.
Not many villages are looked after by a saint!

The men began to trickle back to church; and John
formed the Confraternity of the Blessed Sacrament for
them and the Confraternity of the Holy Rosary for the
women. He started catechism classes for the children, and
had the gift of being able to speak to them in their own
language. Each Sunday there was Mass in the morning

and Vespers with a sermon in the evening. During his nights, instead of sleeping, he would pray for the conversion of his parish. It worked! His whole attitude and the clue to his attitude to everything else are summed up in his words, 'How beautiful, how great, to know, love and serve God. Everything else is a waste of time.'

We may wonder what St John Vianney had against dancing, which seems a rather harmless sort of occupation. Perhaps he believed it to be conducive to sexual fantasy; and we would have to know whether that was in fact the case before we could judge him. Another possibility is that he saw it as an escape into an unreal world. After all, modern people escape from God by living in unreal worlds. Remember that he believed that knowing, loving and serving God is the only worthwhile occupation.

As what made life worth living before he came began to disappear, because more and more people were living a new life centred round the church, so the opposition began to get desperate. One day, his front door was covered with filth. On one occasion a small group of parishioners asked him to leave the parish. For a time, a woman used to come under his window at night and scream accusations that he was the father of her child. However, progress was inexorable. The conversion of the village took about ten years. By that time, people were coming to Ars, first from the area around and then from far and wide. Within the village, there were growing signs of real sanctity. There was old Chaffangeon who remained hours before the tabernacle. When asked by St John Vianney what he said to God, he replied, 'Oh, he just looks at me and I look at him'.

Six years after his arrival at Ars, Fr John spent the money left him by his father to build a house looking on to the square as a refuge for young girls without any means of support. He sent two women, Catherine Lasagne and Benoite Lardet, to a convent to receive basic training and then, with Jeanne-Marie Chanay to do the heavy work, opened the hostel with fifteen girls. The numbers grew to sixty. Any girl in need was accepted, of whatever age. He picked some off the streets, others were recommended, and some turned up of their own accord. At this time, he was not well-known, so the amount of money at his disposal was very small. He begged from the parishioners, and he went further afield to neighbouring towns and to the city of Lyons to ask for money. He called it 'La Providence' and it was well named because it had no guaranteed income.

It was in connection with 'La Providence' that he first began to do miracles. Some time in 1828, his store of grain had almost completely run out. Just a few handfuls were left and he had no money to buy any more. Fr John stormed heaven with his prayers but to no avail. Then he remembered that St Francis Regis, a Jesuit, had miraculously provided food for the poor. Fr John went into the store and buried a relic of St Francis in the handful of grain. He then told everybody to pray. A few hours later, he told Jeanne-Marie Chanay to go to the store and bring what was there. She had difficulty opening the door because the room was filled up to the ceiling. Fr John confessed to the children that he had doubted. On at least three other occasions food or drink were miraculously multiplied.

The infestation of the devil began earlier in 1824. Fr John was very ill and close to death. He obviously suffered from depression, and there entered his head the idea that he was damned. However, he resisted it – which is not normal in depression – and resolutely refused to despair. After his recovery, the attacks became external. Rats gnawed at the curtains of his bed, dogs howled, music played, crowbars struck, people who left no footsteps in the snow knocked at his front door and then at his bedroom door; and, most of all, there was the deadly fear. The devil hammered nails into the floor, used an axe on the walls, shook his bed, and once, dragged him around the room by his ankles. Fr John called the devil '*le grappin*'. I have listed only some of the manifestations, which lasted thirty years.

Many of the diabolic manifestations were witnessed by outsiders. Once, towards the end of his life, Fr John was leading the people in the Forty Hours' Devotion when they smelt smoke. His bed was on fire. The room was a tinderbox, being made of dry wood. The fire climbed the walls, but stopped at the statue of St Philomena. No one could understand why the fire stopped in a straight line under the statue on all four walls and did not burn right up and destroy the roof. He only slept a couple of hours a night; but, quite often, the devil would not allow him to sleep at all and he would leave his bedroom pale with sunken eyes. He spent the time he could not sleep in prayer. He rejoiced when he suffered his worst attacks because, the next day, he would land a 'big fish'; his phrase for absolving a particularly big sinner.

For the saints, the separation between heaven and earth is very thin. After all, it is the Christian vocation to bear witness to the things of heaven in the secular world. Fr John's greatest friends were God, Christ, our Lady and the saints. He filled the church with statues to remind the people that when they pray as Church they approach God together with Christ whose blood cries out louder than that of Abel, together with millions of angels and the spirits of the saints who have been made perfect (Heb. 12.23). In St Gregory the Great's words about the Mass, 'Heaven and earth become one'. As John Vianney progressed in holiness, so the separation became even thinner. Madame Durie, a woman who collected money for the saint's good works, had a large sum to give him on the morning of 8 May 1840. Catherine Lasagne allowed her to go directly to the saint's room. As she ascended the stairs, she heard a conversation. A woman's voice said, 'What do you ask?' The curé's voice replied, 'Most loving Mother, I ask for the conversion of sinners, the consolation of the afflicted, the relief of the sick, and most particularly for someone who suffers much and is now praying for death if she cannot be cured.' This was Madam Durie herself. 'She will be cured, but not yet,' replied the voice.

'What was my surprise', said Madame Durie, 'to see a woman of middle height, standing by the fireplace, clad in dazzling white'. It was the Virgin. There were many other occasions.

He had a special devotion to St Philomena and he built a shrine for her in the church. When people began to come from all over France, he believed that they were visiting her shrine. In fact, they were attracted by him. By 1850, there were twenty thousand people a year visiting Ars. He adapted to this situation by adopting a rigorous timetable. He went to bed at ten at night, but was up at one o'clock when he went into the church. He prayed on his knees a short time, opened the door of the church, and went into the confessional where he heard the confessions of women until six o'clock. He then celebrated Mass and prayed privately. After this, he was at the disposal of the faithful to give advice or to bless images and rosaries and so on. At eight, he went to 'La Providence' to drink half a glass of milk. At half-past eight, he was back in the sacristy, hearing the confessions of the men. At ten o'clock he said the Little Hours before continuing with confessions until eleven. Then he went to 'La Providence' to teach catechism for an hour when he ate lunch, standing up and talking to people who came to him. At half-past twelve he visited the sick; following this with Vespers and Compline and more confessions until eight in the evening. After this, he led rosary and evening prayers from the pulpit. Afterwards, he saw people who needed special direction, said Matins and Lauds, and tried to get to bed by ten, but very often couldn't until later. This was his timetable for thirty years.

The sheer numbers ensured that confessions were brief and to the point. If someone hid any sin, Fr John reminded him; if someone needed to go to confession but sought protection in the anonymity of the crowd, Fr John picked him out. One highway robber came to be cured of an illness, but Fr John took no notice of him. Guessing why, the thief asked to go to confession but edited his confession. Fr John asked if those were all his sins; and the robber said he had confessed all. Fr John then began to tell him what he had left out. He was converted on the spot. One day, Fr John grasped an old man, a free-thinker, by the shoulder. 'When did you last go to confession?' asked the priest. 'Thirty years ago,' replied the man. 'On such and such a day, in such and such a church,' said Fr John. The man, extremely surprised, made his confession. A society woman who was living in sin came to Ars out of curiosity. She was stopped at the door of the church by Fr John who then told her what she had done. She asked to go to confession; but Fr John replied that he saw two demons in her soul, that of impurity and that of pride and that, while she had that disposition, he could not absolve her. However, she would soon be forced against her will to leave Paris, would go to her house in the country and would there receive the grace of conversion.

The penances he gave were aimed at people's weaknesses, which he was able to diagnose without knowing the person before him. A man who did not wish his friends to know that he had been converted was told to take part in a public procession. A person who had been proud of his atheism was told to say his penance publicly before the altar. Someone who was unwilling to renounce his sin was told by Fr John, 'You are damned'; and the saint burst into tears. There were many conversions.

He had no patience for those who went to him to confession because they later wanted to boast that they had been to Fr John Vianney. 'Go to confession to someone else!' he would say. To those who just liked the sound of their own voice, he would say, 'Don't waste my time!' This meant that not everybody left him satisfied; and many were ready to complain loudly of their dissatisfaction. They provided evidence for those priests who could not stomach Fr John's popularity.

As he began to become famous, many priests in the region experienced dwindling congregations as people journeyed to Ars for Mass or confession. Here was this priest who took no pride in his appearance, who wore his cassock until it fell off him, who had a ridiculous three-cornered hat of antique design, who ate potatoes, and hadn't even passed his Moral Theology examination, who let the side down by appearing as the peasant he was, a man of little intelligence and fewer social graces, this disgrace to the priesthood was stealing their people. Some parish priests forbade their people to go to confession to Fr John because he didn't know any theology and could harm them with his ignorance. Many accused him of being merely slovenly or said that his poverty was an affectation. The priests sent a letter to the bishop, asking him to remove Fr John because he was a danger to souls. A copy of the letter was sent round to all the parishes for the priests to sign. Fr John received one, signed it, and sent it to the archbishop.

Fr John did not mind this scorn and had no doubt as to his unworthiness. 'Yes, people do come and consult me; but you know me better than they do. You know that I am neither worthy nor capable.' Once, when he was dangerously ill, he asked his friends to pray for his cure, because he had nothing to show to God for the graces he had received.

The bishop had no doubt as to Fr John's holiness. After a time for consideration, he gave his answer, 'I wish you had a little of the folly that you laugh at. It would do you no harm.' To a priest who doubted Fr John's knowledge he said, 'I do not know if he is well taught, but he is inspired'. After some years, the opposition died down.

In 1845, so many people were coming to Ars that Fr John asked for a curate; and the bishop sent him Fr Raymond. He was a priest who believed in himself. Fr John was old and past it; and the parish needed new blood. He took over Fr John's bedroom, giving him the loft to sleep in. He signed himself, 'Fr Raymond, parish priest'. He set about making changes and he would publicly correct Fr John and would criticize his sermons in his own. A deputation from the village forced Fr Raymond to give Fr John his room back, and he was given a room in the village. Catherine Lasagne declared that God had sent Fr Raymond to the parish 'to try his servant's patience', and the village agreed. Fr Raymond was in an unassailable position because his greatest defender was Fr John himself. 'If Fr Raymond goes, I go,' he said. However, after eight years, Fr Raymond realized how unpopular he was and asked the bishop for a transfer. Fr John said to the new priest who came, 'You do not rebuke me. I am no longer as good as I was.'

The greatest sacrifice that Fr John had to endure was when the Bishop of Bailey took away from him 'La Providence'. The bishop decided that, to ensure its continuance, it should be handed over to sisters. The lay people who had looked after it were dispersed, and the sisters closed the refuge but kept the school attached to it. Like St Seraphim with his convent, St John Vianney had the one human comfort he had retained taken away from him. This was all the more difficult because, like St Seraphim, he probably considered this to be the work that was most particularly his own. On our way to heaven, God often finds it necessary to take away from us even our best projects, those which are, in our minds, our most worthwhile activities because, in the end, nothing, not even our apostolate, can stand in the way of seeking God alone.

God disciplines even the highest ideals and inclination of his saints. Remember Fr John's prayer for solitude when he was eleven years old. An undercurrent in his spiritual life was his wish to be a contemplative religious: he longed for the cloister. In 1827, he asked to be removed. The bishop offered him another parish, but he wanted to become either a Carthusian or a Cistercian. The bishop did not want to release him so he stayed in Ars. In 1840, he could bear it no longer so he decided to escape. One dark night, he set off; but then he asked himself if he was seeking his own will or God's. He returned to the parish.

In 1843, he became ill. Everybody prayed round the clock. Baskets of medals and holy pictures arrived at his bedside for him to bless. He lost consciousness. In a waking moment, he heard the doctor discussing him. The doctor said, 'Thirty minutes, no more.' Later, he told his friends that he prayed, 'My God, must I appear before you empty handed?' He prayed, opened his eyes and began to speak. He was advised to go away for some rest and he decided to use the opportunity to seek a religious house where he could live. He went to Dardilly to his family. A few days later, all the pilgrims at Ars came to Dardilly and asked him to hear their confessions. It was no good.

In 1848, he thought of becoming a Capuchin but it didn't come to anything. Then, his seminary friend, St Marcellin Champagnat, opened a house of perpetual silence for contemplatives. In 1853, Fr John decided to join that house. He confided in Catherine Lasagne that he was going away, officially for a few days, but that he was really going to join the Marist house. Word got round the village so that, when he set out, he found all the villagers blocking his path. He returned to the church, put on his surplice, and began to hear confessions. 'I acted like a child,' he said afterwards.

John had become a living prayer. Many people quote the words, 'Work is prayer', but they rarely realize how costly is the journey to the point where that is true. For most of us, we must have an adequate time for prayer so that we can give God to people in our work. For ordinary folk like us, there is always a conflict between our work and the time we dedicate to prayer, which those on the way to sanctity feel more acutely than most. It is only when absolutely everything is offered to God, even our highest urges, in fact and not just in intention, that prayer and work really become one. To quote 'Work is Prayer' before that, as a reason to give up the conflict, is extremely damaging. Only towards the end of his life, did St John Mary Vianney reach that point of calm.

St John Mary Vianney died in early August in 1859 and was canonized in 1925. Like St Seraphim in Russia, he is known for the charisms he exercised, for his austerity of life and his sufferings and for his great compassion for all with whom he came in contact. His bedroom has been preserved exactly as it was when he died, even to the ashes in the grate. Like St Seraphim, he is a letter, written by the Holy Spirit, who has continued to inspire people down to the present day. It is a terrible tragedy that, if they had ever met, they would have been unable to receive communion at the same altar and would probably have believed of each other things that were not true.

Chapter Thirteen

Two Saints on the Same Road to Joy

Now the Lord is the Spirit, and where the Spirit of the Lord is, there is freedom. And all of us, with unveiled faces, seeing the glory of the Lord as though reflected in a mirror, are being transformed into the same image from one degree of glory to another; for this comes from the Lord, the Spirit. (2 Cor. 3.17–18)

In the lives of St Seraphim and St John Mary Vianney, albeit they were from different spiritual traditions, were separated by schism and were of different nationalities, we see the same image emerging. They suffered similar trials and received similar blessings, and there was the same passionate love of God, the same compassion towards sinners and those in need; most of all, they mirrored the same Christ and saw themselves as children of the same mother, Mary.

In this process of sanctification, they lived the Beatitudes over and over again so that each beatitude became a constant factor in the spirituality of each. Yet their spiritual odysseys were not simply movements in a circle: there was a real progress as – to quote Grisha in his words to St Seraphim – they bored through the block of pride with the tool of obedience. Both felt acutely the conflicting claims of work and human relationships on the one side, and the need to pray on the other; yet, towards the end of their lives, the problem was transcended and their very lives became both work and prayer at the same time. St Seraphim threw open the door of his cell and St John Mary was no longer troubled by the temptation to leave his post to become a monk. They had become peacemakers through and through; complete children of God.

We wrote earlier that the Beatitudes can be read in two ways: when read normally, they give us a programme by which we become transformed through death to resurrection and, when read chiastically, they give us the fundamental characteristics of authentic Christian spirituality at any stage along the road to joy. Just to remind you, a 'chiastic' reading is when we twin the first and last beatitude, the second with the second from last, and so on which leaves one beatitude on its own that has special importance. Here we shall kill two birds with one stone, by referring the Beatitudes to the lives of these two saints. We will show that the Beatitudes are not abstract truths but are actually lived in the real world. We will learn a little more about each beatitude as they are brought into another relationship with the others, by using a chiastic reading.

Blessed are the poor in spirit, for theirs is the kingdom of heaven.
Blessed are those who are persecuted for righteousness' sake,
For theirs is the kingdom of heaven.

We have already connected these two beatitudes because, even when the Beatitudes are read straight, these are related through what scholars call *inclusio*, where the last beatitude explains the first and indicates that all the beatitudes are about being poor in spirit. However, in a chiastic reading, **Blessed are the meek, for they will inherit the earth**, must be included in the first. This indicates that poverty in spirit is shown in three ways: firstly, by our being stripped of or being indifferent to everything in our search for God; secondly, by suffering reverses from those who treat us badly or who speak badly of us; and, thirdly, by our meek acceptance of God's will as shown in the concrete circumstances of our lives. This third factor is taken for granted as operative in the other two. I think we will agree that we all suffer deprivation and are badly treated by others sometimes in our lives, whatever our vocation. These beatitudes are telling us that, if accepted meekly, they are a necessary part of our progress towards God, part of our dying to self that we suffer in union with Christ crucified.

St Seraphim and St John Mary Vianney both reduced their needs to a minimum. St John gave away his mattress, bolster and pillow, sleeping on the bare boards or on the ground with a block of wood as a pillow. He returned the furniture that had been given by the lady of the manor and kept his food down to the minimum. His clothes were always clean but they were of the very poorest and he wore them until they could be worn no longer. Any money he received went to his works, normally to the hostel 'La Providence'. St Seraphim did not have a pillow or mattress to give away. He slept on the ground or on a sack of stones. When in the monastery he would eat the monastery food sometimes, and sometimes not. Like St John, he was careless of his appearance and wore a white smock, summer and winter. His cell in the monastery contained only a table and a log to sit on.

At the same time, neither thought that everybody should follow his example. St John gave away his things so that others would be comfortable. If he had thought that this was against their spiritual good he would not have done it. He was constantly preoccupied with the comfort of his girls in 'La Providence', though he was against luxury. St Seraphim, too, was ever solicitous that his nuns should have enough to eat and enough sleep. He said that holiness does not consist of copying the external details of other people's lives, even those of Christ. What is important is that we offer our lives to God. The external details are for God to decide for each person, part of his or her vocation. He knew that most people do not have the vocation to be hermits, so that he was not eager that they should follow his example. Sanctity consists in saying 'yes' to God in whatever vocation he gives us. Making comparisons or trying to be like someone else is not helpful and is an irrelevant exercise.

Their extreme poverty, carelessness about their appearance and the proprieties of acceptable behaviour and, from a worldly perspective, their eccentricities in general earned them the enmity of many of their brethren in the cloth, and this was compounded by jealousy over their success with the people. This brought about attacks from those who should normally have supported them. This led neither of them to defend himself or feel hostility towards his attackers. On the contrary, they were friendly towards them and, when it was said that they were unworthy, they agreed with their critics. Neither wasted time by criticizing his brethren.

Even when Fr Raymond came to Ars and tried to 'modernize' the parish, publicly criticizing Fr John and re-arranging his life, he earned not hostility but gratitude from the saint. Even when the bishop took away from Fr John his beloved 'La Providence' and the sisters closed his refuge for girls and only kept the school, Fr John accepted all with great meekness and had good relations with the sisters and the bishop. Even when the choirmaster of the monastery took over the running of the convent that St Seraphim had founded, without any authorization from anyone, although it must have caused great pain to the saint who had every reason to complain, he allowed it to happen. Both were models of meekness as God stripped them of their most beloved possessions.

Both of them suffered attacks from the devil of a very similar kind and both took refuge in prayer. As the Curé d'Ars would say, the devil attacks us through our laxity. There is a story from the Desert Fathers about a monk who was always preaching against the devil. One day, the devil appeared to him. 'What do you have against me?'

asked the devil. The monk replied, 'Look about you. See how much fornication, adultery, thieving, dishonesty, violence and murder there are.' The devil answered, 'I have little part in it. Do you think that people need me to commit fornication, adultery or murder? Most of the time, people do my work for themselves.' Most sins arise from our own pride, passions or apathy. The devil has a problem when people humble their pride, control their passions and fight against any apathy they may feel. That is why many of the saints have experienced external attacks. However, they know that his only weapon is illusion, because he has no real power. St Antony the Great was attacked many times by demons. He was asked if he was frightened and replied, 'What is there to be frightened about? In the Gospel, they couldn't even control a herd of pigs! What can they do against someone who is baptized and has the Holy Spirit within him?' Nevertheless illusion can be very seductive or very frightening.

Reading about the hard lives that St Seraphim and St John Mary Vianney embraced with such enthusiasm, it is difficult to understand how happiness was possible. What kind of joy can flourish where people deprive themselves of sleep, comfort and good food? How can people be happy when their neighbours, their brothers and sisters in Christ, criticize them so hurtfully and when they are stripped of the results of the good things they do?

At the very highest level, they were transformed by the joy of Easter, the joy of the risen Christ, the joy of the kingdom fulfilled. St Seraphim's usual greeting was, 'Christ is risen!' His face would light up with a smile that did not begin on his face but deep within: it took over his face and embraced the person he was greeting. During his last days on earth, he was heard singing Easter hymns in his cell. When the Curé d'Ars preached about heaven, his face lit up with joy. He wasn't preaching from books: he was living the truth of it. He would become breathless with awe at the very thought of Christ present in the Eucharist. Then there was the joy of bringing people to Christ.

The only joy that St Seraphim and St John Mary Vianney had was the joy that came from their faith. It was greater than any other possible joy in this life, a foretaste of the joy in heaven. Both were content because they knew that this was only possible for them because they had reduced their earthly needs to the minimum. That was their vocation: to show us where true joy is to be found, to demonstrate the truth of these beatitudes.

Blessed are those who mourn, for they will be comforted.
Blessed are the peacemakers, for they will be called children of God.

Both these beatitudes are about salvation. The first is about those who realize their own weakness, their own unholiness and the grip that sin has on their lives, even their powerlessness in the things of God; and hence that they have an enormous need for God. This does not come from comparing themselves with other people, but from having some intimation of the holiness of God. Hence, it is the result of conversion, rather than its cause, and it is liable to increase the nearer we get to God. The second is about the pure in heart who have become so transformed by Christ's Spirit that they become sources of salvation for others. A chiastic reading of the Beatitudes suggests that there is a direct link between our own realization of our utter dependence on God and our capacity to mediate God to others.

It is true that Christ's Spirit will only transform us to the extent that we ask him to, and that we shall only ask him to the extent that we know we need him, and we shall only know we need him to the extent that we are humble, and we shall only be humble to the extent that we realize how unholy we are, and our unholiness is the cause of our mourning.

In the life of Fr Damian in his leper colony, his relationship with the lepers was transformed when he was able to say, 'We lepers'. As we come closer to God, our ever deeper understanding of our own sinfulness allows us an ever closer identification with all sinners. We are therefore well equipped to become God's contact with them by increasing sorrow for our own sin and by fellow-feeling for all sinners. We will be motivated to fulfil the role of peacemaker by our ever-growing gratitude to God for rescuing us through Christ. Peacemakers do not see any opposition between saints and sinners and know that the only opposition that counts is that between God and the human race, an opposition that was overthrown by Christ on the cross. A peacemaker has no difficulty saying to anybody, 'We sinners'. The difference between him and those yet to be converted is his knowledge of the need for God, and the fact that he has opened himself up to God's Spirit who is at work within him, transforming him into the image of the Son. This process has not yet begun in the unrepentant sinner. However, the peacemaker needs God as much as the active sinner does because, if God were to leave him, his sanctity would vanish as though it had never been: its source is Christ's presence within our repentance, not in the repentance itself.

One of the tasks of a peacemaker is correcting the people who come to him. He may have to point out where they are going wrong and estimate the way they must put things right, and he may even have to rebuke them. We have seen that this is part of St John Mary's vocation as parish priest and also the role of St Seraphim as spiritual guide. How is this possible without falling into the Pharisee's error? How could the two saints avoid becoming self-righteous, dividing the world into 'us' and 'them'? The only way is habitually to practise compunction, and frequently to dwell on one's own sins, failings and limitations. If a Christian cannot say in all honesty, 'we sinners' when he meets a sinner, he is departing from the Gospel. He can honestly say this even when, like St Seraphim and St John Vianney, his life has been transformed by grace. This transformation is God's work, not his own, and he knows that his cooperation with God has been imperfect and that he still has a long way to go.

Perhaps one of the reasons the world is not heeding us or appreciating the Christian message is because we do not appreciate it sufficiently ourselves. Perhaps we cannot convince people of their need for God because we go through the motions without really needing him ourselves. Perhaps one reason why people have lost the sense of sin is that we who teach them have lost it ourselves. Perhaps our pastoral work is less effective than it could be because we put too much emphasis on our own activity, so that our egoism blocks the flow of grace to others.

Indeed, there are versions of Christianity where the need for God is only theoretical, and where the whole emphasis is on things we can do for ourselves, like bringing about social justice, teaching, helping widows and orphans. The secret of successful evangelization is looked for in the right programme or the right argument. When we ask for God's help, we are only asking that our efforts should bear fruit because, in our own minds, all depends on us. This is not a New Testament perspective. Planning, using our own skills, our engagement in social work and fighting against injustice are all necessary; but the emphasis in the New Testament is on God's presence and his power, and we are only instruments of Christ's Spirit. The main target is the elimination of that barrier between God and the human race which we call sin, and sin's true nature can only be appreciated by someone for whom God is very real. When it is seen simply as our personal failings or as social evil, this is very superficial. We begin to mourn when we realize that it blocks our union with God who is the source and goal of our humanity. The human race has always been conscious of human failings and social evil, but it took Christ to convince us of sin. The Christian message is about God doing something through Christ that we cannot do for ourselves and, if we wish to collaborate, it can only be as instruments in God's hands.

While our need for God is only theory and the nitty-gritty of religion is our own activity, we shall never convert anybody because, in fact, our activity is not all that interesting and can be duplicated by non-Christians. To be converted to God people need to meet God, however obscurely. For this to happen we need peace-makers who have been transformed by the Beatitudes so that they both know their radical dependence on God and have become instruments by which God manifests himself to others. Word and sacrament belong to the Church. Peacemakers are the means by which Christ makes human contact with all types of people, both within the Church and outside it. Mother Teresa and Padre Pio are shining examples in our own day. St Seraphim and St John Mary Vianney illuminated the nineteenth century and continue to inspire people a long time after their death. We may not all be canonized but we can all become peacemakers to the extent that we live the Beatitudes. We begin on the road when we realize our dependence on God and know in the deepest recesses of our hearts that we need his mercy.

When they thought of themselves, the two saints hadn't a good word to say for themselves. St John couldn't agree more with his fellow priests when they criticized him to the bishop. If he had been involved with making compar-isons with others, he could easily have said that his methods were more successful than theirs. However, comparing their successes with other people is not what saints do. They are only conscious of the weak response they have made to the grace they have received from God because how we respond to God's grace is, for them, the only thing that matters. For them, God is more real than anything else. In the light of his response to God, St Seraphim called himself 'dust and ashes'. They saw their ministry as God working through them, so they were in no way tempted to believe that their success was an achievement of their own. St John was afraid that he would come to God with empty hands when he arrived at the judgement seat. Knowing their need for God, they both sought him out in earnest prayer, when other people would be sleeping. All this illustrates that their ministries as children of God, as peacemakers, were matched in both cases by an acute sense of their own need for God.

Fr Raymond in the St John Vianney story, and the choirmaster in St Seraphim's story, are examples of people like us who see ourselves in comparison with others. Both saw the saints as out of date in their methods and themselves as the people who were going to put things right. They were nineteenth-century 'progressives' setting about correcting two 'conservatives'. Both had attitudes that were completely irrelevant, because the only progress that matters is progress in holiness. They would have been just as irrelevant if they had been two 'conservatives' trying to restrain two 'progressives'. What mattered to the people and to the Church's apostolate was that these two saints were holy.

If we want to make an impression on the modern world, we must first increase and deepen our relationship with God. To this there is no alternative. Only when we need God with all our soul, will the world come to see through us that God is worth needing. A holy sorrow for our own sin combined with gratitude to God for filling our emptiness, as described in chapter 4 above, is an essential basis for our apostolate as peacemakers. Planning our apostolate takes second place to this.

Blessed are those who hunger and thirst for righteousness, for they will be filled.
Blessed are the pure in heart, for they will see God.

Once again there is a complete parallel between these two beatitudes. When someone is so taken up with the will of God that there is nothing else which motivates his actions, then he is pure in heart. As St John Mary Vianney said, 'Everything else, apart from learning and doing God's will, is a waste of time.' This is why he cut down food and drink to a minimum, why he slept only two hours a night. Any more time concerned with his own needs would be taking time away from the 'one thing necessary', which was to see what God wanted doing and then doing it. Even while he was eating, which he did standing, he would be answering people's questions; and he often spent the time allotted to sleep in prayer. St Seraphim cut down on food and drink and sleep, dedicating his time to prayer. He would stand outside his hut in the forest, not moving for hours, lost in prayer. When he was ordered to leave his beloved hermitage, he did so without complaint. When it was time for him to dedicate himself to people, he did so with a smile. Both saints not only hungered and thirsted to do God's will: it became something that replaced eating and drinking as their constant concern.

Saints are not born ready-made: they are formed by the Holy Spirit, and there is always a certain resistance to this formation. With St John Vianney there was a certain stubbornness, and with St Seraphim there was a certain interior pride. Thus, while their motives were as pure as they could make them from the beginning, they were nevertheless mixed with other less worthy motives, which had to be eradicated before they could reach the full measure of sanctity that God planned for them in this life. I want to take you to one of St Seraphim's moments of crisis and I hope he will forgive me if I try to analyse his thinking at the time. I have said that St Seraphim left his hermitage without a word of complaint when he received his abbot's command. However, the truth is that he did so at his abbot's second call. When the monk was sent to call him back the first time, there was no response. He could have been out in the forest or lost in contemplation. I like to imagine him sitting inside, paralysed by uncertainty.

On the one hand, there were the wonderful encounters with God, the peace and the graces he had received in the hermitage. Each stone, each tree reminded him of them and allowed him to taste them again in his memory. On the other hand, there were the uncharitable criticisms and carpings of his fellow monks, and the weak vacillations of the abbot. He would be returning to a community that did not understand him and in which some heartily disliked him. Would he receive the same favours from God back in the monastery? By granting him these graces in the hermitage, had not God showed him where he wanted him to be? All his instincts, all his feelings were against his leaving the hermitage. Set against that was one small fact which, in the circumstances, appeared cold, abstract, even unreal, not worth noticing: his obligation of obedience meant that it was God's will that he should obey the abbot.

This conclusion appears very obvious to those who are not involved with such a problem, and it is easy for those who believe that emotional satisfaction is the ultimate criterion by which we discern God's will. For Seraphim it was also easy in a way because, deep down, he knew the answer, but he had to burrow through his wishes, his interests and the memories of graces received. As he came out of the struggle with himself he knew that, if he ignored that small, cold voice urging obedience, things would be different in the hermitage. He would be seeking God's favours rather than God in himself and for himself. His time in the hermitage was over, even if his abbot lacked insight, and the saint was never to enjoy true peace of mind again. Faith always urges us to move forward into the unknown, which can be at times very uninviting. The next day, therefore, when the monk called again, he picked up his satchel and walked to the monastery without a word.

We have already seen how St John Vianney had a constant desire to become a contemplative religious, and he made several abortive attempts to become one. It was only when he gave up this desire in favour of God's will that he was able to advance to the highest union with God.

Purity in heart is not something that, once arrived at,

becomes a permanent characteristic. It has to be fought for in every circumstance. Only those will continue to fight who hunger and thirst for God's will.

Blessed are the merciful, for they will receive mercy

In a chiastic reading this beatitude that remains without a pair has special significance. The Beatitudes are written in the context of the proclamation of the kingdom of heaven, which is the definitive manifestation of God's steadfast love. Steadfast love is the motivation behind the kingdom; it fills every element in it; it is its chief characteristic; and it is that which permeates every person who enters it. Thus, no one who refuses to be merciful wants to enter the kingdom. It is by steadfast love that the practice of all the other beatitudes shows itself outwardly.

This is in line with the chiastic reading of the 'Our Father', where 'Thy will be done on earth as it is in heaven' is paralleled with, 'Forgive us our trespasses as we forgive those who trespass against us'. In the time of the kingdom, God's heavenly will is expressed in forgiveness; hence, all people in the kingdom will forgive and make the kingdom visible to the world by doing so.

Christianity is essentially a community religion. Just as God is the Communion of Father, Son and Holy Spirit, so salvation is the communion of human persons together with the angels in the body of Christ. Through Christ by the activity of the Spirit we are brought together into the presence of the Father, and thus share in the trinitarian life of God. Our unity with each other in Christ is destined to reflect the unity of the three divine Persons. Conversion is the process by which we move from the isolation which is sin into the communion with God and with each other for which God has destined us. This salvation is experienced by us subjectively as the peace which the world cannot give, and is manifested in the world as steadfast love which cannot be explained apart from our

Christianity. 'The glory that you have given me I have given them, so that they may be one, as we are one, I in them and you in me, that they may become completely one, so that the world may know that you have sent me and have loved them even as you have loved me.' (John 17.22–3). As Fr C. Spicq OP, the noted Scripture scholar, used to say, commenting on this passage, the Church becomes visible to the world by charity and is rendered invisible, merely one institution among others, when charity is not practised.

If 'Blessed are the merciful' refers to the change of our relationship with others that Christian conversion brings about, and if this is what makes Christian community possible, then its central place among the Beatitudes is obvious. Christian community is the context in which all the other beatitudes are practised. The 'glory' of God is the mutual love of the Divine Persons which was revealed to us in Christ and is reflected in the mutual love of Christians. Of course, the Church pre-exists the love of individual Christians, having been founded by Christ and kept in being by his pre-existent love for us which is manifested in word and sacraments. Hence, the liturgy of the Church is the source of all its activity, even living according to the Beatitudes, and is the goal to which all its activity is directed as our poor efforts are integrated into Christ's sacrifice in the Eucharist. Nevertheless, our witness of the Christian Mystery to the world, what makes it visible to the world so that it can be accepted or rejected, is the quality of our steadfast love. Moreover, the other beatitudes will only be fully appreciated, even by Christians themselves, if their effects are experienced in the Christian community.

Our two saints are shining examples of people who led others to an appreciation of a full Christian life by the practice of steadfast love. After Seraphim had recovered from the attack by thieves he spent much time trying to get them released from prison, and he showed so much love to them that they were converted. When his vocation allowed him to see people, his love for them was palpable; and this formed the context in which he gave them advice, admonished them or looked after their ills and problems. St John Mary Vianney dedicated his whole life to those who came to him, not sparing himself. When he had to admonish or threaten, he did so not as an enemy but as a friend, often with tears. He rejected no one except the insincere and then only to receive them back at the first opportunity. Both saints forgave their enemies. Indeed, they were not even offended by them because they were too aware of their own faults.

The difference between Seraphim and John Vianney on the one hand, and Rasputin on the other, is that although Rasputin did many miracles, as did Seraphim and John Vianney, he did not manifest God in his steadfast love; and, therefore, he was not a child of God in the apocalyptic meaning taken over in the New Testament. Whether he works miracles or not, the true Christian manifests God's presence by the quality of his love.

I have seen two guidelines for the level of our Christian life; and the two are complementary: the level of my Christian life is the quality of my prayer; and the level of my Christian life is the quality of my love. Each guideline reflects the other. The steadfast love of a Christian for the neighbour is rooted in a relationship with God which depends on prayer. Only when this is so can we truly love people who are hostile or indifferent to us, or when they offend us or harm those whom we love. If we forget this, then our love for others will become selective and will cease to be steadfast. It will differ in no way from the love shown by people who are not Christians, a love which may very well be moved by grace and which will secure them a place among the sheep rather than the goats at the Last Judgement, but a love that lacks value as a witness to the world of the presence of Christ in their midst. Our imperfect love for others is constantly being integrated into the love of Christ for his Father and for the world when we celebrate the Eucharist. To the degree that we truly communicate with Christ, our love will gradually be transformed until it takes on the universal quality of Christ's own love and we shall be able to obey his single commandment to love one another as he has loved us. The more we do this, the more Christ is visible among human beings, the more we become salt of the earth and light of the world.

Chapter Fourteen

The Royal Road to Joy

If for this life only we have hoped in Christ, we are of all people most to be pitied.

(1 Cor. 15.19)

No amount of mourning will lead to happiness. The Beatitudes are not self-authenticating. The happiness that Jesus promised is not brought about by the attitude or activity recommended by Jesus, any more than God's promises were achieved by Abraham where he left Ur and began wandering in the desert. Like Abraham, the Christian sets out on the way of the Beatitudes with only Christ's promise, waiting for God to act in his own good time. By themselves the Beatitudes make depressing reading. No one in his right mind can believe that by being deprived of possessions and reputation, by constantly dwelling on past sins, by being meek when suffering hurt or insult and by purposely increasing hunger and thirst for God's will, people can actually achieve happiness; and, of course, they can't in themselves. The happiness that Jesus promises comes from God. Even being pure in heart only holds out the hope of contemplation in this life and the beatific vision in the life to come.

Thus, the Beatitudes stand only if Jesus was telling the truth, and fall if he wasn't. St Paul says that our faith is in vain if Christ is not risen. We can continue this line of thinking: if Christ is not risen, then the Beatitudes are eight pieces of bad advice. Because their lives don't make sense without Christ, those who follow the Beatitudes are, in the words of Charles de Foucauld, 'crying out the Gospel with their lives'.

This is in complete contrast to a certain kind of liberal Catholicism which tries to present to the world a form of Catholic faith that is as self-authenticating as possible. The motive is admirable but the method mistaken. It is an attempt to present the faith to people brought up in a secular environment by showing that Christianity is the true home of their highest ideals; but there is a great danger of distorting the Gospel by changing its emphasis from God's action to our own, and by limiting its scope in concentrating only on those values that are appreciated by the secular world. In fact, the whole exercise can have an effect which is the exact opposite to the one intended.

The impression is too often given that the Gospel is chiefly about fostering, improving, and sometimes correcting human relationships. Jesus showed his love for people by curing the sick, feeding the hungry, identifying himself with sinners and outcasts and, finally, by dying for us on the cross. As his disciples we must also sacrifice ourselves for our neighbour who is our way to God. Often the values and causes which are advocated to receive Christian support are identical to those found in the enlightened secular world. A generation ago many found them in Marxism; nowadays they are found in the centre left: the primary purposes of the sacraments are to encourage and give us the strength to live altruistically and to celebrate the relationship we have with one another in God's sight. Some Protestant liberals go even further. They say that the Christian doctrines which proclaim Jesus as Son of God and that he has risen from the dead are only symbolic and poetic ways of underlining the importance of the values contained in Christ's teaching and example. Both versions, the Catholic and the Protestant ones, put the emphasis on Christian values, and they concentrate on those values that

Christians and secular non-Christians have in common. This is their central religious concern and the main content of their preaching. The difference is that the Protestant version simply denies what is basic and central to the New Testament and can therefore be called post-Christian, while the Catholic version accepts the full Gospel but puts more emphasis on these values. They say that Jesus died for us and therefore we should be prepared to die for one another, but they do not dwell very much on how Christ's death is to our advantage beyond reciting a few formulas from the penny catechism without explanation as they hurry to the real content of their message. The impression is given that the real relevance of the resurrection is that we will go to heaven if we live by the values they preach. Therefore they get excited about feminism or social reform which concerns them now, but not about the resurrection. Perhaps this is because it is tied up with death, a subject that modern secular man prefers to isolate from everyday experience, and because too much emphasis on the resurrection smacks of a 'pie in the sky' religion which is unconcerned with modern problems in this world.

I am sure that the original motive was a good one: to appeal to modern secular people who have little sense of God. It was perhaps hoped that if people agreed with the Church about values, and if they joined together with the Church to solve modern problems, they would accept the resurrection and the divinity of Christ as part of the package and hence remain in the Church or become Christians. After all, there is a logical connection between the religious teaching that God loves each and every person and the secular teaching that each person has inalienable human rights. For this kind of liberal, the Christian minister is primarily a problem solver. The strategy hasn't worked. The consequence of this mistaken emphasis is that people hear a lot of Christian words without ever really hearing the Gospel. The sad thing is that this approach was adopted with starry-eyed enthusiasm after Vatican II by many Catholics who were unaware that it had been the rage among Protestant liberals in the 1920s and 30s and had been found wanting.

The problem is that feminism, left-wing values, helping the poor, and transforming unjust social structures, are ideals which stand or fall by themselves. Unlike the Beatitudes, they do not need Christ's presence to authenticate them, nor his death and resurrection to bring them about. In themselves there is no necessary connection between prayer and sacraments on the one hand and these values and activities on the other. Still less is there a connection between these values and the religious or monastic life. I cannot help but suspect that there is a direct relationship between the crisis in vocations and the liberal Catholic agenda. Non-Christians applaud and agree with these objectives and admire the people who sacrifice themselves by practising them, but they don't become Christians because they see no reason to connect them with Christ. This type of liberal Catholicism is actually contributing to the secularization of a world that it is trying to evangelize.

If Jesus had confined his activities to healing the sick, being friendly to sinners and outcasts and feeding the hungry, he might have been considered eccentric but he would not have been crucified. In the first centuries, the Christians in Rome organized an admirable system of social welfare which was unique in the ancient world. If that had been their message there would have been no martyrs in Rome. The Gospels make it quite clear and beyond dispute that the central content of Jesus' teaching was that God was entering human history in a new and decisive way through him, and that the Christian message is Jesus Christ who died and rose from the dead. Jesus was killed because of who he claimed to be, and the Roman martyrs died because of their belief in him.

Jesus Christ will not mean anything to the modern, secular world unless the people listening receive the grace of conversion, and that is something that not we, but God, gives them. However, it is our job to present him to them.

He is the main substance of our preaching, and to share in his life is the whole of our spirituality. There is no reason to believe that modern people are in a better position to understand the Gospel than were the Jews or Romans of the first century who were challenged by Jesus and the early Church to be converted. In some ways people today are in a worse position, because they have been inoculated against the Christian message and it no longer surprises them.

Assisi was a prosperous Italian town in the Middle Ages. If Francis had paid attention to the opinions, hopes, ideals and values of his fellow townsmen and had tried to build his message around them, there would have been no St Francis of Assisi. He made his impact because he decided to live the Gospel to the full. He was content to be marginalized and lived outside the town in a way that denied everything the place stood for, but he struck a chord and began to have followers. If we take the Gospel to its logical conclusion and strive to live by the Beatitudes, not caring about the impression we make, then the modern world may begin to listen to us because we will be different and will have something original to say. The only way people will come to share our values and our faith is if we live up to them ourselves. The basis of our apostolate is to live in an authentic Christian community which is being formed by living the Beatitudes. Jesus is present in that community, and our communal life witnesses to his presence by reflecting his love. From there we can talk to the world. Some will meet Christ through our words or by sharing in our community's life. They will then be able to say with the Samaritans who were attracted to Jesus by the words of the woman at the well, 'It is no longer because of what you said that we believe, for we have heard for ourselves, and we know that this truly is the Saviour of the world.' (John 4.42) Our function is to witness to Christ because without him we can do nothing.

We need a truly contemporary theology; but all

theology of lasting worth has sprung out of a context where people were living the Gospel. Patristic theology came from a Church vibrant with the love of God. Scholastic theology was made acceptable and of lasting worth by the friars. If we want a contemporary theology that we can put beside Patristic and Scholastic theologies without blushing, we need first to live the Gospel and this means living the Beatitudes. Mere theory-spinning is a waste of time. I had hoped that Liberation Theology would have provided us with such a theology because it sprang out of the Christian experience of the Latin American poor. It began well, and some of the contributions by the poor had a freshness which reminded me of the New Testament and the Acts of the Martyrs. The problem was with some of the professional theologians who did the liberal thing of squeezing the Gospel message into a set of ideas taken from the secular world. This never works. However, the idea of a theology that comes out of the experience of the poor who use the See-Judge-Act method to bring out the relevance of the Gospel to their own lives, a theology that is impregnated with their spirituality, would be a very powerful contribution. Liberation theologians often said very good things. Perhaps there will one day arise a second generation of liberation theologians who will continue the project without making the mistakes of the first. For me, poor people in Peru have helped me as much as any book to understand the Beatitudes. There is a wealth of Christian insight to be tapped among the humble poor.

The Beatitudes are a summary of the marriage contract between Christ and his Church. They are a road to joy, a joy we can experience in this life. There is the joy of forgiveness and self-acceptance, there is the joy of Christian community, and these culminate in the joy of contemplation. All three joys come from our relationship with Christ and are a foretaste of the joy of all joys which is our share in the joy of Christ returning to his Father in heaven which we call the beatific vision.

This road to joy does not imply nor promise that we shall be on a continuous 'high' as we move towards God. These joys come when God wishes to give them to us, in the measure in which he gives them to us. Usually it will be quiet and underlying other experiences, something easily smothered by our cares and by our egoism which is always ready to pop up at any moment; but God is not far away. We shall also experience times of dryness when the only thing that keeps us going is fidelity without any appearance of reward. These times too are privileged ones, when God reminds us of our weakness and tests our resolve. The important thing about joy is that we will never get it if we look for it. If we turn from hungering and thirsting for God to hungering and thirsting for joy we will reach a dead end. Moreover, until the last day our joy will always be mingled with suffering, if not for ourselves, then out of compassion for others.

The motive for living the Beatitudes is to be filled with God; and the more we are filled with God, the more he is present in our contemporary world. It is the active presence of God, Father, Son and Holy Spirit, in the Church that is the true source of the Church's power in evangelization. Now that most of the advantages of living in Christendom no longer exist, we have been given the tremendous grace of having to rely on essentials. Only when this essential goal is clearly understood, and the necessary means of achieving it are being used, can we make common cause with others outside the Church to make this world a better place. We remember the community of Sant' Egidio that has striven to make peace between countries and has negotiated the release of hostages. It has succeeded when others have failed, not because its members are white and members of the European Union, but because those who speak to them know that their sole motive is their Christian faith, which is not an ideology but a spirituality.

Finally, the Beatitudes are the way of the saints. The monastic fathers followed them step by step because the

Bible was, in the beginning practically their only book, and because of the monastic practice of daily using the Scriptures as a means of prayer. As time went on, Catholic spirituality has taken many forms. Particular saints made particular beatitudes their own according to the grace given them by the Spirit. St Francis of Assisi emphasized poverty, St Vincent de Paul and St John Bosco emphasized the works of mercy, St Thérèse de Lisieux made meekness her special virtue, while St Teresa and St John of the Cross sought purity of heart and contemplation. Nevertheless, their progress in sanctity involved all the other steps and became permanent ingredients of their holiness. There are many schools of spirituality to choose from, but they are all different ways of practising the Beatitudes, the only way to joy.

Poverty in spirit leads to thanksgiving and the Church expresses its thanksgiving in the Eucharist. Here we see that grace welds together the conversion process in all Christians into one single self-offering, that of Christ to his Father. To the Eucharist we now turn.

Part II
The Mass

Chapter Fifteen

Introducing the Mass

Before we begin, let us place the Eucharist within its 'kingdom' context. One characteristic of the New Testament is the paradox that local and seemingly unimportant events can have cosmic importance because God is taking part. Thus, Jesus who was born in humble circumstances and lived most of his life in obscurity, who taught and worked miracles for a relatively short time and was then executed by crucifixion, this Jesus is the Word by which the whole cosmos is created and held in being. Moreover, his disciples understood his healing the sick and casting out devils to be skirmishes in a cosmic war between good and evil, in which he eventually won by suffering an ignominious death. Finally, this obscure Jewish rabbi, by resurrection and ascension, became the first to be born from the dead, and he initiated a new level of existence for himself and for the whole human race. He now 'fills all things' and 'holds all things in unity' while he awaits the moment when the whole universe will be transformed into his body, because he will be 'all in all'. All this is absolutely incredible until we come to know Jesus; and then it all falls into place. The events of Christ's life and death are important, not because they impressed observers, but because God dwelt and continues to dwell bodily in him.

The risen and ascended Christ is now the means by which the Father holds all things in existence. He is present in every electron and atom, every planet, every shooting star, and in every event and person in human history. He is working in this universe to encourage what is good, making even evil contribute to what is good by integrating it into his master plan of salvation. He guides the whole universe towards the Parousia which is its ultimate transformation into that new level of creation which was inaugurated by his resurrection. He does this in submission to his Father. His union with the Father is a living memorial of what he did on the cross, a constant plea for us and for the whole universe to share in his resurrected life. In the Letter to the Hebrews, his presence before the Father for our sakes is symbolized by the sprinkling of his blood in the heavenly Holy of Holies. According to the Jewish understanding of sacrifice that the author is using here, the blood is quite literally the life of the victim, which has been released by death and placed at God's disposal to be his instrument for cleansing, consecration or blessing. Thus the life of Jesus has been released by death to be at his Father's disposal and he has become the source of our salvation. (Heb. 9.11–14, 24; 10.19; 12.24). Since the ascension, everything that the Father does in creation and redemption is done 'through Jesus Christ, our Lord', and he is the means by which all approach the Father.

However, although Christ is in heaven, and his presence to the world is in the divine act by which everything is kept in being, he is not in the world as we are, participating in its history. He is present, but not as part of the world, not as an actor in the hustle and bustle of our everyday life. If he wants to participate in our life within history and so prepare the world for the Parousia, he needs a body which belongs to this world but lives by his own resurrected life: this body is the Church. The Church is the historical presence on earth of the Cosmic Christ until he comes again in the Parousia.

Hence the Cosmic Christ is not an afterthought, or just one item in Christian theology: his universal reign is the context in which the Church exists. 'He is the image of the invisible God, the firstborn of all creation; for in him all things in heaven and on earth were created ... all things have been created through him and for him. He himself is before all things, and in him all things hold together. He is the head of the body, the Church; he is the beginning, the first-born from the dead.' (Col. 1.15–20) Just as Christ anticipated 'the new heaven and the new earth' in his own human nature by resurrection, so the Eucharist anticipates the transformation of the whole universe into Christ by consecration, and we anticipate our place in that transformed universe by communion. The same Spirit that brought about the resurrection brings about the Eucharist. While, at an eternal level, Christ is present in all people and all events, the Spirit forms his body at our historical level in the Eucharist by uniting the priest, ministers, choir and people to Christ so that he lives in them and they in him. While Christ is in all books in so far as they are kept in existence, by the Spirit's action the Scriptures become the word of God. While Christ is in all bread and wine because they exist through him, by the Spirit's power they become Christ's body and blood. In the Church which we entered by baptism we feed on the Eucharist so that Christ may be alive on earth as well as in heaven. When Archbishop Cranmer said that Christ could not be present in the Eucharist because he is present in heaven, it was for want of a lively faith in the Cosmic Christ.

As the events of Christ's life were of minor or no importance to the casual observer, but were of cosmic importance for human history and for the whole universe because God was acting in them, so it is true of the Mass because, every time we celebrate it, the whole Mystery of our salvation is present for us to share: we are in the awesome presence of Christ. Christ exercises his priestly office throughout the whole of the liturgy, 'not only in the presence of his minister ... but especially under the Eucharistic species. He is present in His word, since it is

He Himself who speaks when the holy Scriptures are read in the church. He is present, finally, when the Church prays and sings.' (*Const. on the Sacred Liturgy*.) This being the case, the whole liturgy has a sacramental quality, a divine dimension, as well as an ordinary human one. Thus I believe it appropriate to apply to the whole celebration distinctions which scholastic theology applies to the sacraments abstracted from their liturgical context.

When the sacraments are being studied in abstract, these distinctions are normally given their Latin names *sacramentum tantum*, *res et sacramentum* and *res sacramenti*. '*Sacramentum tantum*' means the sacramental sign; '*res et sacramentum*' means that which the sign effectively signifies; and '*res sacramenti*' is the purpose of the sacrament. Hence, for St Thomas Aquinas, the sacramental sign of the Eucharist is bread and wine with the words of consecration, and this signifies the body and blood of Christ which become present by means of the sign, while the overall purpose of the celebration is that it brings about the unity of the Church.

When we talk of the liturgical rite as a whole, instead of the phrase '*sacramentum tantum*' we shall speak of the visible and historical plane. At this level we shall be concerned with the Eucharist's development from its Jewish roots, through the Last Supper and down the ages and describe the rite as it should be celebrated.

Obviously the texts, the prayers and the outward actions of the participants should reflect the inner meaning or spiritual significance of what they are celebrating. It is of the utmost importance that the rite should be celebrated so that participants will know what Christ's Spirit is doing in each part of the Mass. This spiritual significance corresponds to '*res et sacramentum*' and, as it is concerned with the activity of Christ, it is what makes the celebration worthwhile. It is also what distinguishes Christian worship from its Jewish roots. The Sinai covenant was about God's relationship with the Jews only in this world, while the centre of the new covenant is Jesus who rose from the dead and lives with the Father in heaven.

Finally, I hope we shall come to see how, in being united as a community to Christ, we are more deeply united to each other because we are brought together before the throne of the Father. In the Eucharist, the local community is made one in Christ with the angels and saints and with Christians throughout the world. It becomes the visible expression of the whole Church, rather like the tip of an iceberg. This means that the Eucharist is always an act not only of the local church but of the whole Church throughout the world. The whole historical community in all parts of the world is united in its 'kingdom' dimension; and this is essential for it if it is to be the Church. Because of this, we say that 'the Eucharist constitutes the Church'. This is the *'res sacramenti'* of the Eucharist. The historic Christian community becomes Christ's body, the Church, and he works through it and we bear witness to him by living its life. However, this remains mere theory unless our community life is recognizable to ordinary people. We fail to bear witness if we make the doctrine of our heavenly unity with him a substitute for authentic human relationships on earth. On the contrary, authentic human relationships on earth must reflect our Spirit-given unity with Christ in heaven. That is why an ordinary human oneness is an essential note of the visible Church both at a local level and also world-wide; but it must be so real and of such a quality that it directs attention to its source which is Christ. To sum up, it is the Eucharist that makes us the Church because it is by participation in the same bread and the same cup that we form one body with Christ; and this gives the Church the 'kingdom' dimension that is essential to it.

Thus, in a Catholic understanding of the Church, where there is no Eucharist there is no Church. A group of Christians may be totally Catholic in organization, have bishops and jurisdiction and even other sacraments but, if it does not share in the Eucharist of the Catholic Church, it is not a church in the Catholic sense. When these groupings have a communal life of their own based on their faith in Jesus Christ and function in the same way as a church but without the Catholic Eucharist, the Second Vatican Council called them 'ecclesial communities'. They possess essential elements of the Church like baptism and faith, even though their communal life lacks the eucharistic dimension, Also, if a church is out of Catholic communion but celebrates the Eucharist, then the whole Catholic Church is included in its action. This obliges them to enter Catholic communion because it is the nature of the Church to bear witness by its unity in time and place to the 'kingdom' dimension. Their lack of unity with the Catholic Church goes against what they do in the Eucharist, and hence is contrary to their own nature. The schism obscures from the world their essential unity and identity with the universal Church. Of course, this does not mean that the Catholic Church has been free from blame where schism and heresy have occurred; history presents a murky picture. Not all Catholic authorities, even among the popes, have been so advanced in their conversion as to be 'peacemakers', and the Catholic Church as an historical body has not always held the moral high ground, especially at times with our Orthodox brethren. Moreover, the Church is always wounded and impoverished by schism and by the heresy of others when brother Christians and sister churches leave her communion or even have to be expelled from it. Nevertheless, however much the Catholic Church may share in the guilt of the schism or heresy, in our quest for unity with our separated brethren, we do have a clear idea in what direction it must go and the centrality of the Eucharist is non-negotiable; so also is the continued existence of a world-wide Catholic communion.

This theology, that the Eucharist constitutes the Church, seems to downplay the fundamental importance of baptism. Surely, it is objected, faith and baptism are what constitute the Church. However, from earliest times baptism has been seen as the sacrament by which individuals become members of the Eucharistic community. In the time when the Nicene Creed was written and accepted by the Church, the word 'baptism' denoted a ceremony which contained three sacraments. The catechumen, after rejecting Satan and sin, was baptized by immersion, was anointed with chrism to receive the Spirit in the sacrament of confirmation and then entered into the celebration of the Eucharist and received communion for the first time. All this was called 'baptism'.

The Eucharistic celebration is not just a seventh part of the sacramental system: it is its very centre, and all the other sacraments are related to it. Thus, our baptism and confirmation are activated and function every time we participate in the Mass. Obviously this is also true of ordination. The Eucharist is a foretaste of our presence in the marriage feast of the Lamb and, by sharing in the celebration, the Christian couple deepens its participation in the relationship between Christ and the Church of which marriage is a sacramental sign. The sacrament of reconciliation (confession) renews the baptismal conversion of an individual to Christ in the community and so prepares him to participate in the Eucharist. The sacrament of the sick is Christ's blessing on the sick person so that his or her suffering may be united to Christ's own self-offering to the Father, either for the person's cure or so that it may become a means of sanctification for the person and for the whole Church. While the Eucharist is the means by which the community can share in the Christian Mystery and so be the Church, the other sacraments are the application of the Christian Mystery to individual persons so that they can play their full part in the Church. The classical context for blessing and baptismal water is the Easter Vigil and the prayer of the whole Church gathered for the Eucharist. The normal place where the oils for confirmation, ordination and the anointing of the sick are blessed is the Chrism Mass on Maundy Thursday, where the blessing of the bishop is backed up by the prayer of the whole community. While the other sacraments can be validly celebrated outside the Mass, it remains the most fitting context for their celebration. This demonstrates the connection between those sacraments and the Eucharistic Assembly.

There is a debate about which is more basic, the universal Church or the local Eucharistic Assembly. In favour of the universal Church is the fact that it is the Church which celebrates the Eucharist, so that it must have a prior existence. In favour of the Eucharistic Assembly, or rather the local diocese, which is in principle one assembly because the priests celebrate only as the bishop's representatives, is in fact that without the Eucharist there can be no Church. Both facts are accepted by both sides of the argument. Behind this debate seems to be the tension between the centralist tendency of the Vatican and the desire for greater freedom of local bishops to respond pastorally to local conditions. There seem to be people in Rome who believe that without the Vatican's constant vigilance the world-wide unity and consistency of the Catholic Church would come apart at the seams. On the other hand, there are many in the Church, including bishops, who believe that there should be much more freedom for local churches to propose and pursue their own policies without having constantly to refer to Rome. They have adopted opposite sides in this debate.

The Church is like a building that covers an area of ground and thus has width and length, and it also has height. It makes no sense to ask which dimension comes first, the horizontal or the vertical. If it had length and width but did not have height, it would not be a building; neither would it be a building if it had height but no length and width: it needs both even though architects may pay more attention to one or the other dimension. So it is with the Church. Even if the universal Church were a community of communities spread wherever the Gospel has been preached, and which manifested a breath-taking unity of belief and a wonderful common life, but lacked the Eucharistic dimension, it would not be the Catholic Church. It is true that Catholic theologians have until recently chiefly concentrated on the implications of a world-wide Catholic Church, and many Orthodox theologians have concentrated on the Eucharistic dimension. At the level of theologians, such differences are understandable. However, both dimensions are equally essential, and it seems to me that to ask which one is objectively more basic is really meaningless. It follows that the argument between Vatican centralists and some local bishops, as long as they stay within the parameters set by the nature of the Church, which they do, is a normal phenomenon that reflects a different theological emphasis but also a healthy pluralism. In such a situation, mutual love and respect are most important. Then the tension between them can only contribute to the life of the Church, because different aspects of the truth become clear in different theologies.

The Eucharist is the Church's celebration of the Christian Mystery. To bring out different aspects of this Mystery we have the Christian Year. **Advent** reminds us that we are still waiting for the Second Coming as the Jews awaited the Messiah. We are on the way to salvation but are not completely saved yet. Just as the Old Testament was a preparation for the coming of Jesus, so we must prepare ourselves for our next encounter with him and, by our Christian lives, prepare the world for the Parousia. One New Testament theme is that, with the **Incarnation**, heaven has manifested itself on earth. This is symbolized by the host of angels at Jesus' birth in Bethlehem. It is emphasized after the Temptations, when angels and beasts minister to Jesus in the desert. Angels and beasts populate heaven in apocalyptic literature (e.g. Rev. 5.8–13), and here they are in the desert, a place where the Jews considered the lack of life to be a sign that God was relatively absent. It is implied by the Transfiguration on Mount Tabor. In St John's Gospel it is implied when Jesus says that those who see him see the Father, and when the Gospel tells us that from the side of Jesus flowed blood and water, thus indicating him as the true Temple which Jews held to be in heaven. This effect of the Incarnation continues in the Church in the Eucharist, where we sing the Sanctus with the angels and saints, and Christ in heaven manifests his presence on earth. We celebrate the Incarnation at **Christmas** and on the **Epiphany**. **Lent** is the season when we double our efforts at conversion in preparation for Easter. We remember that our true participation in the Mass is measured not by the loudness of our singing or the enthusiasm of our responses, but to the degree we have died and risen with Christ. Hence, by prayer, penance and works of mercy, we strive to deepen our conversion so that we can take our paltry efforts to the Eucharist, where Christ's prayer will include them in his own self-offering. **Holy Week** and **Easter** is the time when we remember with special gratitude those key events of Christ's passion and resurrection, the memory of which we present before God at every Mass in order to share, by the power of the Holy Spirit, in the relationship between God and the human race which was brought about by them. **Pentecost** celebrates the descent of the Holy Spirit on the apostolic community, giving it that relationship with the risen and ascended Christ which made it the Church. This relationship between Christ and the Christian community continues to be sustained by the descent of the Holy Spirit in the Eucharist, making us the body of Christ. The Christian life in all its dimensions and at every level, both in our communal and individual lives, is only made possible by the Holy Spirit.

The Mass is divided into two principal parts, the **Liturgy of the Word** and the **Liturgy of the Eucharist**. The Liturgy of the Word begins with the first reading and ends with the bidding prayers. The Liturgy of the Eucharist begins with the presentation of gifts and ends with the post-communion prayer. God is particularly active in these two parts. In the first, Christ, who is the

Father's Word, comes down and speaks to us through the reading of Scripture as God spoke to Moses: and in the second, we offer a memorial of Christ's death and ascend with him through his death, resurrection and ascension to his Father's throne by becoming one body with him. As we remain on earth, the Mass can be seen also as a theophany, a manifestation of God on earth, and, to the extent that we are transformed by the Mass, we become the light of the world and salt of the earth, the means by which Christ lives in our world.

There are two minor parts of the Liturgy: the **gathering and preparation** of the assembly, which begins with the entrance and ends with the collect; and the short rite of **dismissal**, which comprises of the blessing and the 'Go in peace'. In coming together to celebrate the Mass we are doing more than satisfying our religious needs: we are becoming the Church together in answer to Christ's call, so that we can receive nourishment from the very source of our faith and then go out and fulfil our vocation in the world. When we go out at the end of Mass, we must not think that our religious duties are over because, in a sense, they are only just beginning.

Chapter Sixteen

The Gathering of the Assembly Entrance Rite

St Augustine describes how the people used to greet him with cries of 'Glory to God' and 'God be praised' and other shouts of jubilation. He greeted the people in return and was answered by more loud expressions of joy. When silence had been restored, they had the readings. St John Chrysostom also complains of the large amount of noise that accompanied his prayer for peace at the beginning of Mass. This spontaneity is not common nowadays outside the Charismatic Renewal. The presider greeted the people with 'Peace to you' or 'The Lord be with you', and this was the beginning of Mass. Later on a psalm with refrain was introduced to be sung until the celebrant arrived at the altar. The procession of the celebrant was made more solemn by carrying the Book of the Gospels in front of him. Great devotion and reverence were given to it, because it was the means by which Jesus would reveal himself to the assembly.

The entrance of the bishop or priest is very important. Without his presence, the gathered assembly would not be the Church in the full sense of the word. The Greek word 'ekklesia' meant not just any meeting of citizens: it was an official gathering of all free members of the populace who were called together by the municipal authorities to take part in a civic act. No one was present in a private capacity: they were all exercising their rights as citizens, as parts of a greater whole. While Christ is present whenever two or three are gathered in his name, the Church is most fully itself when the people come together, not as private individuals, but as baptized members to take part in the eucharistic celebration. They have been called together by Christ, who is officially represented by the priest.

By ordination and by communion with his bishop, the priest represents all eucharistic assemblies throughout the world and fulfils the apostolic mission to represent Christ to the gathered assembly. The priest presides, preaches the Gospel, and becomes the voice of the assembly when it prays with one heart and soul to God. He does this because he represents Christ. He does not take the place of Christ, because Christ is present in his Church as its pastor and priest and remains the main celebrant of the whole liturgy; rather, he is the instrument of Christ as the one who presides, just as the readers are instruments of Christ when they read the word of God, and the people are instruments of Christ when they pray and sing. By being one with the priest in the eucharistic celebration, the Christians who have come together are not just a casual group of Christians: they are the holy body of Christ, the whole body being 'joined and knitted together by every ligament with which it is equipped, as each part is working properly'. (Eph. 4.16). They have become the Church.

All theologians agree that the priest acts '*in persona Christi*', in the person of Christ, and '*in persona ecclesiae*' as representative of the Church. However, does the priest represent Christ because he represents his Church, or does he represent the Church because he represents Christ? It seems to me that both propositions are equally true but at different levels.

At the visible, historical level (the equivalent of *sacramentum tantum*), the priest represents Christ because he represents the Church. Thus, by his ordination and his connection with the bishop, he is one with the ministerial priesthood of the universal Church: he is the sign that what is happening is an act of the Church throughout the world and not simply of this local assembly. Moreover, in the Mass he prays the prayer of the Church, presenting the memorial of Christ's Passion, Resurrection and Ascension to the Father in its name and using 'we' rather than 'I' throughout; while the people answer 'Amen', making the prayer their own.

However, it is the Holy Spirit's function to turn the celebration into a 'kingdom event' and thus a manifestation of God's saving power. The Holy Spirit draws the assembly into Christ so that the Church's prayer becomes Christ's prayer. By the Spirit's action, Christ becomes present in the assembly and presides at the Eucharist through the priest. (Christ's action through the Spirit, in any activity which involves the Church's nature such as liturgy or evangelization, is called, when the sacraments are described, *res et sacramentum*). Just as Christ was appointed to represent us by the Father and was enabled to do so by the Spirit, so the priest can only fulfil the role of Christ's representative if he is appointed by Christ and enabled to function by the same Holy Spirit.

Without the Spirit's transforming activity, the Eucharist would simply be a Christian memorial meal, but it would not be a manifestation of God's kingdom; it would remain at the same level as Old Testament sacrifices, and Christ himself would not be actively involved. Thus, while the priest is chosen by the Church and presides and offers in the Church's name, it is necessary for God in Christ to be actively involved in his ordination and in his function as presider of the Eucharist. In the kingdom, God has the initiative and is the main Actor, while the Church functions only as God's willing instrument. Only in this way is the Church the presence of the Kingdom of God on earth.

St Paul followed common Jewish ideas in his anthropology: the human being is body and spirit. This did not refer to two different parts of the person, one material and the other immaterial, but to two different dimensions of the same complete human being. 'Body' referred to human beings in their relationship to all created life-forms as part of the material world, while 'spirit' referred to something which is unique to each human being, his or her relationship with God. As body we are made of organic matter, material for scientific research, but as spirit we are each related to God who makes us human persons. St Paul uses this anthropology in his theology of the body of Christ. 'Body' stands for all that we have in common with Christ and with each other in the new Creation, while 'spirit' stands for the particular vocation or function in the Church which each of us receives from the Father who is acting through Christ's Spirit. It is Christ who is both the source of the Church's unity and the source of the diversity of complementary functions among its members, unity and diversity being aspects of the same Church.

When the people reply to the priest's greeting, 'And with your spirit', they mean, 'The Lord is (or 'be') with that function which you received at ordination'. This is how the Fathers understood the phrase. Narsai of Nisibis wrote, 'He gives the name "spirit" not to the soul of the priest but to the spirit he received through the imposition of hands.' Thus, in whatever way the Church decides to introduce a man into the priesthood – and a uniform way was probably not universally fixed until the fourth century – it is Christ in the Spirit who makes him one.

An eminent Lutheran liturgical scholar, Maxwell E. Johnson, who teaches in St John's University, Collegeville, argues that there is no fundamental differ-ence between the common priesthood of the faithful and the ministerial priesthood.

> There is after all only one priesthood in the Church, that of Jesus Christ, and the 'sacrament of ordination' to this single, common royal priesthood of the faithful is baptism itself. Only by paying attention to this baptismal and, hence, ecclesial foundation of orders and ministry, I believe, will a halt be brought to undue

stress on the role of the ordained in the single action of Christ and his body, the Church, the 'totus Christus', in the Eucharist.[1]

Indeed, we are all members of his priesthood because we have all been baptized into Christ's body which is priestly, and are all introduced into the heavenly Holy of Holies when we receive his resurrected body in holy communion. However, while this is the context in which the ministerial priesthood operates, so that only baptized Christians can become ministerial priests, it is not identical with the ministerial priesthood which is a gift given by the Spirit through the laying on of hands for the building up and knitting together of the Church.

Just as the Incarnation did not make Christ independent of the Father who remained the Source of his Power which is the Holy Spirit, so baptism makes us dependent on Christ's Spirit who is the Source of its efficacy. One function of the Spirit is to give Christians different gifts for the good of the Church. Baptism, and hence membership of the Church, is a necessary condition for receiving these gifts, but the gifts themselves cannot be said to rise directly from the sacrament of baptism. Baptism gives us an ability to open ourselves to the Spirit and receive the gifts, but it is the Spirit who gives them. Someone who has not received the gift of healing, for example, cannot heal, however much he is baptized and however much he tries. The ministerial priesthood is such a gift, and belongs to the very structure of the Church. The priest's function is to represent Christ in the Christian assembly, and thus to promote the assembly from being merely a local group of Christians and make it the Church which is Christ's body.

We said in the last chapter that the Church has a horizontal dimension in time and space, and a vertical dimension, a relationship with the risen Lord which we called the eucharistic dimension. It is the Eucharist, not baptism, that makes the Church the body of Christ. As St Paul says, 'Because there is one bread, we who are many are one body, for we all partake of the one bread' (1 Cor. 10.17). Baptism is a sacramental action of that one body so that individuals may become members of it (1 Cor. 12.13). Hence, in a sense, the eucharistic Church is prior to baptism in that it must already exist for people to be baptized into it. Of course, in order to found a local church it is necessary to preach the Word and baptize those who respond, so that the Word and baptism are essential for the foundation of that church; but if they are not just to remain a group of Christians rather than the Church, they need the Eucharist; and to have the Eucharist they need someone who can pray the Eucharistic Prayer in the name of the whole Church and in the name of Christ. Local churches are not created out of nothing but always in organic relationship with the whole Church. The ministerial priesthood is defined by its function to preside at the Eucharist in which the whole Church in heaven and on earth is involved. As part of the structure of the Church on earth, the two dimensions of unity in time and space and the eucharistic dimensions are essential to it.

The ecumenical problem arises because groups of Christians separated from Catholic unity, and one reason for this was disagreement over the very nature of the Eucharist. This disagreement was one of the things that defined them over against the Catholic Church, and the Church could not recognize in their theology the Eucharist that she celebrates. Therefore it was logical for the Catholic Church not to recognize their ministry as the same as her own, even though many of their ministers' other activities were identical to those of Catholic priests, and not to recognize these communities as churches in the Catholic sense. On the whole, these communities were content to accept that there were important differences between their understanding of the ministry and the Catholic understanding. The ecumenical movement has changed the context in which these problems are discussed; but problems they remain, and it is not legitimate to solve them simply by appealing to baptism. The alternative is congregationalism, which is a totally different understanding of the Church from traditional Christianity.

The priest's vestments portray his role in relation to his baptism. First comes the alb, which is also worn by other ministers at the altar. It is the white robe of baptism which symbolizes what he has in common with every member of the community. It is the white linen garment that the high priest put on before he went behind the veil into the Holy of Holies to pronounce the Name of the Lord and to pour out the blood on the Mercy Seat, and which Christ put on before he washed the feet of his disciples at the Last Supper; it is what Christ's clothes became at the Transfiguration and what he wears for all eternity in the Apocalypse; it is the garment which has been washed white in the blood of the Lamb, worn by those who have passed through the great persecution and through the veil of death, into the life of resurrection where they praise Him who is on the throne and the Lamb. It is the high priestly vestment which all Christians receive at baptism, because they pass through the veil at the Eucharist by sharing in the sacrificed and resurrected life of Christ in the presence of the Father, and then return to the world as sons of God and as a nation of priests to witness and to sanctify it in his name. It is the garment that the young man lost when he fled from the cross, but wore again when he witnessed to the resurrection on Easter Day in the Gospel of St Mark. This is the foundation vestment upon which the priest places stole and chasuble as signs of his ministry. It is only because he is baptized that he can receive this function, and only within the context of the baptized that his function has any meaning.

The priest proceeds to the sanctuary and kisses the altar which symbolizes Christ's presence and then goes to the presider's chair. The gospel book is placed on the altar if it has been carried in, emphasizing that it belongs to Christ. When it is taken off the altar for the Gospel procession, we are acknowledging that we receive the Gospel from Christ, that it is his gift to the Church.

Note

1. 'A Response to Gerard Austin's "Identity of a Eucharistic Church in an Ecumenical Age"' by Maxwell E. Johnson; from *Worship*, vol. 72, no. 1; January 1998.

Chapter Seventeen

The Sign of the Cross
In the Name of the Father
and of the Son
and of the Holy Spirit
People: Amen

This puts us immediately into a 'kingdom' context. Everything that will be said and done is in the name of the Trinity. All prayers are addressed to the Father 'through Jesus Christ our Lord in the unity of the Holy Spirit, one God for ever and ever'. The Holy Trinity is active throughout the Mass. There is the downward movement by which the Father uses his two hands (St Irenaeus), the Word and the Spirit, to speak to us through the Scripture and to bring about the Eucharist; and there is the upward movement of prayer and praise which is expressed in the doxology at the end of the Eucharistic Prayer, 'Through him, with him, in him, in the unity of the Holy Spirit, all glory and honour is yours, almighty Father, for ever and ever'. From the very first moment, we are participating in the kingdom which is God in action. The Byzantine Liturgy puts it more explicitly, 'Blessed is the kingdom of the Father, the Son and the Holy Spirit, now and for ever, and unto ages of ages'.

The Father's Ministry
The Father, as Unoriginate, is both the Source of all that is significant in what happens in the Mass, and all prayer and praise are directed towards him as its Ultimate Goal.

Even the words of consecration are part of a prayer to the Father which manifests Christ's dependence on him. In the Mass, the Father is in Christ reconciling the world to himself.

The Spirit's Ministry

The Holy Spirit is the Enabler. It is through the Spirit that Scripture becomes the Word of God for us and the Church's memorial meal becomes the Christian Eucharist. His activity is threefold: firstly, he manifests Christ and puts people on Christ's wavelength so that they may recognize and accept him; secondly, he transforms a whole situation into a sacramental one; and, thirdly, he brings about communion in Christ. These three functions are operative throughout the rite and, indeed, in our ordinary Christian lives while we 'live' the Mass. However, they are associated especially with particular moments in the liturgy. The first has its clearest expression in the Liturgy of the Word; the second at the consecration; and the third at communion.

The first function of the Spirit is to present Christ to us, challenging that part of us to change which is not yet converted.

The second function of the Spirit is to transform the celebration into a sacramental one. At the visible level, the Mass is a memorial meal in which the Church thanks God for his wonderful deeds in the past, for creation and for Christ's death and resurrection, and it looks forward to his Second Coming. If that is all that the Mass is, then it differs from Jewish sacred meals only in the content of its memorial. However, the Holy Spirit transforms this rite, making it into a Christian celebration. 'Heaven and earth become one', as St Gregory the Great says. Christ presides at the Mass, using the priest as his instrument, proclaims his Word and leads the congregation in prayer. The Holy Spirit makes the Eucharistic Prayer a participation in Christ's prayer in heaven, thus changing the bread and wine into Christ's body and blood. The priest is not just the presider over a local congregation: he represents Christ who offers his Passion for the Church and the whole world from the beginning of the human race to the end of time. Priest and people are not just a local community: they become the local manifestation of the Catholic Church in all times and places, and are united to Christ's liturgical action, together with the angels and saints in heaven. (Heb. 8 and 9).

The third function of the Holy Spirit is to bring about and deepen our communion with Christ. Communion (*koinonia* in Greek) has its roots in the common life of the Holy Trinity into which we have been introduced by baptism. At a purely human level, people come together to celebrate Mass because they are members of the same parish, because it is the nearest church to their home, because they belong to the same institution, because they are taking part in a common activity, out of a sense of obligation, or because they have some need. It is the Holy Spirit's function to make them a community of faith which receives its unity, not principally from these factors, but from their common unity in Christ.

As Christians, we are called by God to be witnesses to the risen Christ, but our community life can only fulfil this purpose if our unity is rooted in him; 'that they may all be one. As you, Father, are in me and I am in you, may they also be in us, so that the world may believe that you have sent me'. (John 17.21). As long as we simply remain a like-minded group who enjoy celebrating Mass together or are together simply because it is convenient, we will never truly be witnesses. Hence, in one form or other, we ask the Father at Mass:

> Grant that we, who are nourished by his body and blood, may be filled with his Holy Spirit, and become one body, one spirit in Christ.[1]

St Paul has two ways of looking at the body of Christ: a) From the point of view of the Church's relationship with the world, we are all one body because we share in the one loaf and the one cup; Christ is the real subject of our Christian activity and lives in us who are simply organs of his body. What people do to us because we are Christians is really done to him. b) However, when St Paul deals with our personal relationship with Christ, he likens it to the marriage act. Only sexual union in which man and woman become one body is intimate enough for him to describe the union between Christ and the Christian. So when St Paul says that we are 'in' Christ and Christ is 'in' us he is expressing the most intimate union imaginable; and then what we can imagine is only a pale image of the reality. Christ can say to the Church and to each member of it: 'This at last is bone of my bones and flesh of my flesh'. (Gen. 2.23) It is the function of the Spirit to bring about this union with Christ.

As the unity in Christ's body is a union of persons and not the sanctification of a crowd, the Spirit works at two levels: he unites us with Christ and hence with each other in a visible unity, and he works within each of us. The most intense moment of our common sharing in Christ is holy communion. However, each person benefits from Christ's body and blood according to his openness to receive him. We have mapped this process of interior transformation in our commentary on the Beatitudes, and it is also the work of the Holy Spirit. It is a process of death and resurrection, which he works in us to the extent that we are willing to accept and do God's will for us from moment to moment.

Just as God is a perfect union of three persons, so the Church becomes, little by little, a communion of persons in the one body of Christ. Even though each person has his own salvation history and not all are equally united to Christ at any one time, in the Mass our personal lives become and are seen to be a sharing in the one life of Christ through death and resurrection as members of his body. In the Mass we become Church together, and this is the work of the Holy Spirit.

Christ's Ministry

If the Holy Spirit is the Enabler, Christ is the Revelation
of the Father. In the Mass, he is the celebrant, host, priest
and sacrifice: he is the giver and the gift, through the
power of the Spirit. Here we shall look at his role as Celebrant and Host.

> You prepare a table before me in the presence of my
> enemies; you anoint my head with oil; my cup over-
> flows. (Ps. 23.5)

> Wisdom has built her house, she has hewn her seven
> pillars. She has slaughtered her animals, she has mixed
> her wine, she has also set her table. She has sent out her
> servant girls, she calls from the highest places in the
> town, 'You that are simple, turn in here'. To those
> without sense she says, 'Come, eat of my bread and
> drink of the wine I have mixed. Lay aside immaturity,
> and live, and walk in the way of insight.' (Prov. 9.1–6)

> 'Let us rejoice and exult and give him the glory, for the
> marriage of the Lamb has come, and his bride has
> made herself ready; to her it has been granted to be
> clothed with fine linen, bright and pure' – for the fine
> linen is the righteous deeds of the saints.
> And the angel said to me, 'Write this: Blessed are
> those who are invited to the marriage supper of the
> Lamb.' (Rev. 19.7–9)

The early Church used these texts to feed their eucharistic piety. Christ is the Wisdom who invites us to eat and
drink. Typical is a text from St John Chrysostom: 'This
our Table is the same as that (of old) and holds nothing
less ... he prepares it ... when you see how the priest
hands you communion, then do not think that it is the
priest who does this; but it is the hand of Christ which
extends itself to you'.[2] St Augustine said, 'That table is
great where the Lord of the table is himself the meal. No

one feeds guests with himself as food, but this is exactly what the Lord Christ does; he himself is the host who invites; he himself is the food and drink.' Theophilus of Alexandria, St John Chrysostom's contemporary, puts it this way: 'Together let us hasten to the Mystical Supper. Today Christ feasts us, today Christ serves us, Christ, the Lover-of-mankind, refreshes us.'[3] St John Chrysostom says again: 'You should believe that today also is the same meal over which Christ presides.'[4]

The meal to which Wisdom invites us is Jesus who is the Bread of Life. He offers himself through word and sacrament. In the word he comes down to us and speaks with us, addressing himself to our reality, whilst in the Eucharist he raises us up to share in his own reality.

Thus the Eucharist is a manifestation of the Holy Trinity at work. What is important is that, in the kingdom, we are so united to Christ by the Holy Spirit that we share in his relationship with the Father and thus share in God's own life.

Thus, when we say, 'In the name of the Father ...' we are truly putting the celebration of the Eucharist in its 'kingdom' context: the Father is giving and receiving; the Son is manifesting himself as our Saviour and presiding as the revelation of God and as our priest before the Father, as Giver and Gift, and the Spirit is transforming and enabling. There is little wonder that the people answer, 'Amen.'

Notes

1. Eucharistic Prayer III.
2. 'Heavenly and Earthly Liturgies: Patristic Prototypes, Mediaeval Perspectives and Contemporary Application', by Mary M. Schaefer. *Worship*, vol. 70, No. 6, November 1996.
3. ibid.
4. ibid.

Chapter Eighteen

The Lord Be With You –
And With Your Spirit

Then the priest greets the people:

The Lord be with you (or) The grace of the Lord Jesus Christ, the love of God and the fellowship of the Holy Spirit be with you all.

And the people answer: And with your Spirit (or) And also with you.

To illustrate the meaning of the 'The Lord be with you', and 'And with your spirit', I am going to take an incident from *The Cross and the Switchblade*, by David Wilkerson. David Wilkerson had invited the Harlem gangs to a meeting in a large sports arena, and it didn't seem to be working out all that well. They were jeering and stamping their feet, and it was obvious that they were getting nowhere. He decided to have a collection and put the task of collecting in the hands of one of the most hardened criminals called Nicky Cruz. This caused even more jeering: only a fool would trust Nicky Cruz. However, as everybody was frightened of him, Nicky and his team collected a large amount of money. Then came the moment when they mounted the stage and went behind a curtain where there was an open door to the street. Meanwhile David Wilkerson prayed silently.

There was a long delay and the jeering turned to laughter: it was clear that the group of boys had gone off with the money. Behind the curtain, Nicky was rooted to the spot, unable to make up his mind. On the one hand, he knew what everybody expected him to do; on the other, it was the first time in his life that someone had trusted him. He ordered the group to return to the preacher with the money. This absolutely dumbfounded the audience. Soon there was a large number of criminal youths kneeling down to give their lives to Christ. Nicky later became a pastor.

What was happening there? There was David Wilkerson, moved by the Spirit to preach the Gospel to these gangs, but he could do nothing unless the Spirit entered them too. Once this happened, he was able to minister to them. When a Christian mediates grace to another, he can only do so if Christ, through his Spirit, is present working in that person, because our mediation is only a function of Christ's mediation. Christ mediates between God and the human race at the visible, historical level through the charisms the Spirit gives to the Church. When the Church responds in faith to the Spirit's action it becomes the instrument of Christ's mediation. Thus there is only one Mediator, but if we are in Christ, then we can share in this mediation role because Christ lives and acts in us. We become channels of the Spirit at a certain level, only if Christ is active in us and in those to whom we minister. An electric cable can only pass electricity if it is plugged in at the mains, and can only give electricity to objects capable of receiving it. God's Spirit plugs us into the mains and gives the grace to respond, thus bringing about a unity between the minister and those to whom he ministers.

Thus, the community can share in the eucharistic action only if Christ is present in its members through the Spirit, and the priest can only function as priest if Christ is active through his ministry. This is because we are all in the kingdom which is a manifestation of God's saving power. When this is forgotten, we get stories of apostate priests consecrating bread shops, or a crate of champagne during a party, or celebrating satanic masses. When the sacraments are studied outside their liturgical and kingdom context, certain aspects become obscured.

'The Lord be with you'. 'And with your spirit' or 'And also with you' are said, often in an extended form, at the beginning of Mass as well as before the proclamation of the Gospel, in the dialogue before the Eucharistic Prayer, and before the final blessing. Outside the Mass, it is said whenever a priest or deacon greets the people – he can say, 'Peace be with you', or some other greeting which means the same thing – and before a blessing. It is a sign that we are in kingdom territory. If Christ is not with the people they will not hear the Gospel as the Word of God, and it is because he is using the minister as an instrument that the Word is proclaimed. If Christ were not with the priest who presides on behalf of the whole Church, the latter's role of speaking for the whole Church would be inoperative. It is only because of Christ's presence in and with the people that they can act as body of Christ and so take part in the liturgy. If Christ is not with the priest when he blesses, then he cannot bless; if he is not with the people, then they cannot receive the blessing.

The fact that, if the priest celebrates a sacrament intending to do what the Church does, the effect is guaranteed by Christ's promise and hence does not depend on the priest's worthiness, does not take away his radical dependence on Christ; and this greeting clearly states this dependence. In the classical reply, 'And with your spirit', there is a distinction which is obscured by 'And also with you'. When the priest says, 'The Lord be with you', he is referring to the people's openness to Christ in faith. When the people reply, 'And with your spirit', they are referring to his function in the Church which has been given to him by the laying on of hands. Of course, as a baptized person, the priest's growth in holiness depends on his openness to Christ in faith; but his functioning as a priest depends on fulfilling his role rather than on his inner disposition.

'The Lord be with you'. 'And also with you' can teach us

something else. Mother Teresa of Calcutta looked at the destitute of India and saw in them the suffering face of Christ, and she dedicated her life to assuaging their suffering. The more she saw Christ in them, the more they saw Christ in her. That is the rule: people see Christ in us to the extent that we see Christ in them. If a priest really sees Christ in his congregation and is not drunk with his own authority and expertise, then the people will find it easier to see Christ in him. If he knows them well, he will also recognize the different gifts they have which God has given to them for the building up of the Church. In a stable Christian community there are a variety of gifts and ministries to be discovered and utilized. He is not a solo player; he is like the conductor of an orchestra whose job it is to bring out the best in the player of each instrument and to make sure that they all play as one.

It adds something to a celebration to give liturgical recognition to the different groups and ministries from time to time. In the very large parishes to be found in Peru, some parishes have a Mass every few months where the different groups and ministries take part, each behind a placard bearing the group's name. In other parishes, each group organizes and provides altar servers, readers and so on, in turn for the main Mass on Sunday. There is something very impressive in Lourdes when on each pilgrimage, the nurses, doctors and the sick are all identifiable: it gives the true impression that this is a community and not just a crowd.

We are not only interdependent in mutual service; we are also spiritually interdependent because the Christian life of one belongs to all as members of the same body. Thus St Paul writes, 'I pray therefore that you do not lose heart over my sufferings for you: they are your glory', (Eph. 3.13) and, 'On the day of the Lord Jesus we are your boast (glory) even as you are our boast (glory).' (2 Cor. 1.14) Protestants, in order to give due emphasis to the unique mediatorship of Christ, have tended to deny that there is any form of mediatorship between members of the Church. Yet it is their experience as much as ours that Christ uses people as channels of grace for other people. We have seen how St John Vianney and St Seraphim of Sarov transformed the lives of thousands of people. Their sanctity was catching, and people with high degrees of holiness flourished round them. Yet they were the first to acknowledge that they could have done nothing if Christ had not worked through them: an electric cable does not generate its own electricity.

The New Testament portrays the life of the Church on earth as a foretaste of the kingdom of heaven; yet many people imagine that, after rejecting the values of consumerism and living lives of self-sacrifice in which 'in giving we receive', they will settle down to a consumer's paradise in the life to come. Is it not true that those who live the Beatitudes find joy, where previously they would only have found misery? God wishes to change our tastes so that we will be happy with him for ever in the next life. The giving and receiving within the Church on earth is a foretaste of our life in heaven.

Protestants often say that, as Christ is the unique Mediator, there is no need for others such as the Virgin Mary and the saints. They are quite right: God is perfectly capable of working our salvation without the help of any saint, and Christ has done everything necessary for our salvation. However, is it possible that the saints' need to minister to one another and to us arises, not from any inadequacy in Christ's redemptive work, nor from a need in God, but because Christ has perfectly restored in them the image of God who, in the Blessed Trinity, is all Self-Gift? Just as we need to learn to give ourselves, to love one another as he has loved us, so the saints in heaven do this spontaneously as a direct result of Christ's redemptive work. They have entered the kingdom in which to serve is to rule, and happiness is gained only by forgetting themselves, where their love of God and of neighbour has been perfected. They have been transformed into images of him who is in heaven to make intercession for us. Their mediatorship, like ours, is not additional to that of Christ, but is a way in which Christ's mediatorship works; just as their holiness, like ours, is not additional to Christ's holiness. Christ is the sun and they are the planets, who have no light of their own but shine with the light of Christ; and the holiness of one is the joy of all, when each saint recognizes Christ's presence in the others. To use St Paul's vocabulary, they, like ourselves, are Christ's glory, as St Paul's Christians were his glory and he was theirs. That is what salvation brings about: an interdependence among ourselves precisely because we are all dependent on Christ and Christ lives in us. Our total dependence on Christ and our interdependence with each other is expressed in 'The Lord be with you'. 'And with your spirit', and is a foretaste of salvation and our life in heaven.

'The Lord be with you'. 'And with your spirit' are translations of 'Dominus vobiscum'. 'Et cum spiritu tuo', where the verb is missing. This follows Jewish usage. Hence, the phrase can also mean, 'The Lord **is** with you', and many liturgists believe that this is the intended meaning. More probably, it means both: it is a statement that Christ is in the community and at work through the sacrament of ordination in the priest. It is an act of faith that Christ is present, and it is a prayer that he will deign to be more actively present; and thus it is a humble acknowledgement of our dependence on him. As a pilgrim Church we are on the way to salvation, but our union with Christ is not yet complete, and Christ can be more present or less present to us according to our capacity to receive him, which depends on the depth of our faith. By continuing to leave out the verb, the Church is able to express both Christ's presence and the fragility of our own hold on him.

Chapter Nineteen

The Penitential Rite, Gloria and Collect

The Act of Penance

This part of the entrance rite owes its origin to a private preparation of the priest which used to be said in the sacristy before entering the church, and was later placed at the foot of the altar. Therefore there are liturgists who argue that penance is something to be done before taking part in the Mass, and that we would be more faithful to the sources if the act of penance were abolished. However, the *Didache*[1], a book of prayers which was probably written towards the end of the first century, began the Eucharist with an act of penance, 'so that our sacrifice may be pure', and I believe there is a strong pastoral argument for keeping it.

The *Didache* was Jewish–Christian and spoke out of the tradition of the Old Testament. The Bible insists that a sacrifice was acceptable to God only if offered with a humble and contrite heart. Indeed, when the offering of sacrifices was not possible, the psalmist asks God to accept this interior disposition of contrition and humility in their place. When the woman with a bad reputation came to Jesus while he was eating in the house of Simon the Pharisee and washed his feet with her tears, dried them with her hair and anointed them with precious ointment, Jesus said that the more that people are forgiven, the more they will love. Contrition and humility are essential dispositions for offering sacrifice, and repentant love and forgiveness form the context and give the motive for our love for and gratitude to God. In the Eucharist, which is basically a communion sacrifice of thanksgiving, these dispositions are essential for anyone who wishes to make the sacrifice of the Church his own.

Jesus came to convince the world of sin. Before conversion people may have a great sense of unworthiness because they have done something against their own self-image, or unacceptable to those around them. This is not identical to a sense of sin, though it may be a good basis for forming one. Sin only makes sense to those who know they are called to have a relationship with God and realize that sin blocks or weakens that relationship. Hence, we are conscious of sin only in so far as God is a reality for us. The more we are united to God, the more we are aware of our unworthiness, of our unfittingness to become saints, which is our destiny. As our awareness of God's holiness increases, our awareness of how unholy we are also grows. We saw in our commentary on the Beatitudes how poverty of spirit and mourning lead to meekness where we become more like Christ, the Paschal Lamb; and that the greater our humility, the more our giving thanks to God is genuine and heartfelt.

Certainly the common tradition of the Church in both East and West had no public act of penance at the beginning of the Eucharistic rite until the twentieth century. It was assumed that people would prepare for their participation in the Mass either by going to confession or, at least, by an act of contrition before the Mass started. The people began to join in the priest's private act of penance when the dialogue Mass was introduced in the years before the Council, and this was carried over into the new rite. Those liturgists who want to abolish the act of penance say that it was simply a liturgical mistake that should be rectified. However, I suspect that the mistake, if mistake it was, was providential. Someone has said that we belong to the first generation who do not feel the need

to be redeemed, which implies that it is the first generation for whom God is not real. To give authentic thanksgiving to God we must have a sense of sin, and faith in our
forgiveness, and to offer sacrifice we must have a humble
and contrite heart. To eliminate or ignore this would lead
us to participate in the Mass in a superficial way. If we
give up the act of penance, just at a time when awareness
of sin is so vague and even non-existent in many, we
would be going with the secularist tide and strengthening
in people the very tendencies in modern society which
lead them away from God. It would be a pastoral disaster.
Christianity without any sense of sin and forgiveness is
not Christianity at all. The main motivation for our giving
thanks, for making eucharist, is that, while we know we
are sinners, we also know that we are loved by God, that
Christ died for us, and that we are members of his body.
Therefore the priest prays with confidence:

**May Almighty God have mercy on us, forgive us our
sins, and bring us to everlasting life.**
The people respond: **Amen**.

Kyrie eleison   **Christe eleison**   **Kyrie eleison**
Lord have mercy   *Christ have mercy*   *Lord have mercy*

This prayer can be sung in English or Greek and pleads
mercy from God. In the commentary on the Beatitudes,
we have seen that 'mercy' is God's constant love for
mankind, because of which he is always seeking what is
best for us. This petition is often included in the Act of
Penance, but may originally have been the response to a
litany. The Greeks use it very often during their Mass as
the standard response to almost all their petitions. When
it is not used in the penitential rite, other petitions may be
made, but it can be said or sung on its own: pleading with
God for his constant love is a prayer full of meaning by
itself.

The Gloria

This is an ancient Christian canticle in which the Church praises and worships the Father and the Son, and asks the Son to have mercy on us and to receive our prayer.

It opens with the words of the angels at the Nativity (Luke 2.14). The words 'Glory to God in the highest and peace to his people on earth' echo the 'Our Father' which says, 'Thy kingdom come; thy will be done on earth as it is in heaven'. In the kingdom, the same conditions which exist in heaven are being brought about on earth. When God became man, this brought about a new and close relationship between heaven and earth, even though this is happening in an imperfect and provisional manner. This is symbolized by the presence of the angels in Bethlehem. This relationship continues to be enjoyed by the Church, especially in the Mass which we celebrate with the angels and saints, as we continue to worship the Father and his Son, in whom heaven and the Church have become a single entity.

In Scripture, a person's 'glory' is that by which his or her greatness or high position or beauty is recognized. To 'give glory' to someone is to recognize and acclaim his or her qualities, power or rank. Christ, as Word made flesh, is the Father's 'glory' on earth, especially when he revealed God as a God of love on the cross, and by sharing in Christ's salvation we become Christ's 'glory' by which he can be recognized. The peace for which we and the angels pray is 'not as the world gives', but is the harmony among God's creatures which is brought about by harmony with God; it is the experience of salvation. In the Beatitudes of St Matthew we have seen the steps which we have to take to deepen that peace within ourselves until we become 'peacemakers'. It is the same peace that we wish on each other as we are about to receive communion.

As in the cosmic liturgy in the Book of Revelation, we direct our prayer and praise both to the Father and to the Lamb who was slain. We make our pleas for mercy to

Christ who sits at the right hand of the Father, as we remember the heavenly liturgy in the Letter to the Hebrews. By participating in the Eucharist we are taking part in that liturgy. 'But you have come to Mount Zion and to the city of the living God, the heavenly Jerusalem, and to innumerable angels in festal gathering, and to the assembly of the firstborn who are enrolled in heaven, and to God the judge of all, and to the spirits of the righteous made perfect, and to Jesus, the mediator of a new covenant, and to the sprinkled blood that speaks a better word than the blood of Abel.' (Heb. 12.22–4)

Precisely because we are expressing our joy as members of that assembly of heaven – as St Paul says, we are citizens of heaven – we do not sing the Gloria in Advent and Lent: in Advent because we remind ourselves that we have not yet arrived; we are on the road to salvation but are not saved yet and the Parousia has not yet come about; and in Lent because we are in penitence for our failure to live up to the grace we have received. During these two seasons, we sing the Gloria only on feastdays which are important enough for us to lay aside Advent or Lent for a day.

The Collect

This prayer brings the entrance rite to an end. The priest says, 'Let us pray', and there should be a short silence, long enough for people to recollect themselves and short enough not to be burdensome. Then the priest says a prayer, usually to the Father, in which he collects together and sums up the interior prayer of all the faithful and associates it with the prayer of the whole Church on that day. The prayer of all is expressed through one mouth because the priest and people are now one body. He prays 'through our Lord Jesus Christ, who lives and reigns with you in the unity of the Holy Spirit, one God, for ever and ever'. The people answer, '**Amen**', which means that they accept the prayer as their own.

Some Protestant traditions prefer heartfelt spontaneous prayer to a liturgical formula because they believe that it is more likely that such prayer is from the heart. The ancient rabbis were very conscious of the danger of empty formalism when carrying out liturgical rites and many insisted, just as much as the New Testament, that prayer should come from the heart. To combat this danger of a superficial wording of texts and to help use the set prayers as vehicles for raising the heart and mind to God, they recommended that people should use the liturgical formula in their private devotions prior to any celebration so that the liturgical text really became the personal prayer of each one. This seems pretty good advice for us whose liturgy has descended from Jewish prayer forms. Spontaneous prayer is a good complement to liturgical prayer; but the danger when liturgy is neglected is that the church service becomes limited by the restricted insights of those who speak, while the liturgy is an expression of Catholic Tradition over two thousand years and is a wonderful source of spirituality. However, the challenge remains that we must internalize it, and this is the work of a lifetime.

The purpose of the entrance rite is to prepare us for what is to follow. For a good reason, the act of penance and the Gloria may be dispensed with. We have seen that the Gloria is not used in Advent or Lent, and it is not used on ordinary days during the week. A blessing of water and sprinkling of the people, called the *Asperges*, can take the place of the penitential rite on Sundays. As it is a remembrance of our baptism, it is very fitting for the feast of the Baptism of our Lord and for the Sundays of Eastertide. Lauds and Vespers are the official morning and evening prayer of the Church and are mainly made up of some psalms and a New Testament canticle. If one of these services is to be integrated with the Mass, then the psalms take the place of the penitential rite. The first part of the baptism rite can take the place of the penitential rite if Baptism is going to be celebrated during the Mass.

Note

1. The *Didache* was probably written around AD 90 and for some centuries was considered part of the New Testament by the Church in Egypt. It would be anachronistic to call it a missal because such a book did not appear until the early Middle Ages. In the early Church, the common prayers were memorized and there was a certain amount of freedom to invent prayers within the framework of a common tradition. Books were reserved for prayers they had no reason to memorize. In those days, books took too long to write and were too costly to be used for what the Christians already knew by heart. The prayers of the *Didache* are Jewish in character; some were adapted to the Christian faith or were of Christian composition while others are identical to those used in the synagogue of that time.

Chapter Twenty

The Liturgy of the Word

One of the Fathers said that, when the Scriptures are read, God is speaking to us and when we pray we are speaking to God. The Constitution on the Liturgy says that Christ is speaking when the Scriptures are read in church. In the Old Testament, only Moses was allowed to ascend Mount Sinai to listen to God's voice and to converse with him, while in the New Testament we all 'have come to Mount Zion'. To us the Letter to the Hebrews (12.29) says, 'See that you do not refuse the one who is speaking'. In the Sermon on the Mount, Christ is the voice of God and his disciples take the place of Moses. This new intimacy and dialogue between God and us, brought about by the Incarnation, made universal throughout the Church by the Ascension, and made possible for us by the Spirit, is the source of Tradition and pervades the whole of the liturgy. It provides the basic structure of the whole eucharistic rite where the Liturgy of the Word is followed by the Liturgy of the Eucharist. Both the downward movement of God speaking to us in the Word, and the upward movement by which we are raised to the throne of the Father by our inclusion in Christ, are the work of Christ's Spirit.

If we really believe that God speaks to us in the Word, then every effort must be made in the eucharistic celebration to make this clear. Too often people regard the readings as a liturgical chore and are oblivious to the sacredness of what is taking place. To accentuate the special nature of scripture reading in the liturgy, the readings have traditionally been sung, and the Gospel book honoured and incensed, Anglican clergy have used the parsonic voice, and evangelicals have often tended to speak very dramatically. These practices may seem rather ridiculous to people outside these traditions but if they make their listeners aware that it is God who is speaking, they are not in vain.

Our rubrics recommend that Scripture be read from an *ambo* or reading desk which is permanent, dignified, and is a natural focal point, so that the people can easily see and hear what is going on. It should be used only for the reading of Scripture, the homily and for prayer. Choir leaders, commentators and cantors should use something else, and the priest should not read the notices from it because it is a sacred place from which God speaks. Moreover, those who read should be spiritually prepared so that they know what they are doing, and they should prepare the reading so that they do it well; they should not read the Scriptures from a leaflet but from a proper book. A young man from Mexico City told me that readers in his parish are not only prepared and trained: they are expected to go to confession before starting their period of reading. If possible, the Gospel should be read from a Gospel book which looks particularly dignified. Above all, nothing should be done to give the impression that reading Scripture is haphazard or no different from reading anything else: I once celebrated a Mass for sisters in which they substituted other readings for those of Scripture. It is clear that they did not appreciate what is happening during the Liturgy of the Word. God is speaking and we have the enormous privilege to be his instruments and to listen to him.

God is speaking, but he infinitely transcends the words that are spoken and the minds of those who understand. The whole process would be a waste of time or only of academic interest if God were not communicating himself. The Fathers used to say that it is necessary to read and to listen with great humility and to seek God's guidance in prayer before we begin. God cannot fill a mind which is already full of other things. The poorer in spirit we are, the more receptive we will be to God's word, and the deeper we will be able to enter God's mystery. Perhaps if we do not spontaneously pray before we read or listen, it is a sign that we either lack humility or that we are not participating in the Liturgy of the Word with faith.

We must remember that the Scripture is a means and not an end, a means by which God in Christ teaches us and communicates himself to us; but although he communicates himself through the words, the purpose is so that we may know and love him. The Fathers warn us not so to concentrate on the words that we fail to be aware of him who is speaking. They saw four levels of understanding Scripture: the actual literal meaning of the text; what it teaches about Christ and Christian doctrine; a guide to Christian living; and a means to pass through the words to the contemplation of God himself. All this is the work of the Spirit according to our purity in heart. St Gregory the Great says that the wonderful thing about Scripture is that it speaks to each person according to his spiritual state: it speaks simply to the least advanced and yet is deep enough to challenge even the most perfect.

It seems that in the early Church there were readings from the Old Testament, the epistles and Acts, and a reading from the Gospels, and that these readings began at the beginning and went through the whole of each book, the readers starting where they left off the week before. The exception was the Easter Vigil which had its own extensive readings. However, as the Christian Year began to fill up and as the saints' days multiplied, each feast needing its own readings, presenting the whole Bible to the faithful became impossible and the need to do so was forgotten. The revision of the lectionary after Vatican II has as its aim to present to the faithful a knowledge of the whole of God's word. The compilers had to balance semi-continuous reading with the need to harmonize the lessons with each other according to themes, especially with those provided by the liturgical seasons and great feasts.

For Sundays and important feast days, there are three lessons: the first is normally from the Old Testament, though there are readings from the Acts during Eastertide and from the Apocalypse towards the end of the liturgical year; and the second is from the letters of the Apostles; and the third is the Gospel. Taking a lead from the Jewish tradition, the readings are in a three-year cycle with, for instance, St Matthew's Gospel during Year A, St Mark's Gospel in Year B, and St Luke's Gospel in Year C. St John's Gospel is read every year at Christmas in a semi-continuous way, during Lent, starting on the Monday after the fourth Sunday, on Maundy Thursday and notably during Eastertide. There is also a section of St John's Gospel in Year B to make up for the shortness of St Mark's Gospel.

Weekday Masses have only two readings: the first is from the Old Testament or from the letters of the apostles; and the second is the Gospel. There is a two-year cycle of the first reading, while the Gospel is the same every year. No effort was made to harmonize the readings with each other.

On Sundays, the first reading harmonizes with the Gospel so that they shed light on each other, while the second lesson usually presents us with another idea because the apostolic letters are read semi-continuously. The harmony is intensified during Advent, at Christmas and for the Epiphany and the Baptism of our Lord, during Lent, Holy Week and Eastertide. Important feasts, Masses for the dead and Masses for particular occasions have their own readings.

The Old Testament Reading
The Old Testament reading is chosen to harmonize with

the Gospel on Sundays. For Christians, Christ is the key to open the spiritual meaning of the Old Testament. Origen says that the Scriptures (by which he meant the Old Testament) are like an almond, the bitter rind being the letter, the protecting shell being the ethical teaching which brings about our purification, and the nut is the treasury or wisdom and knowledge which nourishes the souls of the faithful. Origen believed in the inspiration of all Scripture, but he was not a fundamentalist and knew that having a religion which sticks to the letter of the Law, or which wishes to copy the outward conditions of those who people its pages, can only lead to a narrow and dead religion. He had Jesus to guide him to see the wisdom beneath even the most seemingly irrelevant passages. He said that reading the Scriptures before the coming of Christ was like drinking water; but Christ's presence changed the water into wine. Only the Holy Spirit can enable us to understand the Scriptures with the mind of Christ. In this Origen voiced the general teaching of the Fathers. Thus, when we read the Old Testament on Sundays and great feasts, the Old Testament readings harmonize with the Gospel to make it easier for us to understand them with a Christian mind.

The Psalm

In the early Church, the psalm was sung by a cantor with a refrain sung by the people, and it was a very important element in the Liturgy of the Word. The psalms had been Christ's own prayer during his life, and if we want to form in ourselves a Christian mentality then their use is important. The word 'meditation' originally meant learning passages of the Bible, and especially the psalms, off by heart so that they could become part of our spontaneous prayer as well. It was so important that, even when the practice of reading a lesson from the Old Testament began to drop out in the Byzantine Rite some time in the fourth century, they kept the psalm which is now sung before the Epistle. St Augustine would sometimes base his sermon on the psalm, thus treating it as a reading.

The psalm is a song and really should be sung. As the centuries progressed, the music became longer, the people's participation became rare, and the psalm was reduced to a few lines. In the new missal, the ancient practice of a psalm with an antiphon sung or said by the people was restored. However, many churches replaced it with a hymn from their hymnal, which rarely had anything to do with the preceding reading. One of the functions of the psalm is as a kind of meditation on the reading. For this reason and so that our minds can be formed by God's word, I am very glad to notice that more and more churches are now using it. However, in parish churches they usually read it. In so far as it is possible, it would be much better to take the trouble to sing it. There are now many simple and easily-learned tunes for both psalms and refrains for every Sunday and feast day of the year and I am sure that, once they get into it, parishes will benefit from the practice.

The importance of the psalms and canticles to help us to have biblical minds, and to pray as Christ prayed, has led the Church to use them extensively throughout the liturgy, and they are the largest component of the Divine Office. It has also led many people to use them in their private prayer and thus to internalize them. When this happens, the distinction between biblical prayer and spontaneous prayer simply vanishes. Thus Jesus cried out, 'My God, my God, why have you forsaken me?' which is a quotation from Psalm 22. Both the Benedictus, the prayer of Zechariah, father of St John the Baptist (Luke 1.68–79), and the Magnificat (the prayer of the Blessed Virgin (Luke 1.46–55), are given as spontaneous prayer, yet they are strings of biblical quotations. Before the use of paper and the printing press, most people could only savour Holy Scripture by learning it off by heart anyway; but long after their invention, monks at least continued to learn psalms and other favourite passages by heart so that these prayers could become their own.

There is much emphasis nowadays on the importance of being ourselves; and this has led many to prefer their own spontaneous prayers to 'something out of a book', even when that book is the Bible. But the Christian life consists of adapting ourselves to Christ as he adapted himself to us, and one way of doing this is to make biblical prayer our own. Striving 'to be ourselves' before we are transformed in Christ can be an obstacle to discovering our true selves in Christ.

If we use the psalms extensively in our prayer we are going to find some psalms which express the self-satisfaction of the author in his own righteousness, and there are passages which are extremely bloodthirsty, more like the religion of religious terrorists than our own. How can they be the word of God, and how can they benefit us spiritually by using them? Here we must follow Origen's advice to tear away the bitter rind of the letter. This entails realizing the difference between the religion of the author and our own, and how much further and deeper is the religion revealed by Jesus.

Perhaps the author's idea of righteousness was easily quantifiable, reduced to following a number of religious rules, but rather superficial, and this enabled him to be satisfied with his own righteousness. Jesus looked deeper into his heart, into our shadow-selves, and saw how unfit we are before the holiness of God. He taught us to forgive and love our enemies, something we will find easier to do once we realize that the difference between us and even the worst of them is rather small in comparison with God. We know that God loves them as much as he loves us. Even though it seems they are not in the grace of God, we do not know what God is doing in them, and we should be more anxious that his will be done than indulge in our own feelings of enmity, however natural those feelings may be. I am conscious that I have my own shadow side and that what is said about the just and what is said about the wicked in the Bible show up a division that runs right through me. Therefore I find no difficulty in applying to my faults what God says about the wicked. This is how St Benedict interprets the psalms. This motivates us always to pray 'Lord have mercy'. What does God wish to teach us in these prayers, once we have rejected as impossible the literal meaning of the text? Christ is without sin, so we apply the psalms which tell of the author's righteousness to him and pray them as his mouthpieces. If we cannot wish harm to our enemies, then what can we drastically reject? Surely, occasions of sin. If our right hand should be a stumbling block to our salvation, then we must cut it off, said Jesus. Hence we make the praying of these blood-thirsty passages an occasion internally to reject all within us that is not of Christ.

The Reading from the Apostolic Letters
There is a semi-continuous reading from the letters of St Paul and St James, while those of St Peter and St John are read during the Christmas and Easter seasons. Because it is very long and varied in its subject matter, First Corinthians is spread out over the three-year cycle. The Letter to the Hebrews is divided between Year B and Year C.

It is not necessary to write of the importance of these letters to any Christian who has read them. By listening and absorbing the doctrine contained in them we remain in touch with our apostolic roots, allowing the Church of apostolic times to bear witness to us who share its faith. The Church is one, holy, catholic and apostolic, and it belongs to the nature of the Church that each of these essential characteristics has two dimensions. This is because the Church is the kingdom of God in time and place, in the intervening period between Christ's death and resurrection and the Last Day. Hence the Church is apostolic historically, and also in relation to the risen and ascended Christ through the Holy Spirit.

The Church is apostolic in time and space because it has spread through the world by means of the apostolic preaching and its acceptance by people in each generation.

The apostolic message is contained in the New Testament, which has been handed down from one generation to the next by those who have inherited the apostolic mandate to be Christ's heralds and to proclaim the Word. The words of the New Testament are not only the words of the apostles or of their immediate followers; they are a vehicle for the Word who is Christ himself to address those who listen. St Paul, one of the greatest of those apostolic preachers, was very sensitive to the need to allow Christ and the power of the Cross to contact people through his words, and so he avoided ingenious arguments or anything that would distract people's attention from Christ to his own person. In that spirit, the Christian message is proclaimed to the people through the apostolic letters at this point in the Mass. In the Acts of the Apostles, and in the Apostolic letters, we learn the central message of the Apostolic Church, which we call the *kerygma*, the baptism, death, resurrection, and ascension of Christ. This continues to be the central theme of our preaching and the substance of our memorial in the Eucharist.

The Church is also apostolic because the same Spirit that fell upon the apostles at Pentecost is operative in the Church now, never more than when it gathers together to celebrate the Eucharist. The Holy Spirit transcends history, uniting past, present and future with God's eternity. He does not make past and future present to us because that would annihilate history, but he does give us a relationship with Christ's death and resurrection and with the Last Day, as well as with past and future generations of Christians, which would have been impossible without him. Moreover, he brings us into a relationship with the risen and ascended Christ which is so intimate that we and all other Christians have become one body with him. Therefore the eucharistic community is a manifestation in space and time of the whole Church rather like the tip of an iceberg. It is the general teaching of the post-apostolic fathers like St Ignatius who was martyred around AD 110, and Tertullian in the next century, that the Holy Spirit brings each local church into communion with the apostles, and hence it is sensitive to the true meaning of the apostolic writings and makes the faith of the community the proper place to find an authentic understanding of the apostolic message. Of course, this is only true if the Church is functioning properly. Lack of purity in heart can be an obstacle as can idiosyncratic ideas. Hence there has always been a local church which has acted as a God-given model of orthodoxy. In St Paul's time it was the church in Jerusalem but, by the time of St Irenaeus in the second century, it had become the church in Rome. It is the function of the homily to place the readings in their proper setting which is Catholic Tradition, a growing and developing thing because the Holy Spirit is operative continuously throughout the Church in every generation.

Alleluia

This cry of praise, 'God be praised', was taken over by the East from the Jewish synagogue and began to be a part of western worship around the time of St Gregory the Great.

The late Fr A. Schmemann, an eminent Orthodox theologian, says that there are two types of sung texts in the liturgy: what he calls *psalmodic* chants, in which the words are the most important and dictate the structure of the music, and *melismatic* chant, where the sound or melody is more important for prayer than the words. In the Latin tradition. *melismatic* chant is called *jubilus*, from which we get the word 'jubilant', which expresses the dominant tone of this kind of music.

When we cheer on our football team we are expressing an attitude and an emotion rather than a concept; and this emotion is intensified by our cheering, as is our unity as fans when we cheer together. **Alleluia** can be called a liturgical cheer, though it is used within a very different context, and expresses a wider set of emotions which comes from the very depths of the worshipper.

In our relationship with God words are very necessary,

both God's words to us and our words to God, because that is how we are made. Nevertheless, God is above words and concepts, and concepts are too restricted to express our whole attitude towards God because they are only cerebral. Hence there is a natural tendency sometimes to use words in our prayer to God which have a meaning we only know vaguely, enough to ensure that they are appropriate in the circumstances, but which are too vague for us to pay much attention to them. We use these words to express the attitude of the whole person towards God who transcends words. Other examples are **amen** and **glory**. I suspect that the reason why many people have missed the Latin liturgy is that Latin partly suppressed meaning and so became a good vehicle for a prayer that transcends words. Singing in tongues fulfils the same function with the Charismatic Renewal.

We associate Alleluia with our paschal joy at greeting the risen Christ. According to the mood, it can be like a long-drawn-out sigh, or it can be a shout of joy. We are not paying attention to the meaning of the word but to the presence of him who is about to manifest himself to us in the reading of the Gospel. Jesus appeared to the eleven after his resurrection while they were at table. His presence among us is just as real. We have reached the climax of the Liturgy of the Word when Christ reveals himself in person. The Alleluia is sung during the procession of the Gospel book, and there is a verse which illustrates the main theme of the Gospel reading. If there is no singing, all this can be omitted.

As Alleluia is associated with paschal joy, it disappears from the liturgy in Lent. This increases the impact when it is sung for the first time at the Easter Vigil. During Lent the verse is sung without 'alleluia', but a suitable refrain can be put in its place.

The Gospel

If there is incense, it is blessed at the beginning of the Alleluia verse; then, where there is a deacon, the celebrant blesses him, asking the Lord to cleanse his heart and his lips so that he may worthily proclaim the Gospel. If the priest is alone, he asks the same thing from God for himself.

This is a reference to what happened when Isaiah saw God sitting on his throne surrounded by seraphs (Isaiah 6.5–7). Isaiah says, 'Woe is me! I am lost, for I am a man of unclean lips, and I live among a people of unclean lips; yet my eyes have seen the King, the Lord of hosts!' Then one of the seraphs touched his mouth with a red-hot coal and said, 'Now that this has touched your lips, your guilt has departed and your sin is blotted out.' Then the Lord asked, 'Whom shall I send, and who will go for us?' Isaiah replied, 'Here am I; send me.'

This is appropriate because Christ is about to use the proclaimer of the Gospel as his instrument, using his lips to manifest his own presence. To fulfil this function worthily, the priest or deacon must be without sin, and hence the petition.

Traditionally, there is now a procession to the *ambo* led by processional cross and candles, though the Gospel can be proclaimed from a separate pulpit or even in the midst of the congregation. When a procession is not practical, the priest or deacon takes the book from the altar and carries it aloft to the *ambo* where there are two servers with lighted candles waiting for him.

'The Lord be with you.' 'And also with you.' This announces the need for Christ to be with the proclaimer and also with the people if the revelation contained in the reading is going to take place.

'A Reading from the Holy Gospel according to N.' The people answer, **'Glory to you, Lord.'** The Gospel book is incensed.

The Gospel is received standing to show respect, and to nudge people into attentiveness if they have tended to go to sleep during the other lessons. The Gospel reading is unique among the Scriptures in that it is concerned directly with showing us, through his actions and words, a portrait of Jesus himself and thus reveals to us what Bishop Robinson called the 'human face of God'. We meet the person of Christ, who has been with us since the beginning of the celebration, and whom we are going to accompany and communicate with in the Eucharist.

The proclaimer ends with **'This is the Gospel of the Lord'**, and the people answer: **'Praise to you, Lord Jesus Christ',** and the priest kisses the book. The official instruction recommends that we sing the introduction, 'The Lord be with you' and the announcement of the Gospel as well as 'This is the Gospel of the Lord' at the end, even if the Gospel is read. This emphasizes the special sacredness of the Gospel proclamation. It is a good practice for the people or choir to repeat the Alleluia verse or some other short acclamation which reflects the Gospel at the end of the reading.

Chapter Twenty-one

Our Reaction to the Word, the Homily, Creed and Prayers of the Faithful

Thoughts on the Word of God

Before we go on to the homily, it is worth while to pause a moment and think about the word of God which we listen to in the Liturgy of the Word and which, hopefully, we continue to read outside the Mass. Let us look at some principles which the Fathers have left us that are based on the essentially dialogical character of our contact with the Word of God. They reflect the fact that when the Spirit-filled Scriptures reach into the souls of Spirit-filled Christians, a conversation takes place between God and man. These principles can be used to teach us something about the homily as well as help us when we read the Bible privately.

The Letter to the Hebrews tells us:

> The word of God is living and active, sharper than any two-edged sword, piercing until it divides soul from spirit, joints from marrow; it is able to judge the thoughts and intentions of the heart. And before him no creature is hidden, but all are naked and laid bare to the eyes of the one to whom we must render an account. (Heb. 4.12–13)

We should always begin our contact with Scripture by renewing our faith in him in whose company we are going to listen to the Word. As we have done in the Act of

Penance in the Mass, we should always express sorrow for our sinfulness; and we should acknowledge our need, asking the Lord's help in the process which is about to take place. Then we begin. Acquainting ourselves with the text as well as we can, using all the help that modern scientific studies can offer us, is a good preliminary for our participation in the Liturgy and for using the scriptural text as the word of God. Here I want to concentrate on Scripture as a means of dialogue with God, and then we shall go on to Scripture as a means to interpret what is happening in the world around us.

The Scriptures are rather like a bag of seeds: while they remain in the bag the seeds cannot function. They can only produce living plants when they are planted. Equally, Scripture can only give life when it is planted in the human soul, and it stays inert while it remains within the pages of a book. Within the soul it brings forth things old and new. Let us look at how this process takes place.

It is useful to remind ourselves what we should not be doing when Scripture is used as a means of dialogue with God. Firstly, we are not 'studying the Bible'. It is very worthwhile to study the Bible, but that is not what we are doing when we receive the Scriptures as the Word of God. Such study is a preparation for what we are doing here, where we are seeking God as he is seeking us. Secondly, we are not composing our own biblically-based theology. This is an admirable exercise, but it would be a temptation if we tried to do this here. Still less are we trying to build a belief system. This is already provided by what the Fathers called the Rule of Faith and what we call the teaching of the Church. This Rule of Faith is not taken from the Bible alone, but is a product of the Church's dialogue with the Word of God contained in the Bible. This is only possible if Christ speaks through the Scriptures to the Church and illuminates the same dialogue in which we are taking part, but we are reading the Scriptures and taking part in the dialogue as members of the Church and are not starting from zero.

Without the Holy Spirit, we tend to find our own reflection in the Scriptures rather than have genuine contact with the Word of God. There have always been many sects very certain of their particular but eccentric interpretation of the Bible. St Irenaeus (second century) has a parable of a man who had a mosaic portrait of a king. Someone rearranged the stones to portray a fox and claimed it was the same mosaic because it was made up of the same stones. St Irenaeus said that only the Church can know the basic pattern of the Scriptural revelation because it has the 'charism of truth', given by the Spirit. Only Christ himself is capable of refashioning Scripture in his own image and likeness. Any attempt on our part to do so is infidelity. Relieved of the necessity to build up our own belief system, we can concentrate on the main function of Scripture: bringing about a dialogue with God. Before anything else, Scripture is a means of salvation, a place of encounter with God.

We are not satisfying our curiosity about the scriptural text. We should consider a temptation any tendency to read on simply because we want to know what happens next, which is like skimming over the surface at a time when we should be going down deep. If we are going to use a text which is unknown to us, perhaps we should satisfy our curiosity first before getting down to praying it.

So we must approach Scripture humbly, aware of our unworthiness; we should ask God's assistance; we should beware of simply satisfying our own intellectual curiosity, and we should be receptive, not imposing on the text our own ideas. The danger is that we will use the text to build up our own ego and then all possibility of dialogue is lost. We are in 'kingdom' territory in which God initiates the dialogue, using the text.

A successful reading or listening to the text depends on everything we have discovered in our commentary on the Beatitudes because, as St Bernard says, the Holy Spirit enlightens the person to the degree that he is thirsty for God. What is important is that we receive the text into ourselves, that we accept it as God's message for us. Our model is the Blessed Virgin who said, 'Here am I, the servant of the Lord; let it be done with me according to your word' and 'His mother treasured all these things in her heart.' If, during the reading or listening, some phrase sticks out or appears particularly significant, we should not only let it speak to us then: we should also save it up for later and use it even after the readings are over, treating it like a cow chewing the cud. This was called 'meditation' in the Middle Ages. We should try to respond to what we hear from God in the text with short prayers; but sometimes the text itself can be used as a prayer.

We should have no agenda of our own, no presupposition about how God is going to treat us during this exercise. Like everything else, if we practise this with any regularity, there are going to be times when we are not in the mood, or when there seems no contact between us and God, or there is even a positive repugnance against it; and we cannot hear unless we are listening to God telling us by means of a stark silence to remain faithful, and that there is no resurrection without the cross. There will be other times of great sweetness; but even these may be tinged with a little sadness because our union with the Lord is not complete. I remember a monk of Belmont, whom I did not think was particularly holy, who became positively excited when he knew he was going to die because he was going to Christ. He was like a child going to a party. This could well be the fruit of such faithful reading.

Another way of using Scripture is to use it to interpret a certain situation or as a guide to action. In this method, our main attention is directed at the situation or activity and we ask the Lord, 'What shall we do?' If we are constantly praying the Bible in the way we have described, we may not have to look for a particular text, our biblical minds simply coming to biblical conclusions; and, even if we do need a text, we will know where to look. Probably we will need help and discussion. Or we can read a text and apply it to the situation in which we live, either our own personal situation or another which we are in a position to influence. When Christians became kings, they had to look to the Old Testament for role models; but an Old Testament read through Christian eyes. They were sometimes successful in this.

When I was chaplain to some Young Christian Student groups, we used the 'See–Judge–Act' method, sometimes to good effect. In the way of using the Bible we have been looking at, the 'See' is the text, the 'Judge' is meditation, and the 'Act' is prayer; though they all take place more or less at the same time. In the present method, the 'See' is a meticulous and accurate examination of a situation that needs changing, the 'Judge' is the application of biblical thought to the situation, which results in the 'Act' to help bring about the desired change. All three steps are important: the 'act' is only appropriate as the 'see' is accurate, and only as Christian as the 'judge', but neither of the first two steps is useful unless it leads to action. I told you earlier how this method has transformed families in Peru where it is used in family catechesis. It works.

These two ways of using Scripture are not opposed. The first is contemplative and the second is active; but contemplation and action require one another. In the Beatitudes, the contemplative experience of 'the pure in heart' naturally leads to the role of 'peacemakers'. Thomas Merton uses the image of 'the spring and the stream'. If a spring ceases to flow outward it becomes stagnant; if the stream loses contact with its spring, it dries up. It follows that, if prayer does not express itself in action, it becomes inauthentic; and if action is not rooted in prayer, it loses its Christian character.

These two ways of using Scripture point to two different kinds of sermon. We are now in a position to look at the homily in the Mass.

The Homily

A homily is required on all Sundays and holy days of

obligation, and when Masses are celebrated for children and special groups. It is strongly recommended on the weekdays of Advent and Lent and during the Easter season, on big feasts and at other Masses when the congregation is large. It is a good practice to give a homily at all Masses when there are people attending. It is usually given by the presiding priest or by a concelebrant. It must be completely separate from making announcements and giving the notices. These have their place at the end of the Mass, before the blessing.

The homily sets forth the mysteries of faith and the standards of Christian life, through an explanation of the Word of God proclaimed in the readings or expressed in some other liturgical text that is being used in the celebration. It should be the fruit of the priest's own meditation and should be carefully prepared. It is to be neither too long nor too short, and must be geared to the mentality and situation of the people who are listening.

The priest must be very conscious that his sermon is a vehicle by which Christ speaks to the people. This makes it different from a class or a lecture. As in all 'kingdom' activities, humility is required for the priest to be a willing instrument of Christ's Gospel. If all the people remember is that the priest is an excellent speaker, if all they remember are his jokes and stories, then he is a bad preacher: in fact, he hasn't preached at all. A good preacher uses his skills to deliver a message rather than to advertise himself. There is an element of self-denial, even in preaching. St Paul writes:

> When I came to you, brothers and sisters, I did not come proclaiming the mystery of God to you in lofty words of wisdom. For I decided to know nothing among you except Jesus Christ, and him crucified. And I came to you in weakness and fear and in much trembling. My speech and my proclamation were not with plausible words of wisdom, but with a demonstration of the Spirit and of power, so that your faith might rest

not on human wisdom but on the power of God. (1 Cor. 2.1–5)

The shortest homily in Christian history was given by Jesus in the synagogue at Nazareth, 'Today this scripture has been fulfilled in your hearing'. (Luke 4.21) It is true that he expanded on it as a result of their reaction, but even that speech was short and poignant. All sermons are versions of that 'today'. It is of the nature of the Word of God to make a difference, and it is the function of the homily to apply the Word of God to the condition and circumstances of those who listen in such a way as to make a difference. This means that it has a particular aim, an object in view which has been clearly thought out. It must challenge the people in some way. And what must challenge is God's Word, not some crusade of the priest's own making nor some fashionable cause, however worthy, which does not flow from the Word. We must be careful not to fall into the temptations that Christ resisted in the desert.

The main subject of the homily is the Christian Mystery, the *kerygma*, God's saving love revealed in the life, death and resurrection of Christ, together with its implications for us. All sermons must be grounded in it and all activities recommended by them must lead to our participation in it. Anything else is not a homily. That being said, there is a great variety of ways of preaching it because it is not a little message but a great mystery, and human life has many facets.

There are the two types of sermon based on the two ways that Scripture can be used. These correspond to the two commandments, to love God with our whole being, and to love our neighbour as ourselves. After having proclaimed the Gospel, we then take an aspect of it – this corresponds to 'meditation' in our private reading – and then so relate it to the lives of the hearers that they absorb the truth contained in it, with the object of increasing their participation in the Mass and sacraments, deepening their prayer life and, in general, increasing their love of God. We can examine some aspect of their lives, family relationships, their work practices, or we can look at something in the news that affects them or affects other people whom they should help, with the object of challenging them to change or giving them encouragement to persevere, applying the reading or text to their circumstances. We can introduce the theme and make it more concrete by using true or fictitious stories, and we can use the lives of the saints.

An important thing to remember is that the Christian community at Mass is the body of Christ, and the priest does not have a monopoly on the Holy Spirit. Thus a good preacher's sermon is not only the fruit of his own meditation on the word of God: it is also the fruit of listening to the people. A good sermon is a work of mediation between the reality of God's word and the reality of the people. He can say to the congregation, 'This is the Spirit of truth, whom the world cannot receive, because it neither sees him nor knows him. You know him, because he abides with you, and he will be in you.' (John 14.17). I have known priests who discussed the theme of the next Sunday's homily with a group of parishioners and the sermon came out of that discussion. Even if we do not go to those lengths, the habit of listening to the people and knowing their reality is the mark of a good preacher.

Silence

If the Mass is being celebrated properly, then a dialogue is taking place between God and the community. Every opportunity must be given for priest and people to interiorize God's word: hence the importance of silence. The General Instruction of the Roman Missal 1975 strongly recommends silence after the homily. People should be instructed how to handle silence in a prayerful way because it doesn't come naturally.

Profession of Faith

The Creed is obligatory on Sundays and Solemnities and can be used on days that are important to the local community.

Originally the Creed was recited in the Baptismal Liturgy, and it came into the Mass during the Christological controversies in the East. It was then adopted in Spain during the sixth century. Then the Frankish Empire took it over during the Adoptionist heresy in the eighth century and added the famous 'filioque' clause to combat the heretics' claim that Christ was in some way inferior to the Father. Only in the eleventh century was the Creed adopted in the Roman Mass, somewhat reluctantly, due to imperial pressure.

Long use has convinced the Church that this is a fitting response to the Word of God. It demonstrates that the community has listened and accepted it within the context of Catholic Tradition and Catholic faith.

The Prayer of the Faithful

The whole community exercises its priestly function to intercede for the Church and for the whole world. There may be prayers for private needs, but this is not the main thrust of these prayers. We are participating in Christ's intercession in heaven and, therefore, it is fitting for our starting point to be what most concerns Christ rather than what most concerns us. That having been said, there is nothing wrong with praying for our needs as well; and, at least in English-speaking countries, there is a short silence at the end of the intercessions which gives people the opportunity to make their own petitions. It is fitting to have these intercessions whenever there is a congregation.

The intercessions normally follow a pattern:

a) for the needs of the Church
b) for public authorities and the salvation of the whole world

c) for the oppressed and those in need
d) for the local community.

In England and Wales, there is a Hail Mary to ask our Lady's intercession.

The priest introduces the prayers with an exhortation to prayer and ends them with a concluding prayer.

In the celebration of other sacraments during the Mass, in Requiems and on particular occasions, the prayers are adapted to these occasions; but the intercessions are never only about the people present or about the person who is dead. This is because we attend Mass specifically as members of the Church and not merely as private individuals. There are always petitions for others as well.

Chapter Twenty-two

The Liturgy of the Eucharist

In the Liturgy of the Word, God has spoken to us as he spoke to Moses, and we have spoken to God. In the Liturgy of the Eucharist, we shall take part in a meal in which the presiding priest will give thanks to the Father over bread and wine for Christ's life and especially for the Last Supper, his death and resurrection in anticipation of his second coming, and then we shall eat and drink this blessed food so that we may receive the blessing that the Father bestows on those who remember his Son in faith.

If this were all that happens, it would still remain a celebration at the Old Testament level: the kingdom would not have come, because the kingdom is God's work, and the main emphasis of the rite would be on what we do rather than on the action of the Holy Spirit. An important aspect of the kingdom is the new covenant relationship between God and the human race, and this has been established in Christ's own body by his death and resurrection so that, to enter into this covenant, we must enter into Christ himself. In the Eucharist, the Father sends his Spirit who transforms a merely human sacred rite belonging to this world into a 'kingdom' event in which the Church is united to Christ in heaven.

We noted earlier that it is a characteristic of 'kingdom' situations that particular historical events have cosmic implications. Let us put the eucharistic sacrifice into its cosmic context. Sacrifice is the fundamental law of the universe and is based on the life of the Blessed Trinity. The Father gives his whole being to his Son, and the Son gives his whole being to the Father, and this personal communion in self-giving is the Holy Spirit. God created our world in one act of self-giving love in order to bring us into existence, and so to let it be a revelation of himself to humankind. In a world without sin, the universe would have revealed to us the Word by which the Father created it. It would have been God's gift to us and a manifestation of the Father's love for us. In our turn, our very participation in the world and our wonder at its beauties would have been our gift to God, a hymn of praise and thanksgiving to him.

However, we looked only at the gift and grasped it to ourselves, wanting it for its own sake, thereby marginalizing God. We are the mind of the universe, entrusted by God to give it at the created level the same meaning that it has for him as its Creator. As sin had separated us from God, we could no longer do this and the universe became meaningless for us who were the only creatures that could give it meaning. At our created level, it was no longer an expression of God's love for us nor of our love for him. We could only invent false meanings which were expressions of our own ego, of our false ideas, beliefs and ignorance. The distortion of the universe's mind was a distortion of the universe itself because it had ceased to be a mutual gift in the relationship between God and man, and the human race lost its function as nature's priest in relation to God.

Jesus Christ gave himself entirely to his Father and to us on the cross and became the kernel of the New Creation at the resurrection. By the resurrection–ascension, he has changed the relationship between creation and its Creator, between the human race and the Father, through the transformation of his own human nature. This has made possible the transformation of the whole human race and, indeed, of the whole cosmos because, as man, he is a minute part of everything that has been made, but also the new mind of the universe who gives it new meaning, and as the incarnate Word of God he holds everything in existence. He is present in heaven before his Father, making intercession for us with his blood; and is related to the whole universe because he 'fills all things'. He is also present in time and space through the Church which the Spirit brings into being by word and sacrament. All this comes together in the Eucharist. Christ is much more than what the universe would have been had there been no sin, but he fulfils the function of the old creation before the Fall in a more wonderful way because he is both the perfect gift of God to us and the expression of our praise and thanksgiving to God. By our union with him Christ has restored to us the priestly function which sin denied us, but we can exercise this priesthood only in Christ.

Later Judaism was willing to call any exterior action a sacrifice if it manifested an interior sacrificial attitude. Almsgiving, burying the dead, and prayer had a sacrificial character and a memorial of these actions was taken up into the divine Presence by angels, who were the priests of the heavenly Temple. After the destruction of the Temple in Jerusalem, this justified those Jews who believed the only way to approach God in his special covenanted presence was through sacrifice, to decide that the ritual meals which presented to God a memorial of his past deeds were sacrifices of sufficient holiness to replace those of the Temple. The food over which the thanksgiving prayers of memorial were chanted was made available to God, in order to make it a vehicle of his favours to those who participated. The same enlargement of the idea of sacrifice permitted the first Christians to interpret Christ's death as a sacrifice and to interpret the Eucharist in the same manner.

Although sacrificial language is used in New Testament accounts of the Last Supper, the first time that the Eucharist is unambiguously called the Church's sacrifice is in the *Didache*, written around AD 90 twenty years after the destruction of the Temple, when many Jews were coming to the same conclusion about their sacred meals.

The Eucharist takes place when a Jewish-type memorial meal becomes Christ's sacrifice. The thanksgiving prayer presents before the Father a memorial of Christ's obedience unto death, and of God's saving power as manifested in the resurrection and ascension, thankfully acknowledging that we may approach him because Christ had paid the price for sin on our behalf. In the light of Christ's death, it also presents to God a memorial of the saints and what God has done in them, and it intercedes for the living and the dead. This prayer is said over bread and wine which has been made available for God's use. In line with Jewish ideas of sacrifice, we benefit from this rise to the extent that these gifts of bread and wine represent our own humble and contrite hearts, our own conversion from sin, and the extent to which we have been changed by our acceptance of Jesus Christ. This is where the Beatitudes come in because they describe the change that is necessary. To the extent that we have changed, we are open to receive the blessings of the kingdom which the Father will give us when we eat the consecrated bread and wine. However, just as bread and wine in themselves are unable to give us any sort of blessing, so the changes of basic attitude described in the Beatitudes by themselves are incapable of bringing about their promised consequences. Both the bread and wine and the inner attitude in us that they symbolize await God's gift. The Church's gift, useless in themselves, and our own self-offering must be included in Christ's gift of self to the Father. When this happens, our thanksgiving prayer becomes Christ's prayer, our gifts become Christ himself. This is done through the prayer of the priest who represents both the whole Church, and the risen Christ who is present in the Church by the power of the Holy Spirit. If the thanksgiving for God's saving deeds in Christ over bread and wine are sufficient to express the Church's self-offering, we may ask what in the rite expresses Christ's own self-offering which reached its full perfection of the cross. We need to go no further than Christ offering himself as food and drink. On the cross, Christ offered himself to the Father by putting himself entirely in the hands of men, which is what he is doing here. If, according to Ecclesiasticus, giving alms is a sacrifice, then surely giving himself to us is even more so. He becomes our sacrifice, the one that God has provided.

In the early Church, Christians saw, in the story of Abraham's sacrifice of Isaac, a prophetic insight into the Christian Mystery. One only had to look deeper into the story to discover the Word who is the author behind all biblical authors and the principle of unity of the whole Bible.

Abraham goes up with his son Isaac to the place of sacrifice. Isaac asks his father where the lamb is for the burnt offering and Abraham replies that the Lord will provide. After binding his son ready to sacrifice him, an angel stops his hand and tells him not to sacrifice his son. Being without anything to offer, Abraham finds a ram which has been caught by his horns in a thicket. He sacrifices the ram and afterwards calls this place 'The Lord will provide'. God does in the Eucharist what he would not allow Abraham to do: he offers his Son to us; Jesus is the lamb or ram that the Lord provided, and Abraham is ourselves who have nothing to offer to the Lord unless the Lord himself provides.

How does all this square with the insistence of the Letter to the Hebrews that Christ died once and for all for sin and does not have to offer himself again and again, otherwise he would have had to suffer again and again since the foundation of the world?

The need for the eucharistic sacrifice does not become apparent if we consider the death of Christ simply as a legal transaction by which Christ won for us the legal right to salvation. This is only one of the metaphors used to explain to us the meaning of the Cross. The Letter to the Hebrews uses a different imagery, based on Temple theology and the ceremony of the Day of Atonement.

In Jewish thought, *korban* or 'sacrifice' came from a verb which meant 'coming close' and was about approaching God who had himself approached Israel by making himself present in an intimate way in the Temple. Other kinds of prayer to God were suitable elsewhere but, wherever he revealed himself in a special way to those whom he chose, sacrifice was necessary. In the Temple was his intimate presence, the result of his covenant with Moses, and the only way he could be approached was by sacrifice. Killing the animal had two functions. Firstly, it was a ritual expression of repentance and, secondly, they were also handing over the blood to God so that he could use it as a means by which he purified and blessed his people. Killing the animal was a recognition by the offerers that they could not survive a meeting with God unless he mercifully protected them, because death is the natural consequence of sinfulness when it meets the holiness of God. Hence it was an expression of a humble and contrite heart. They also killed it because they needed the blood to offer to God, not so much as a gift because God owned it anyway, but as a symbol of their own self-offering and so that he could use it. They did not offer the death of the animal to God because God is the God of life. Still less would they offer the death of a human being, because they considered human death to be a consequence of sin and hence positively antipathetic to God. Thus, any contact with a corpse rendered a person ritually unclean. They believed that the life of an animal is quite literally contained in the blood, and when the priest poured blood at the foot of the altar he was actually handing over its life to God, a life that was only made available by the animal's death. Killing was not a priestly function, though they were often asked to do so because they were experts. In the sacrifice of the lambs for the paschal feast, the killing of the animal was not the work of priests because the families usually did it themselves. The priests' function was to pour out the blood at the foot of the altar.

On the Day of the Atonement the high priest killed the animals, but the highlight was sprinkling and pouring some of the blood in the Holy of Holies, while the rest of the blood was used to purify and heal the Temple from the effects of the people's sin. This made it possible for God to remain in his sanctuary in covenant relationship with his people so that they could 'approach' him during the rest of the year. If the sacrifices of the Day of the Atonement were not to take place, the danger was that God would abandon his sanctuary and the covenant relationship would be broken. The exile in Babylon taught them that the covenant did not depend on the Temple. Nevertheless, most believed that sacrifice was the normal way of approaching God where he specially manifested his presence, and they took pains to build another Temple at the first opportunity.

The problem came when the Temple was finally destroyed by the Romans in AD 70. There had always been an anti-royalist faction who saw the insistence of the Temple's necessity as royalist exaggeration to support the king's authority. During the exile these people put all their emphasis on the Torah, the five books of the Law, as the true manifestation of God's presence and they believed that keeping the Law rather than the Temple was the guarantee of God's continual presence among his people. They accepted the Temple, or at least many of them did, because it was the successor to the Tent of Meeting which was important in the Torah. However, they did not consider it essential to the covenant. This faction came into its own after the Romans destroyed the Temple. They met in a place called Jamnia some time afterwards, and established the foundations of the modern Jewish religion.

Nevertheless, by no means all Jews were happy with this solution or accepted their version of Jewish life. Many Jews still believed that the only way to approach God when he manifests his presence is through sacrifice. Therefore they had to accept either that there was no

longer a special presence of God in Israel, or that some
other observance had taken the place of the sacrifices in
the Temple. They looked around in their religion for
observances which could take on the important role that
sacrifices had had when there was the Temple, and many
decided on their sacred ritual meals. They justified this by
saying that the prophecy of Malachi was being fulfilled:
'From the rising of the sun to its setting my name is great
among the nations, and in every place incense is offered
to my name, and a pure offering; for my name is great
among the nations, says the Lord of hosts'. (Mal. 1.11)
The central importance of sacred meals which were seen
as a foretaste of the Last Time when God would establish
a succulent feast together with the Messiah in the
kingdom had already been a feature of the Essenes at
Qumran. This idea of the sacred meals as the purest of
sacrifices is supported by the Rabbi Trypho in his
dialogue with St Justin Martyr in the second century.
Among those who followed this tradition was the Christian Church, which remained part of the Jewish world for
much longer than the polemic on either side would lead
us to believe. You will recognize the text from Malachi in
Eucharistic Prayer III.

The Letters to the Hebrews was probably written by a
Christian convert from the priestly tradition. He considers the Temple sacrificial system as a reflection, a shadow
of the Christian mystery. This was in accordance with
Temple theology which considered the Temple rites as a
reflection of heaven. Thus, while the author believed that
Christ's death and resurrection–ascension had replaced
the Temple and had made it obsolete, nevertheless he
considered it legitimate to use the ritual of the Temple to
help us understand the Christian mystery.

According to the Christian theology of the Atonement,
the death of Christ is a result of sin in two senses. Firstly,
because humankind had rejected God's place in its life,
human biological life simply took over, and we die like
any other animal. Thus death became a natural

consequence of sin which Christ accepted for our sake. Secondly, Jesus was rejected by his own people who collaborated with the Romans to kill him, so he was a victim of a particular sin of rejection and this he also accepted for our sake.

What was acceptable to God was his obedience unto death, his total giving himself to the Father in love. His death was permitted by God as a means of achieving this result; but it was not pleasing in itself. By dying, Christ repudiated sin by suffering the consequences in loving obedience, and this is the very opposite of sin. This is his offering to the Father. The cross was the occasion and means by which he became perfect, as Hebrews says. He is the perfect gift. The lambs, goats and bullocks were not gifts to God, because God already owned them. What he did not own in the same way is that which could be freely given, the perfect, humble love and obedience of Christ under the most extreme conditions.

While his humble obedience made him acceptable as a perfect sacrifice, his death made the risen Christ available to the Father to be the means of salvation for all. On the Day of the Atonement, the goat and bullock were killed so that their blood was made available, and God could use it for the purification and healing of the Temple. Christ in heaven became available so that his Father could use him for the salvation of humankind. However, as he is human and not a goat or a bullock, this making himself available is pure gift to the Father. The Letter to the Hebrews sees him enter the heavenly 'Holy of Holies' with his blood, by which is meant that Christ is pure gift, a living memorial of his loving obedience on the cross.

Christ died, and he does not need to die again. Christ approached the Father, entering the heavenly 'Holy of Holies' and is there eternally, so he does not need to enter again. He does not have to approach God again, but we do. The same Letter talks of us approaching Mount Zion '... to God the judge of all ... and to Jesus with his blood'. The Mass is a thanksgiving memorial of these unrepeatable events enabling us to approach God; it is effective because Christ makes our prayer his own, and our offering himself. In this way we approach God where he is most specially present and, instead of killing an animal, which would now be an empty symbol, we offer to the Father a memorial of Christ's perfect sacrifice. By this we proclaim Christ's loving obedience unto death as our sacrifice because we have become one body with him.

In the Liturgy of the Word, Jesus 'goes up the mountain' and we, his disciples, come to him. He speaks to us as he did to the first disciples in the Sermon on the Mount and as God did to Moses, and we speak to him through prayer. In the Liturgy of the Eucharist, the Spirit comes down on our gifts and on ourselves, so that we may become one with Christ who is the Lamb slain but standing in heaven before the throne of the Father. The Eucharist is our way of approaching the Father where he is specially present: it is our Temple and our sacrifice, because it is our sharing in Christ.

The altar in the Temple was nothing like altars in our experience. It was very high and, to reach the top, one had to climb up steps or a ramp. On the top there was a fire. On Christian altars, the fire is the Holy Spirit by whom the bread and wine become the body and blood of Christ. The biblical image is that of Elijah on Mount Carmel who prepared a bull for sacrifice, and then prayed to God who sent down fire from heaven to consume the sacrifice. (1 Kings 18.36–9).

The bread and wine become the succulent food and drink prophesied by Isaiah (Isa. 25.6); succulent because it is Christ who is the source of everlasting life: 'Those who eat my flesh and drink my blood have eternal life, and I will raise them up on the last day; for my flesh is true food and my blood is true drink. Those who eat my flesh abide in me, and I in them.' (John 6.54–6)

The whole universe is a system of processes, and everything in it is related to something else within the system. Anything which bears no relation to some process within the system is deemed fictional. Thus there are neuro-scientists who study the brain and have come to the conclusion that the immortal soul is a fiction, because they are getting near to explaining all the functions of the brain in a way that leaves no room for a soul within the system. Within the observable world, the human person seems to be the product of a biological system which is doomed to die and, as violin music dies when the strings stop vibrating, so the human person will cease to exist when the biological system breaks down. However, the Eucharist bears witness to another dimension of the universe, and to another set of relationships, which are not observable by Science, because it was never designed to observe them. This dimension is the relationship between the whole universe and God, which explains why it is something and not pure nothingness, and the relationships are those between human beings and God who has called us to eternal life.

In the Eucharist, we see through faith the human person being drawn into a new set of relationships, with Christ and hence with the other two Persons of the Blessed Trinity, and also with each other. This is eternal life, the new creation, the kingdom, the direct result of belonging to the body of Christ which, since the resurrection, is a reality of the New Creation. God has called all human beings to this, and it is our call to a relationship with God that gives substance to us as persons of a kind that will survive death. Persons are made for relationships and are even constituted by these relationships; and to have no relationships at all would be a kind of living death. It is the Christian vocation to live in these relationships on earth and to bear witness to them before the world, because all human beings are called by God to live in them in heaven. To fulfil this vocation we need to be constantly brought up into these relationships; and that is the role of the Eucharist.

The relationship between the Blessed Trinity and us, and of us with each other in the kingdom, can be described as self-giving in love, a good enough definition of Christian sacrifice. The fundamental rule for us is, 'in giving we receive, in dying we are born to eternal life'. We must become 'living sacrifices' as we love God with everything we are and have, and love our neighbours as ourselves. The Eucharist is the weekly or daily expression of daily self-giving which gradually turns us into images of Christ. The Father gives himself to us through Christ; we give ourselves to the Father in Christ; and we give ourselves to our brothers and sisters in fraternal love because we see Christ in each other. On behalf of all creation, we adore the Father by offering him Christ, even as Christ offers us to the Father as members of his body. We give thanks to God, pleading Christ's sacrifice on the cross for our sins and for those of the whole world, even as Christ pours out his blood on the mercy seat for the same intention; and we pray for our needs and those of all humankind, knowing that our prayers are taken up by Christ who makes them his own. The Eucharist is the supreme manifestation on earth of Christ's mediatorship in heaven.

The Liturgy of the Eucharist is divided into three parts:

1 The Presentation of Gifts: 'Jesus took a loaf of bread ... Then he took a cup ...' (Matt. 26.26–27). In this we present on the altar the bread and wine which are our contribution to the sacrifice. With these we present any other gifts we wish to give to the Church or to those in need. All this symbolizes our own self-giving.

2 The Eucharistic Prayer: 'And after blessing ... After giving thanks ...' This is the thanksgiving over bread and wine which places before God the 'memorial' of his wonderful deeds, Christ's death, resurrection and ascension, in anticipation of his coming again on the last day; and the bread and wine become Christ's body and blood.

3 Communion: 'he broke it, gave it to his disciples ... he gave it to them.' We receive the body which has been broken for us, the blood which has been poured out for us, becoming one body with Christ.

Chapter Twenty-three

The Presentation of the Gifts

The only miracle found in all four Gospels is the Multiplication of Loaves, five times if we include the Feeding of
the Four Thousand. The repetition of the phrase, 'Taking
the five loaves and two fish ... [he] blessed (gave thanks)
and broke the loaves (the fish having been forgotten in
Matthew and Mark) and gave them to his disciples', in all
accounts cannot be a coincidence, and links the miracle
with the Last Supper. This miracle was popular because it
was used in the apostolic Church's exposition of the
Eucharist. For the Jews, it was a messianic sign of the
coming of the kingdom and they wanted to make Jesus
king (John 6.15) and, for Christians, the Eucharist is the
sacrament of the kingdom.

Jesus saw a large crowd and had compassion on them
and cured their sick. When evening approached, the
disciples suggested that the people should be sent away so
that they could eat, but Jesus told them to supply the food
themselves. The disciples protested that they only had
five loaves and two fish. Jesus took the loaves and fish,
looked up to heaven, and blessed (gave thanks) and broke
the loaves, and gave them to the disciples who, in their
turn, distributed the pieces to the people. All ate to the
full, and there were twelve baskets of left-overs. In all,
there were five thousand men, besides women and children. (Matt. 14.14–21)

Jesus did not create the food for such a large crowd out

of nothing. He took what the disciples had, only five loaves and two fish, and used them to work his miracle. The disciples gave him all they had, which was not a solution to the problem; but Jesus made it adequate by giving thanks.

The twelve baskets of bread that were left over are a symbolic reference by suggestion to the twelve loaves of 'showbread' that were kept in the Temple. Originally, these were probably a food sacrifice to the Deity, but they became a mute petition to the Lord to remember and protect the twelve tribes of Israel. The loaves were stacked in the Temple, and between them were herbs, normally aloes and myrrh. This bread could only be eaten by the priests, and the rule was broken by David and his companions out of necessity, as Jesus reminded the Pharisees. St John describes Jesus embalmed with aloes and myrrh, suggesting that, by his death on the cross, Jesus had become the new 'showbread' which asks God to remember and protect the New Israel. In St John's account of the Multiplication of Loaves, Jesus goes on to say that he is the bread of life and to talk about the Eucharist, using another Old Testament image, *manna* in the desert. This grouping together of Old Testament themes in expounding the Gospel is typical of St John. The twelve baskets could also signify that the twelve apostles were given the task to distribute the bread the Lord had provided in their mission to the whole world.

The five loaves and two fish illustrate the place of the presentation of gifts in the eucharistic liturgy. There is nothing in bread and wine to make them worthy gifts to the Father, nor can they spiritually nourish us. Like the disciples, we can only hand them over to Christ. When he blesses them through the priest, they become his body and blood and hence an adequate sacrifice and true communion with the Father. Our offerings become Christ's own gift of himself to the Father and to us. As with Abraham, the Lord provides the lamb for the sacrifice. (Gen. 22.1–14)

It is almost certain that there was no formal ceremonial attached to the placing of bread and wine on the altar before the eucharistic celebration until at least the second century. However, one of the earliest heresies denied that the material world is good, and also that Jesus had a material body. This led the Church fathers like St Irenaeus to put emphasis on the material nature of the bread and wine before, and the true presence of Christ's body and blood after the consecration. We shall see that later generations became conscious of a moment of consecration, not, as Fr A. Schmemann and others say, during the Scholastic Period, but in East and West during the fourth century. Here we must concentrate on the significance of bread and wine before the consecration.

Once Jews began to see the paschal meal as a sacrifice in itself rather than communion in the sacrifice that had taken place earlier in the day in the Temple, they would have seen the food, not only as their memorial of the events by which God established his covenant relationship with Israel, but also as a ritual expression of their own humble and contrite hearts and a symbol of their own self-offering which they made available to God to become a vehicle of his blessing. This would also be true when they celebrated the *seder* or sacred meal on other occasions. Christians saw the bread and wine as the witness before God to their faith that Christ's death was the means by which God saved the world and as a sign of their own gift of self. However, the bread and wine before the act of thanksgiving received greater significance because they were encouraged by over-spiritual heretics to meditate on the value of matter and of the fundamental goodness of natural human life and work. For Christians everything material, including human works, remains God's creation even after sin has entered the world. Catholic Tradition came to see that the bread and wine represent the natural world and human work which are sustained by God's creative act. This makes them good in themselves even though they are in need of transformation into Christ. This is admirably expressed in the priest's prayers over the bread and wine after they have been brought to the altar.

> **Blessed are you, Lord, God of all creation.**
> **Through your goodness we have this bread to offer,**
> **which earth has given and human hands have made.**
> **It will become for us the bread of life.**
>
> **Blessed are you, Lord, God of all creation.**
> **Through your goodness we have this wine to offer,**
> **fruit of the vine and work of human hands.**
> **It will become our spiritual drink.**

If our sacrifice has been provided for us by God and it is none other than the sacrifice of Christ, why does the priest ask the people:

> **Pray, brethren, that our sacrifice may be acceptable**
> **to God, the almighty Father.**

And the people reply:

> **May the Lord accept the sacrifice at your hands for**
> **the praise and glory of his name, for our good and the**
> **good of all his Church.**

Is the acceptance of Christ's sacrifice in doubt?

Since the time of Isaiah, the People of God has realized that a sacrifice is only as genuine as the sacrificial attitude of those who offer it. If, on the contrary, we are orientated away from God, ignoring the call to conversion, our own sacrifice is an empty ceremony signifying nothing even though, as the Eucharist is the sacrifice of the whole Church, it is fruitful for others. We fail to rise above the visible ceremony and do not participate in what it signifies because of our lack of commitment. The prayer we have quoted implies that Christ's sacrifice only becomes ours to the extent that we humbly orientate ourselves towards the

Father and thus share in Christ's sacrificial attitude. If we want to share in Christ's sacrifice, we ourselves must become 'living sacrifices', but it is his sacrifice that gives value to ours rather than the other way about. This being the case, as a preparation for the sacrifice, it is necessary to have a place where we express our own self-offering to God, in which we present before God ourselves, one another and the whole world of nature and of human work, so that it may become God's world. We also present our almsgiving and acts of charity, our Christian works, to the Lord. All this is represented by the bread and wine.

Like the five loaves and two fish, what we offer is wholly without Christian value in itself unless included in Christ's offering, and we await his prayer which will make his sacrifice our own. In the Old Testament, the sacrificial attitudes and works gave the ritual sacrifices value, while in the New Covenant it is Christ's sacrifice which gives our attitudes, works and prayers Christian value. At the Presentation of gifts we place our useless gifts of bread and wine on the altar and wait for the Lord to act.

To present ourselves to the Lord, to become personally involved in Christ's sacrifice, we need more than an external participation in the celebration. The psalmist says, 'The sacrifice acceptable to God is a broken spirit, a broken and contrite heart he does not despise.' In other words, the extent of our participation in the Mass is the extent to which we have become poor in spirit, is the extent to which our conversion is real. Thus, the Mass is the sacrifice of all Christians who practise the Beatitudes, of all who have a 'broken and contrite spirit', even of those who do not believe in the Mass and are excluded from receiving communion, because we cannot admit their tradition as it stands into the Catholic Church. On the other hand, as a Catholic priest, I can celebrate the Mass with the Catholic assembly and have no spiritual part in it because my heart is not, even remotely, 'broken and contrite'. For this reason, the priest asks God quietly, before incensing or washing his hands:

Lord God, we ask you to receive us and be pleased with the sacrifice we offer you with humble and contrite hearts.

In the second century, the people brought the bread and wine for the Eucharist, and these were carried to the altar at this point in the Mass together with the paten and the cup. Hippolytus says that this was done by the deacons. Later, people brought food from their homes for the Christian community or to give to the poor. In some places, these 'sacrifices' were carried in the procession and comparisons were made with what happens at communion. In other places, the food was placed in the sacristy or in some other suitable place. It became a practice for a deacon to read out the names of those who made offerings, and this led to caustic comments from St Jerome in the fourth century. Sometimes, as in Rome, the names were read in the Eucharistic Prayer itself. This was the nearest thing that the early Church came to having special intentions at Mass.

In Gaul, the carrying of the eucharistic gifts to the altar was accompanied by great signs of reverence, almost akin to a Blessed Sacrament procession nowadays. In the Orthodox East, there still is an immense respect and awareness of the holiness of gifts. They sing the Cherubic Hymn: 'We who symbolize the Cherubim and sing the thrice holy to the life-giving Trinity, lay aside all worldly cares that we may welcome the King of heaven and earth, who is invisibly accompanied by legions of angels'. This used to be sung as the bread and wine passed through the congregation as they bowed down in reverence.[1]

We do not go quite so far but, on occasions when incense is used, the priest incenses the gifts. Afterwards, the priest incenses the altar and then priest and people are incensed. In this way, Christ is honoured in the gifts and in the participants as we prepare for his sacramental manifestation. Christ is present through everything in the cosmos because God holds it in existence through him.

The bread and wine represent this cosmic presence, especially in our human life and work, and we honour this presence with incense. We also honour the bread and wine because the Church has chosen them to represent Christ in his suffering and death and to be vehicles by which Christ enters into our historical lives to be our sustenance. Statues and icons are honoured because of whom they represent and because we use them in our dialogue with heaven. Still more do we honour the bread and wine.

It is highly recommended that members of the faithful should bring the gifts to the altar and that they should be received by the priest or by a deacon. It is in keeping with this moment that money and any other gifts for the poor or for the church should also be brought, but these must not be placed on the altar but apart in the sanctuary. A suitable psalm with a refrain is sung by the people or a hymn in keeping with the moment. If it is not sung, the presentation antiphon is omitted.

After the incensing or, if incense is not used, immediately after the prayers, the priest washes his hands as a sign of his need for inner cleansing worthily to fulfil his task. Ritual washing was a feature of Jewish sacred meals and clearly took place at the Last Supper, though it is referred to for the first time in the Christian Liturgy by St Cyril of Jerusalem in the fourth century. Anything which emphasizes the sacredness of what is about to take place has pastoral value.

The Presentation of Gifts ends with the priest inviting the people to pray that our sacrifice should be acceptable to God, to which they respond. The priest says or sings a final prayer which, on Sundays, feastdays and in the more important seasons, is proper to the day.

Notes

Information from 'The Eucharist', by Robert Cabie; *The Church at Prayer* vol. 2; ed. A.G. Martimort; trans. Matthew J. O'Connell (Geoffrey Chapman, 1986).

1. *The Eucharist. Sacrament of the Kingdom* by Alexander Schmemann (St Vladimir's Seminary Press, Crestwood, New York,
   1988).

Chapter Twenty-four

The Eucharistic Prayer

Before we make our commentary, it is a good idea to record why it was thought necessary after the Second Vatican Council to change the tradition in the Roman Rite of having only one Eucharistic prayer with a variable preface. There may well have been the motive to keep people's interest, now that people were going to listen to the Eucharistic Prayer and understand it, but this was not the main motive. Nor were they trying to 'protestantize' the new Liturgy. It was for reasons of liturgical ecology and pastoral opportunity.

If the liturgy is the main organ of the ordinary magisterium, as Pius XI said, this is not true of the Roman Liturgy alone. Catholic Tradition embraces many liturgical families. Just as the New Testament has four Gospels, and any attempt to harmonize them into one single account has been resisted by the Church, so the Catholic Tradition comprises a healthy number of liturgical traditions which cannot be formed into one without impoverishment, nor can many of them be allowed to die out. Catholic scholars at the time were anxious that liturgical traditions which have either been swamped by the advance of the Roman Rite, severely curtailed, or which are important but unknown to the majority of Catholics, would be able to make their contribution to our liturgical renewal. These rites are all equally valid expressions of Catholic Tradition, even though some had disappeared and others were little known outside the areas where they are celebrated. For these scholars who had been entrusted to work with the bishops in the task of reform and who were internationally respected for their knowledge of catholic liturgical tradition, 'more Catholic' meant 'less exclusively Roman'.

This was not an attempt to provide a hotch-potch of traditions, unifying them so that there would be eventually only one composite tradition, comprising elements of them all. This is not possible. Each rite is the liturgical expression of the way one people has lived the Gospel over a long period. There is a Benedictine monastery in Belgium called Chevetogne which celebrates the liturgy according to the Russian Orthodox use. It does this perfectly, as Benedictine monasteries are accustomed to celebrate our own Roman liturgy in western Europe. A Russian Orthodox archimandrite (abbot) once said to me that Chevetogne celebrates the liturgy with a precision, an exactitude, which is quite foreign to the way the Orthodox celebrate it. That is not Chevetogne's fault: it is doing its best, a very beautiful best, and it is fulfilling a very important liturgical and ecumenical function; but it does not belong to the culture of which the Russian Orthodox liturgy is the religious expression. When we say that Catholic Tradition is made up of a number of liturgical traditions, we mean that no culture is foreign to the Church, and that the Church has various liturgical cultures, each with its own spirituality.

Nevertheless, Liturgy is not a branch of archaeology, nor are liturgical traditions islands. Each tradition is a historically-conditioned but living expression of the faith of the whole Church, and cannot be isolated from other traditions which are expressions of the same faith. It only closes in on itself if it is weak and feels threatened by the other traditions. In renewing the Roman Rite, the liturgical scholars looked to other sources for the three other eucharistic prayers. Eucharistic Prayer I is the old Roman Canon; Eucharistic Prayer II is based on that of St

Hippolytus of Rome; Eucharistic Prayer III is formed from Spanish (Mozarabic) and Gallican sources; and Eucharistic Prayer IV is based on the Byzantine Liturgy of St Basil with a little help from the Liturgy of St James.

Once the idea of several eucharistic prayers had been accepted, there rose to the surface another motive, the motive which underlay the whole project of liturgical reform: so to adapt the liturgy that people would enter more deeply into the Christian Mystery. The two eucharistic prayers of Reconciliation emphasize the role of the Mass in reconciling us with God and with each other. The children's eucharistic prayers adapt the tradition to their vocabulary and understanding and, by breaking up the eucharistic prayer with acclamations, take into account the tendency of children to concentrate only for very short periods. This practice the liturgists borrowed from the Orient. The three forms of the Eucharistic Prayer for Masses for Various Needs and Occasions make reference to St Luke's account of the two disciples' meeting with Christ on the road to Emmaus.

We are now in a position to do our commentary on the Eucharistic Prayer. We shall begin by looking at the dialogue which introduces the Prayer. Then we shall have a look at the Preface. Afterwards we shall give a short commentary on the Roman Canon because it is in many ways unique, and we shall follow up with a generalized commentary on the other eucharistic prayers. We shall base much of this on L. Bouyer's book, *Eucharist*.

The Lord be with you.	**And also with you.**
Lift up your hearts.	**We have lifted them up to the Lord.**
Let us give thanks to the Lord our God	**It is right to give him thanks and praise.**

This dialogue goes right back to the earliest Christian worship and has retained its Jewish character. We have already looked at the implications of 'The Lord be with you', so we shall concentrate on the other two.

The Jews prayed towards Jerusalem, and the Christians prayed with their faces towards the rising sun, because they imagined that Christ would come from there as he manifested himself on the last day, bringing about a new dawn for the whole of creation. Nevertheless, they were conscious of being citizens of the new Jerusalem, which they located for liturgical reasons in the sky.

'Lift up your hearts' means 'Concentrate on what is above'. We are present at a theophany, a manifestation of God. We are going to pass some time with Jesus before the throne of his Father, together with the angels and the saints. Hence we must put ourselves in the right frame of mind. Also, we must do what the prophets insisted on: we must put ourselves completely at God's disposal so that this sacrifice may truly be ours.

'Let us give thanks to the Lord our God'. This states the principal theme of the whole eucharistic prayer. We must give 'eucharist' (thanks) to God, even become 'eucharist' (a thanksgiving offering) to God. The priest is the mouthpiece of the people, giving thanks for the wonderful works of God in Christ; but this assumes that he is expressing the attitude of the whole community. The phrase 'the Lord our God' reflects the covenant relationship between God and his people: 'I will be their God and they shall be my people'. (Jer. 31.33) L. Bouyer believes that this dates from the time in the first century when Christians heard the word of God in the synagogue and then went to someone's private house to celebrate the Eucharist as a meal of the Christian family. This invitation corresponds to what was said at a Jewish ritual meal when fewer than ten people were present.

The Preface

The 'preface' originated in the *berakah* or blessing which was chanted after the reading of the Torah or five books of the Law of Moses in the synagogue. At least, that was where it was put after the destruction of the Temple.

Perhaps it played some role in Temple worship before that. The 'Holy, holy, holy' is certainly associated with the theophanies in prophetic literature which are modelled on the Temple. This prayer is called the *Yozer*. It praises God for creating light and giving it to the earth which is full of his works and which he has made in wisdom. It asks God who made the rays of the sun to have mercy on us. He is praised for the creation of ministering spirits and tells how they interact with one another, giving each other leave to praise God; and the prayer ends with the angels saying in awe the *Qedushah*: 'Holy, Holy, Holy is YHWH of hosts; the whole earth is full of your glory'. Everybody in the synagogue joins in with this angelic hymn of praise.

In Jewish theology, God's glory is manifested in his wonderful deeds of creation and salvation and then naturally reflects back to him. However, in the angels' case, it is returned through their conscious acts of thankful praise. This is the natural response of creatures to their Creator for the gift of their existence. Because God has given the Jews the Torah, they can join with the angels in reflecting back his glory through their praise. The Christians put Christ in the Torah's place and therefore give thanks for Christ where the Jews thank God for the Torah.

The *Yozer* concentrated on praising God for creation, especially the creation of light; while the *berakoth* or blessings in Jewish ritual meals were more concerned with God's deeds in favour of the people of Israel. This pattern is followed very clearly in Eucharistic Prayer IV, where the preface says:

Father in heaven, it is right that we should give you
thanks and glory:
you are the one God, living and true.
Through all eternity you live in unapproachable
light.
Source of life and goodness, you have created all
things,

**to fill your creatures with every blessing and lead all
men to the joyful vision of your light.
Countless hosts of angels stand before you to do
your will;
they look upon your splendour and praise you night
and day.
United with them, and in the name of every creature
under heaven,
we too praise your glory as we say ...**

This is very close to the *Yozer* prayer, so much so that it is
enlightening to make a comparison. In the Christian
prayer, God is addressed as 'Father in heaven' while in
the *Yozer* he is addressed as 'YHWH God, king of the
universe'. In the Jewish prayer, God is praised for creating light, the rays of the sun, and filling the world with his
works; but in Jewish thought, the light of the sun
suggested the light of God which is his glory. In the Christian prayer, there is the same theme of light, but it is the
'unapproachable light' which is the internal life of the
Trinity, and the 'joyful vision of your light' which is God
as he reveals himself to us and shares with us his life. Both
prayers praise God for filling this world with his gifts and
both prayers speak of the angels who are constantly praising God, though the Jewish prayer, along with the Oriental Christian tradition, goes into more detail about the
kinds of angels involved. Both prayers end up with the
angels in heaven and human beings on earth praising
God together and so reflecting God's glory back to him.

The reason why it is forbidden to use another preface
with Eucharistic Prayer IV is that it has preserved this
pattern, which is based on Jewish liturgical practice of
praising God for creation in the preface and thanking
God for salvation after the Sanctus. Any other preface
would disturb this balance.

When the preface and Sanctus from the liturgy of the
word in the synagogue was joined by Christians to the
prayers of thanksgiving in the eucharistic meal, then it

was not long before there came a certain fluidity about where commemorations were made, especially as preface, Sanctus and canon were seen as making up one single prayer. In the Roman rite, the variable preface probably came about because the presiding bishop or priest used to make it up. There were unwritten but strict rules which came from tradition as to how he was to do it. Gradually, by a process of trial and error, a good collection of prefaces was collected. When the liturgical year was formed, these prefaces were allotted to the different feasts and seasons. We shall now look at one of the prefaces for Easter which is very ancient and was probably used at any time originally, but then, with an addition, became the preface for the greatest feast of the year.

> **Father, all powerful and ever-living God,**
> **we do well always and everywhere to give you thanks**
> **through Jesus Christ our Lord.**
> **We praise you with greater joy than ever**
> **on this Easter night (day),**
> **when Christ became our paschal sacrifice.**
> **He is the true Lamb who took away the sins of the world.**
> **By dying he destroyed our death;**
> **by rising he restored our life.**
> **And so, with all the choirs of angels in heaven**
> **we proclaim your glory**
> **and join in their unending hymn of praise:**

It is the genius of classical Roman liturgical prayers that they managed to combine precision, clarity and depth in the smallest number of words.

The Sanctus
The biblical text which inspires the *Qedushah* and Sanctus is from Isaiah, chapter 6.

> I saw the Lord sitting on a throne, high and lofty; and the hem of his robe filled the temple. Seraphs were in

attendance above him; each had six wings: with two
they covered their faces, and with two they covered
their feet, and with two they flew. And one called to
another and said: 'Holy, holy, holy is the Lord of hosts;
the whole earth is full of his glory.'

There is an echo of this prayer in the Book of Revelation,
where the four living creatures that are charged with the
care of the universe sing day and night without ceasing:

Holy, holy, holy, the Lord God the Almighty, who was
and is and is to come.

St John Chrysostom comments that 'the priest is himself
at that solemn moment surrounded by angels, and the
choir of the heavenly host unite with him; they occupy the
entire space around the altar, to honour him who lies
there as sacrificed'. It is a common teaching of the Fathers
that the Eucharist is a theophany, a manifestation of God
among men; and they described it in terms of the theophanies in the Old Testament. In this they are completely
in agreement with Jewish liturgical thought which considered the Temple worship as a theophany and, at least
after the destruction of the Temple, the reading of the
Torah in the synagogue as a theophany. In the Letter to
the Hebrews, chapter 12, we are in the company of angels
and saints as we present ourselves with Christ who bears
his blood before the throne of the Father.

   Soon the Church added the text, 'Blessed is he who
comes in the name of the Lord'. This is taken from Psalm
118 (117 in some Bibles) which is considered THE
messianic psalm. On the feast of Tabernacles, the Jews
processed seven times round the altar, singing this psalm,
bearing boughs; and when they came to verses 25 and 26,
they danced and sang, *'Hosanna, hosanna'*, waving their
palms. The text reads, 'Save us, we beseech you' (*Hosanna*
in Hebrew). 'O Lord, we beseech you, give us success!
Blessed is the one who comes in the name of the Lord. We

beseech you from the house of the Lord.' The entrance of Christ into Jerusalem, prior to his Passion, is seen as a celebration of the feast of the Tabernacles. The people carry boughs and cry out, '*Hosanna!* Blessed is the one who comes in the name of the Lord! Blessed is the coming kingdom of our ancestor David! *Hosanna* in the highest heaven!' (Mark 11.9–10). Jesus tells the Jews, 'You will not see me again until you say, "Blessed is the one who comes in the name of the Lord."' (Matt. 23.39)

Hence, 'Holy, holy, holy Lord, God of power and might, heaven and earth are full of your glory' is a cry of adoration to the Father who is manifesting himself to us through his Son, and 'Blessed is he who comes in the name of the Lord' is a cry of recognition addressed to the Messiah, to Christ. '*Hosanna*, which means 'Save, we beseech you', is a cry of those who know that it is a terrible thing to fall into the hands of the living God because God is a consuming fire; yet it is sung in joy because this is a theophany of God's love: hence it expresses a mixture of conflicting emotions, of awe and confidence, which is quite natural in someone who knows something of the reality of God but believes in his mercy.

The Canon

It is no longer the custom to call that part of the eucharistic prayer after the *Sanctus* 'the canon' because we are anxious to preserve the unity of the prayer as a whole. Nevertheless, it differs in origin from the preface and, in this context, I have to call it something while insisting that, when the two *berakoth* were joined up, they came to form a single entity.

In the ritual meals of the Jews there was a short blessing (*berakah*) to be said over each cup and plate that was served. Just before the meal, a cup of wine was blessed with a short prayer before being passed round. The meal officially began when the father of the family or the senior person present broke bread and passed it round with the words, 'Blessed art thou, YHWH (Lord), our God, King of

the Universe, who bringest forth bread from the earth'.
After this sharing in the one loaf, no one else was allowed
to join the table. The blessing over each plate was said by
the participants in turn. At the end of the meal, a servant
or the youngest member of the group brought water to
the person presiding who washed the hands of all.
Perhaps it is here that Jesus washed his disciples' feet.
Then a cup of wine mixed with water was brought to the
presider and, bowing, he said, 'Let us give thanks to the
Lord our God', to which the rest replied, 'Blessed is he
whose generosity has given us food and whose kindness
has given us life'. Then the presider solemnly chanted a
number of *berakoth* (blessings). He first blessed God for
giving them food and for his mercy. The second blessed
God for the land he had given them, for the covenant
which they enjoyed with him, and for the Torah which
ruled their lives; the third *berakah* pleads for Jerusalem,
for the house of David and for the Temple. He asks mercy
that God will continue to provide for them and relieve
them from anxiety; he asks that Elijah and the Messiah
should come during their lifetime, that the kingdom of
the house of David should be established, and that they
should enjoy living in Zion, God's city. The people
respond with, 'Blessed be thou, YHWH (Lord), who
rebuildest Jerusalem'.

The festive form of the third *berakah* is worth quoting in
full:

> Our God, and the God of our fathers, may the remem-
> brance of ourselves and of our fathers, and the remem-
> brance of Jerusalem, thy city, and the remembrance of
> the Messiah the son of David, thy servant, and the
> remembrance of thy people, the whole house of Israel,
> arise and come, come to pass, be seen and accepted and
> heard, be remembered and be mentioned before thee
> for deliverance, for good, for grace, for loving kindness
> and for mercy on this (such and such) day. Remember
> us YHWH (Lord), our God, on it for good and visit us,

on it for blessing and save us, on it unto life by a word
of salvation and mercy; and spare, favour and show us
mercy, for thou art a gracious and merciful God and
King.

Berakah with its plural *berakoth* means equally 'blessing'
and 'thanksgiving'; so that when we say, 'Jesus blessed' or
'Jesus gave thanks', we are simply translating the same
Hebrew word in two different ways. When the word
'remembrance' or 'memorial' is used in a cultic setting, it
always means bringing the memory of some deed before
God so that God will 'remember' it. Thus when Jesus says,
'Do this in memory of me', he does not mean primarily
that the Eucharist is the means by which we remember
what he has done for us, but that in this rite we present
before God the memorial of what Christ has done for us
so that we may receive the fruits of the New Covenant. In
Tobit (12.12–13) we see the same use of the word 'memorial'. 'So now when you and Sarah prayed, it was I who
brought the record (memorial) of your prayer before the
glory of the Lord, and likewise whenever you would bury
the dead. And that time when you did not hesitate to get
up and leave your dinner to go and bury the dead ...'
   The Paschal meal was a memorial meal of the covenant,
of the mighty deeds by which God established Israel as a
covenant people. They believed that, by eating and drinking food over which the *berakah* had been prayed, they
participated in the blessings of the covenant; and they
knew this because God is always faithful.
   These *berakoth* are the ancestor of the eucharistic canon,
just as the paschal meal is the ancestor of the Mass. I
believe it a waste of time to argue whether the Last
Supper was the paschal meal as we read in the synoptic
Gospels, or another ritual meal as related in St John. Both
sources have good, theological reasons for putting it
where they did; and theological reasons have precedence
over historical detail. What is certain is that the synoptic
Gospels want us to understand the Eucharist in the light

of the paschal meal. In the paschal meal they ate the lamb which had been sacrificed in the Temple earlier to make a memorial before God of the covenant he had made with them. They did this so that they could participate in that covenant. In the eucharistic meal Christians present to God a memorial of his deeds in Christ, praying over bread and wine, and they participate in the body and blood of Christ in order to participate in the new covenant that Christ's death inaugurated.

In place of the memorial of Israel's rescue from Egypt and their entrance into the Promised Land, Christians make a memorial of the Last Supper and of the death, resurrection and ascension of Christ until he comes again. As Tobit's deeds were brought before God by Raphael, so we ask that the bread and wine over which our *berakah* or thanksgiving is said should be taken up by an angel to the Father that it may become Christ's body and blood, because Christ himself is the blessing of the New Covenant.

The Roman Canon

The Roman Canon is different from the other main Eucharistic prayers in common use in that it is made up of a series of quite distinct shorter prayers and because there is no explicit petition to the Father to send his Spirit to make the bread and wine the body and blood of Christ. Both these differences lead L. Bouyer to believe that, in some ways, this canon is more ancient in its structure than any of the others, in spite of the fact that, like them, it has undergone development during the course of its history.

The Hebrew language was very poor in prepositions and did not allow for long, flowing prayers. The longer, more solemn blessing over the cup at the end of the Jewish sacred meal was, in fact, a series of shorter prayers. While the Roman Church rearranged the blessings and heavily christianized their content, it kept the canon as a series of prayers, some ending, 'through Christ our Lord', to which the people presumably answered, 'Amen'.

A thanksgiving prayer interspersed with petitions is made to the Father for what he has done in Christ. There is an extended memorial of the Last Supper which forms the centrepiece of the canon, and this is followed by a remembrance of Christ's death, resurrection and ascension. Our gifts of bread and wine are a 'holy and perfect sacrifice; the bread of life and the cup of eternal salvation' within the context of this memorial. It is also our offering, and needs acceptance as such, as God once accepted the gifts of his servant Abel, the sacrifice of Abraham, our father in faith, and the bread and wine offered by his priest Melchisedech. For Christians, all the blessings of the New Covenant are contained in Christ as their source. Hence, while the Jewish food was simply a vehicle of God's blessing, the bread and wine in the Mass are communion in Christ's body and blood.

The Roman Canon is focused on heaven where Christ is. This is a particularly Christian orientation. We have already seen how the theme of created light in the *Yozer* was changed into the theme of the divine light, in the preface of Eucharistic Prayer IV. The Roman Canon always looks upwards. There is no reference to the Spirit coming down or to the second coming of Christ. In the words of institution, Jesus 'looking up to heaven' takes the bread, and God is asked that his angel may take the bread and wine up to the heavenly altar so that we may receive Christ's body and blood on our own altar.

The canon is in two parts, before and after the words of institution. The first part asks God to bless our gifts and is then dedicated to prayers for the living. A list of saints is given both before and after the memorial (Greek: *anamnesis*) of the Last Supper, but there is a subtle difference between them. The list before the words of institution is noting the fact that this assembly is the Church of the apostles and martyrs and can thus benefit from their merits and prayers. The words of institution seem to be a launching pad for heaven because, in the second part, which begins with Christ's journey upward through death to resurrection and ascension to the Father's presence, there is a request that our offerings, the bread and wine, may be carried into the Father's presence by an angel so that we may receive the body and blood of Christ; there are prayers for the dead, 'those who have gone before us', and this is immediately followed by another list of saints, but the accent here is on actually sharing in their fellowship. It reaches a climax with the doxology, 'Through him, with him, in him ...', and the people answer with the Great Amen.

The Church's sacrifice of bread and wine is made acceptable by being identified with Christ's body and blood because Jesus is the source of our salvation in the presence of the Father. The Eucharist becomes our entrance into the heavenly kingdom, as portrayed in the Letter to the Hebrews and the Book of Revelation. The Roman martyrs were well aware that Christians are citizens of heaven who not only share in the merits and prayers of the saints in heaven, but even share in their fellowship. As citizens of heaven they were filled with joy as they went to their deaths; they were going home. The spirit of the martyrs impregnates these prayers and is illustrated in the choice of saints.

The central piece, to which the first part of the canon leads and from which the second part goes on its journey to heaven, is the *anamnesis* or memorial of the Last Supper where Jesus first ordered his disciples to celebrate the Mass and told us what his death is about. The Mass is not simply a repetition of the Last Supper seen as part of the Passion story where Jesus made a prophetic sign with the bread and wine which instituted his death as an act of sacrifice. Hence, while being the origin of the Mass, there is an aspect of it which belongs to that moment in history. The Church makes a memorial of it, as it does of Christ's death and resurrection. This raises the question: Are the words of institution merely an extended memorial, or are they the words of consecration as well?

While the Mass was thought of as offering a memorial of

Christ and his saving deeds to the Father over bread and
wine by which they became Christ's body and blood, there
was no need to look for the moment of consecration.
Hence the statement, made often by liturgists, that the
whole eucharistic prayer is consecratory. However, when
events led the Church to emphasize the reality of the
bread and wine before the consecration, and the reality of
Christ's body and blood after the consecration, it became
natural to concentrate on the change itself. This is probably when the Eastern Fathers developed the theology of
the Holy Spirit as maker of this change. As they still
regarded the main purpose of the eucharistic prayer to be
presenting a memorial before God, the most natural place
to put the *epiklesis*, or prayer for the Spirit, was where they
would be remembering Pentecost: after the passion,
resurrection and ascension, and hence after the words of
institution.

The next step was to wonder when in the liturgy the
change takes place. In the fourth century, St Ambrose of
Milan firmly placed the moment of consecration when
Christ's own words are pronounced. He writes:

> Look at each detail. The day before his passion, he took
> bread in his sacred hands. Before he consecrated it, it
> is bread, but after the words of Christ had been said, it
> is the body of Christ. Therefore hear him say, 'Take
> this, all of you, and eat it: for this is my body.' And
> before the words of Christ, the chalice is full of wine
> and water, but after the words of Christ have been said,
> it has become the blood that redeemed the people.
>
> (*De Sacramentis* IV)

Two centuries later, St Gregory the Great describes the
moment of consecration:

> For, who of the faithful can have any doubt that at the
> moment of immolation, at the sound of the priest's
> voice, the heavens stand open and choirs of angels are

present at the mystery of Jesus Christ. There at the altar the lowliest is united to the most sublime, earth is joined to heaven, the visible and the invisible merge into one.

Both in East and West, there was agreement that the bread and wine become Christ's body and blood because of what he said at the Last Supper, but there is a difference of emphasis. St John Chrysostom in the fourth century says that, just as God said, 'Let there be light', and this word is effective up to the present day, so, when Christ said, 'This is my body ... This is my blood', his words at the Last Supper effect the change in all Masses. This is valuable in that it shows how there is only one Mass at the eternal level, even though there are many at the level of history. However, it is not clear whether he is aware of a moment of consecration. He stresses that we are offering to God the memorial of Christ's sacrifice on the cross; there was no urgency to find such a moment among people who thought of the Eucharist primarily as the offering of a memorial.

Nevertheless, in the same century, St Cyril of Jerusalem, speaking to people who have recently been baptized, describes the Mass from the presentation of gifts to the end, in which he also speaks of a moment of consecration. In the previous talk, he gave a commentary on the words of institution:

Since then he himself has declared and said of the bread, 'This is my body', who shall dare to doubt any longer? And since he has affirmed and said, 'This is my blood', who shall ever hesitate, saying that this is not his blood? He once turned water into wine, in Cana of Galilee, at his own will, and is it incredible that he should have turned wine into blood? ... Therefore with fullest assurance let us partake as of the body and blood of Christ: for in the figure of bread is given to you his body, and in the figure of wine his blood.

In his next talk, he begins with a description of the Preface as a thanksgiving for creation which ends with bringing in the angels with whom the assembly sing the Sanctus. This looks like a straight description of the *Yozer* ending with the *Qedushah* from the Jewish synagogue. He then goes on to say:

> Then having sanctified ourselves by these spiritual hymns, we call upon the merciful God to send forth his Holy Spirit upon the gifts lying before him; that he may make the bread the body of Christ and the wine the blood of Christ, for whatsoever the Holy Spirit has touched, is sanctified and changed.

That he is speaking of a moment of consecration during the eucharistic prayer is clear, because he goes on to describe the rest of the eucharistic prayer in other talks.

St Ambrose's teaching has entered the doctrinal teaching of the West, while the East sees the moment of consecration in the *epiklesis* or petition for the Spirit. Both agree that the bread and wine become the body and blood of Christ because of what Christ said at the Last Supper; and both agree that the consecration is effected by the Holy Spirit.

How can we reconcile two views of the Eucharist? Firstly, there is the older Jewish teaching that consecration is God's response to a prayer that he should remember his past deeds, the present relationship he has with his people and his promises of the future. This prayer was made in the form of a thanksgiving over food, and the food was seen as embodying the blessing that had been asked for in the prayer. Thus the whole prayer was significant and there was no urge to look within it for a moment in which the food became charged with the blessing. Secondly, when the emphasis ceased to be put on the eucharistic prayer as a memorial of past, present and future and people concentrated on the consecration of bread and wine, the significance of the memorial prayers or *anamnesis* was overshadowed and the moment of change became important. On the one hand, we have the liturgical scholars who speak of the importance of the whole eucharistic prayer, and on the other hand, we have the piety of the people and the way the Church in the west gives special importance and reverence to the moment of consecration. How can we reconcile history with Catholic piety?

While we concentrate exclusively on what the priest is doing, or oppose artificially 'consecration' and 'memorial', this is impossible. However, if we stress the importance of the fact that Christ, acting through his Spirit, is the main celebrant of the whole liturgy and is present throughout the rite, and if we remember that the consecration is only properly understood within the context of 'memorial', then there is a way forward.

Christ is present throughout the rite and is therefore exercising his mediatorial role during the whole of the eucharistic prayer. This is expressed six times in the Roman Canon when individual prayers end with 'through Christ our Lord'. Therefore there in a very real sense Christ makes the whole prayer his own. There is continuity between the words of institution and the rest of the prayer because, grammatically, it is an integral part of the whole, and because Christ is speaking through the ministry of the Church throughout the prayer and not just during the words of institution.

The purpose of consecration is so that the memorial of the Church can be literally identified with Christ in heaven, who is the living memorial to his own obedience unto death in his presence before the Father. Our prayer, the whole eucharistic prayer, becomes him at prayer, and it does this at the moment of consecration.

Hence, the difference between the moment of consecration and the rest of the eucharistic prayer is one of sacramental intensity. Christ, through his Spirit, uses the voice of the priest to express his word by which the bread and wine are consecrated. The words of institution are not addressed to the bread and wine, nor, primarily, to the people, but to the Father: they are a prayer because Christ exercises his power in submission to the Father – a kingdom theme. This, together with the *epiklesis* before the words of institution in the eucharistic prayers composed after Vatican II, make clear that the consecration at Mass is a joint action of the Blessed Trinity in which each Person has his distinct role in accomplishing this single divine act. However, it is the whole prayer that has been united to Christ in prayer, because the Church has been declared his body.

Once the words of institution are isolated from the eucharistic prayer, then certain dimensions of the Eucharist become obscured and can even be forgotten or denied. It is no longer clear to whom the words are addressed; the relationship between these words and the rest of the prayer is obscured, as is the relationship between consecration and memorial; the continuous activity of Christ throughout the liturgy and especially in the eucharistic prayer is forgotten because of the exaggerated difference made between the sacraments and everything else in the liturgy; and, worst of all, the conditions are present for someone to place the words of institution into a foreign context outside any eucharistic prayer, as at the Protestant Reformation.

We may now look at the structure of the other eucharistic prayers celebrated among Catholics of the Roman tradition since Vatican II, leaving out what has been covered already.

The Other Eucharistic Prayers

a) The **Preface** is an integral part of the eucharistic prayer, even when it is variable and can be used with several of them. There are proper prefaces for EP II and EP IV and for the new eucharistic prayers. There is an extremely rich collection of prefaces which can be used with EP I, II and III but not with the others. Thus EP II is the only one with a proper preface that can be changed in favour of the other prefaces.

All prefaces end with the **Sanctus**.

b) The priest continues with the theme of the Sanctus, praising God for his deeds. I suppose this can be called the **Post-Sanctus** which is normally short.

c) This leads into the **Epiklesis**, where the priest asks the Father to send his Spirit to make the bread and wine the body and blood of Christ.

d) The **Institution Narrative** follows, in which the **Consecration** takes place. The whole eucharistic prayer is holy because Christ is taking up the prayer of the Church and presenting it to the Father, but this is the moment of greatest sacramental intensity where Christ speaks through the mouth of the priest to make the bread and wine his body and blood.

Many liturgists believe that the people should remain standing, because kneeling interrupts the flow of the eucharistic prayer. Some of these liturgists would really like to do away with the idea of a moment of consecration altogether, because it is not primitive and is not indicated by the grammar of the prayer. However, if it is not primitive, it is certainly very ancient; the development has its own logic, and there are dogmas of the Church which do not go back so far. Moreover, our belief that the Holy Spirit is as active in the humble faithful today as in apostolic times means that we cannot simply dismiss as irrelevant what members of the Church do, even if what they do arose in the Middle Ages or in the twentieth century. We are not Orthodox or Orientals who manage to imbue the whole celebration with an aura of the sacred. We are western Europeans who are in danger of losing any sense of the sacred. Where it is still present, let us not rob this moment of consecration of the special reverence due to it. If the people kneel, let them kneel: (The eucharistic prayer is 'interrupted' anyway by the acclamation.) if they stand, let them make a profound bow.

e) The priest invites the people: **Let us proclaim the**

Mystery of Faith, to which the people reply with a proclamation of the central truth of our faith, addressing Christ. There are several versions and here is one of them: **Dying you destroyed our death; rising you restored our life; Lord Jesus, come in glory**. The word 'mystery' was taken from the words of institution in the old Roman Missal and may well have recovered its original use as part of a proclamation. Here the people are taking an active part in the *anamnesis* or memorial by proclaiming the central Christian Mystery. It is quite wrong to substitute a hymn to the Blessed Sacrament or a pious charismatic hymn to Jesus, for in these acclamations we are proclaiming the Gospel, the deeds by which Christ brought about our salvation, not directly expressing devotion to his Person.

f) The **Anamnesis:** The priest takes up the theme of the acclamation, expressing to the Father the memory of what Christ has done for us and, in some eucharistic prayers, his Second Coming. It would not make sense for him to address this memorial to Christ because his role is to present this memorial to the Father in Jesus's name; hence there is a 'division of labour', with the people expressing their gratitude to Christ while the priest addresses the Father.

g) **Intercessions:** Following the Jewish custom in their **berakoth**, the priest intercedes for the people. The Pope and the bishop are mentioned as we express our communion with them, as well as clergy and people. In Christian worship, we present a memorial of the living and the dead because God's people embraces both the Church on earth and those who have died, even those who did not belong to the Church on earth but 'whose faith is known to God alone'. We intercede for each other, even though separated by death, because we are all one in Christ.

h) The memorial of the dead leads to the **Memorial of the Saints**: This has two functions; Moses prayed to God to 'Remember Abraham, Isaac and Jacob' (Exodus 31.13), asking that he and the people may have the same favour with God that they had. We present the memorial of the

264264264264264264264 Royal Road to Joy*

aints, remembering the graces they received and, by implication, asking that God will do the same for us. The other motive is to ask God that we may benefit from their intercession. In the kingdom, the angels, the saints, the living and the dead interact with one another in the love of Christ.

i) The whole eucharistic prayer is summed up in the **Doxology: 'Through him, with him, in him, in the unity of the Holy Spirit, all honour and glory are yours, Almighty Father, for ever and ever.'** Here we join the angels and saints in praising the Father, 'He who is on the throne'. We are able to do so in such illustrious company because Christ has taken us up in the unity of the Holy Spirit. If the Father has made the Mass possible by sending his Son in the power of the Spirit, the Father is also the goal of the whole operation. A door has opened in heaven, and we praise him as only the Son is capable, because the Son has included us in himself.

j) **The Great Amen:** This is the response of all the people. They are saying that the eucharistic prayer is their prayer. It is important that this should be given emphasis. It is probably the most important response that they make in all the Mass. Too often it is a mere grunt which is hardly noticed. If possible, it should be sung. The trouble is that it is so short. It is better that they sing it to a special tune, and that it is either elongated or, more practical perhaps, repeated several times.

Chapter Twenty-five

The Communion Rite

The Lord's Prayer
Our Father who art in heaven
Hallowed be thy Name
Thy Kingdom come
Thy will be done on earth as it is in heaven.
Give us this day our daily bread;
And forgive us our trespasses
As we forgive those who trespass against us;
And lead us not into temptation,
But deliver us from evil.

General Remarks. Tertullian, a second century Christian writer, called the Lord's Prayer a summary of the whole Gospel. Certainly, in St Matthew's Gospel, it is a work of incredible theological density. Only St John's Gospel has the same ability as St Matthew in the Beatitudes and the Our Father to cram so much meaning into his text; but St Matthew manages to do it using words which are clear, short and memorable. The Our Father is a simple prayer, based on Jewish texts, and is used daily by Christians all over the world. At the same time, it is a succinct summary of Christ's teaching on the kingdom.

The petitions, 'Hallowed be thy name. Thy Kingdom come', are found in an Aramaic prayer which is used, even now, in the synagogue service:

Magnified and sanctified be his great name. Amen. In the world which he has created according to his will. And may he establish his kingdom during your life and during your days and during the life of all the house of Israel, even speedily and at a near time. Amen.

This, in turn, reflects temple worship. On the most important feast of the Jewish liturgical year, the Day of the Atonement, as the High Priest was preparing the bullock which would be offered for his own sins and those of his family, and the two rams, one 'for the Lord' and one 'for Azazel' or scapegoat, he would utter the personal Name of God. Each time he pronounced the Name, the congregation would respond, 'Blessed be the Name of his glorious kingdom'. Thus the Name, which was pronounced only on the Day of the Atonement, and the coming of the Kingdom were bound up together in the Jewish mind.

In the Gospel of St Matthew, it comes in the Sermon on the Mount during a warning against hypocrisy in religious matters, which takes many forms. On prayer, Jesus teaches us that it should be sincere communion with God. Private prayer should be done in private where there is no danger that people might see and praise us. If we pray in order to be praised by people, it is no longer prayer because it is only apparently addressed to God. Those who do so will find their reward in people's praise and not from God. When we make petitions, we should not go into detail as though God doesn't know what we need: the value of prayer is not measured by its length but by the 'purity of heart' of those who say it, by its sincerity.

All this insistence on interiority and sincerity was common teaching among Pharisee rabbis, as it was with Jesus. The impression is sometimes given that the rabbis were all hypocrites, only concerned with appearances; but this was not so. However, that they, along with Jesus, spent so much time condemning hypocrisy and empty ritualism does indicate that these were common vices.

The Our Father is a very Jewish prayer, and the theme of each petition can be traced to many places in the Old Testament. Two petitions show particular Christian characteristics: the use of 'Father' as the common way of addressing God, and forgiving each other as a condition for being forgiven by God.

It is generally considered that St Luke's version of the Our Father is closer to the original. The simple address 'Father' is Christ's own vocabulary. St Luke is generally very scrupulous about preserving his sources in their original style, while St Matthew's version shows every sign of being adapted to liturgical use and as a summary of Christ's teaching on the kingdom.

We shall use St Luke's version to help us interpret the prayer in Matthew.

> Father,
> Hallowed be your name.
> Your kingdom come.
> Give us each day our daily bread.
> And forgive us our sins, for we forgive everyone
>   indebted to us.
> And do not bring us to the time of trial.

'Our Father who art in heaven'. This means simply, 'Our Father who is God'; 'heaven' being St Matthew's normal title for 'God'. In the religious imagination of the Jews, God dwells in the heavens. This symbolizes the utter transcendence of God, his otherness, his holiness. They counted seven heavens that ranged from the world's atmosphere where the wind blows, the rain falls and the birds fly; then came the firmament with the sun, the moon and the stars; then there were the different courts where heavenly beings dwell; and finally there was the heaven of heavens or highest heaven, which is the divine level of existence where God sits on his throne. To sit at the same level as God implies sharing in a level of existence which belongs uniquely to God. Hence, when

Jesus at his trial told the high priest, 'You will see the Son of Man seated at the right hand of the Power', and when Stephen said, 'I see the heavens opened and the Son of Man standing at the right hand of God', their judges tore their garments or covered their ears because this implied that Christ is on the same level as God. When we talk about our going to heaven, we are really saying our destiny is to share in the very life of God.

One of God's titles is *El Shaddai*, the mountain God. As mountains rise up to heaven, they are the natural places where God and people meet, places where one may expect a theophany or manifestation of God, and where sacrifice should be offered. This is a constant theme throughout the Bible, from the sacrifice of Abraham on the mountain appointed by God, to Mount Sinai where God spoke to Moses, to Mount Tabor, where God manifested himself in the Transfiguration. As we said earlier, by putting the summary of Christ's teaching on a mountain, St Matthew is implying that to listen to Christ is to listen to God.

The world is unaware of its relationship with God because of sin. In our look at the lives of St Seraphim of Sarov and St John Vianney, we saw that, where there is sanctity, the veil between ordinary everyday life and the divine dimension becomes very thin: both these holy men saw and conversed with our Lady, angels and the saints in heaven. For the Jews, the Temple on Mount Zion was the place in which this was specially so. It was there that God manifested his presence to his People, where his Name was pronounced and hallowed, where everything was done according to his revealed will as in heaven. By following the Law, this was prolonged into daily life; but it was in the Temple where the covenant relationship which God had established with Moses was centred. To quote Vatican II on the Christian Liturgy, we can apply these words to the Temple in Christ's time, it is 'the summit towards which the activity of the [Jewish People] is directed; at the same time it is the fountain from which all her power flows'. If our liturgy fulfils this function for us, it is specially so in the Eucharist: hence the aptness of using this prayer at this point.

Of course, the Jews knew that God is not contained in space and that, in fact, he is everywhere, so that we cannot escape from his presence, no matter where we may hide ourselves (Ps. 139). They also believe that he is far from the proud and very close to the humble. Nevertheless, we can only think in spatial terms; and therefore it is helpful for us in our weakness to be able to imagine God as present in a particular place. At least after the destruction of the Temple, Jews prayed facing Jerusalem, while Christians faced east and upwards. 'Lift up your hearts' orientates our minds towards heaven, while the Roman Canon imagines the eucharistic consecration as the bread and wine being taken up by an angel to the heavenly altar. For St Paul, we must be mindful of those things which are above because our lives are hidden with Christ in God.

'Hallowed be thy Name'. God's revelation of his name to Moses was given enormous importance in Jewish thought. It indicated that God not only gave orders to his covenant people but revealed himself in the covenant relationship. As God's revelation of himself, the name came to be treated with great awe; and, in later times, the Jews ceased to pronounce the word YHWH out of reverence, substituting the word *Adonai*, which is the Hebrew for 'Lord', whenever they came across it in the Bible text. Only on the Day of Atonement was it pronounced ten times by the high priest; but, before he did so in the Holy of Holies, he filled the sanctuary with incense smoke so that, if the pronouncing of the sacred Name provoked God to reveal himself, the high priest would have some kind of protection because 'no man can see God and live'.

The meaning of YHWH is disputed: 'I am who I am', 'I will be that I will be', or any combination of present tense with future. It is not meant as a metaphysical statement of Pure Being; this is quite foreign to Hebrew thought. It probably means that God can always be relied on, is constant in his care for his people, and will be with them wherever they happen to find themselves, whether they are wandering in the desert or in the Babylonian exile or at home.

The idea of God's Name as the revelation of himself in covenant relationship is very close to the concept of 'Logos' or 'Word' in the Gospel of St John. Jesus is the revelation of the Father. He says, 'I have made your name known to those you gave me from the world.' (John 17.6) Here are two equivalent formulas: 'Father, glorify your name'. (John 12.28) and, 'So now, Father, glorify me in your own presence with the glory that I had in your presence before the world existed'. (John 17.5) In the Letter of St James, he asks about the rich, 'Is it not they who blaspheme the excellent name that was invoked over you?' (Jas. 2.7) When he writes about the anointing of the sick, he says, 'They should call for the elders of the church and have them pray over them, anointing them with oil in the name of the Lord'. (Jas. 5.14) The first text is probably referring to baptism and the second to anointing, and both are pointing to the cultic use of the name. However, this name is Jesus. St Paul says that Christ has received a name which is above all other names, so that all creatures will bow the knee and call him 'Lord'. (Phil. 2.9–11) The name above all other names, in a Jewish context, is YHWH whom all Jews call 'Lord'. Paul is saying that the risen Christ is now the supreme self-revelation of the Father to all creatures. The rabbis said that God's Name sustains the whole of creation: Paul is saying that this is now Christ's role. It was not long before early Christian writers began referring to Jesus as the Name of God.

'Thy Kingdom come'. The Father's name will only be glorified in a complete way when his kingdom is manifested on earth in the *Parousia*, when his full relationship to the universe will be clear, when Christ is 'all in all'. St Paul has no really thought-out theology of death. We enter into Christ by baptism, and our life which is hidden in Christ will be manifested in the Parousia. For him, death is an inconvenience which some people will have to suffer before the End. In the Book of Revelation, even the Christian dead cry out, 'How long?' *'Maranatha'*, 'Come, Lord Jesus', and these are the constant cries of the early Church. Nothing will be absolutely perfect until God's kingdom is fully manifest at the end of time: hence, this petition.

According to Jeremiah and, especially, Ezekiel, the coming of the kingdom is marked by the coming of God's Holy Spirit. The kingdom will have arrived when God's Spirit is poured out on all flesh. Therefore, to ask for the coming of the kingdom is to ask for the coming of the Spirit. So bound up with each other are these two petitions that there is a variant reading of the Our Father which asks, 'Your Spirit come' in place of Luke's 'Your kingdom come'.

Thus, Maximus the Confessor writes of the first petitions of the Our Father:

> By these words the Lord is teaching those who pray to begin with the very mystery of God ... The words of the prayer really point to the Father, the Father's name, and the kingdom, to teach us ... to honour, to call upon and to adore the One Trinity, For the name of God the Father, in its essential subsistence, is the only-begotten Son. And the kingdom of God the Father, in its essential subsistence, is the Holy Spirit. For what Matthew calls 'Kingdom' another evangelist calls Holy Spirit: 'Thy Spirit come'. (O. Clement op. cit. p. 62)

'Thy will be done on earth as it is in heaven'. However, this is St Matthew's own definition of the kingdom: God rules where his will is done. It will only be done perfectly and universally in the Parousia; but, as the kingdom has already been inaugurated by Christ's death and resurrection with the coming of the Spirit at Pentecost, it needs people whose only agenda is humbly to do God's will. The kingdom was present in Christ because he was obedient unto death. It will continue to be present in the world where people take up their cross daily, accepting what happens to them as the will of God, as Jesus did, and follow in his footsteps. The kingdom needs people who will live the Beatitudes, who are poor in spirit because they grasp to themselves nothing but the will of God. If we live in humble obedience to Christ, with no other desire apart from doing whatever he wants us to do, then we shall not save the world; but we shall be his instruments by which he saves the world in his own way.

In the Garden of Gethsemane, Jesus prayed, 'My Father, if it is possible, let this cup pass from me; yet not what I want but what you want'. Again he said, 'My Father, if this cannot pass unless I drink it, your will be done'. (Matt. 26.36–42) It is sometimes asked how anyone knew what Jesus said to his Father if Peter and the sons of Zebedee were asleep. It is probable that Matthew put these words in his mouth because they were typical prayers of Christ, showing his habitual attitude towards the will of his Father. They remind us of this petition in the Our Father. By praying it, we make Christ's prayer our own.

'Give us this day our daily bread'. This and the final three petitions are governed by 'this day'. They are requests that God would help us now, in contrast to the more generalized petitions which have gone before.

This petition is not as clear in the Greek as it appears to be in English. The problem is the word *epiousion* which we normally translate as 'daily', even though the meaning of *epiousion* is not very clear nor is it the usual word for 'daily'. There are two possible roots for this word: *epi-ousion*: from the verb *eimi*, meaning 'I am', and *ep-iousion* from *eimi*, 'I come' or 'I go'. If it comes from the verb 'to be', then it can mean either the bread that is sufficient, or the supersubstantial bread (as in the Latin Vulgate), or (just possibly) 'daily bread'. If it is from the verb 'to come or to go', then it can mean 'bread of the coming', perhaps the 'coming day' or the 'coming kingdom'. *Epi* means 'on top of', but when used with the participles, it simply adds emphasis to the meaning.

Since the Jews just loved to combine many meanings in one phrase, and their language was well suited to this because words had multiple meanings, and as sentences were without punctuation, they could change a meaning by imaginatively rearranging the sentence. It is quite possible that 'Give us this day our *epiousion* bread' could mean all these things. Even if it is in Greek, it was written by a Jewish Christian with a strong Semitic mentality, and he is writing for Jewish Christians.

However, I still believe that there is a dominant meaning. Considering all that has gone before and at least two of the three petitions that are yet to come, there is a strong argument that the petition is related to the coming of the kingdom, and hence to the 'bread of the Coming'; that it is a request that we should today participate in the banquet of the kingdom.

In St Luke's version, there are reasons to believe that the 'bread of the Coming' is a symbol for the Holy Spirit. Immediately after the Our Father he goes on to give a parable of the man who asks for three loaves of bread from a friend and, because of his persistence, finally receives it. 'Ask and it will be given you; search, and you will find,' and the final phrase is, 'If you then, who are evil, know how to give good gifts to your children, how much more will the heavenly Father give the Holy Spirit to those who ask him'. (Luke 11.5–13) If this is so, then there is a continuity of thought between the request for the coming of the kingdom, which is associated with the coming of the Spirit, and this request that those who pray should receive the Spirit today.

In St Matthew's version, Jesus goes on to talk of the need for forgiving those who offend us. Later on he tells us not to worry about what we are to eat, drink or wear because the Father will make sure that our needs will be met. We must strive first for the kingdom and his righteousness, 'and all these things will be given to you as well'. (Matt. 6.31–33) This reminds us of the beatitude, 'Blessed are those who hunger and thirst for righteousness, for they will be filled'. (Matt. 5.6) There is also the text in the temptation of Jesus, 'One does not live by bread alone, but by every word that comes from the mouth of God'. (Matt. 4.4) Thus there is a continuity of thought between this petition and the last, that God's will be done on earth as in heaven.

The Eucharist, which is the bread of the Coming, our foretaste of the banquet to which we shall be invited when the Lord comes, is included in both Matthew's version and that of Luke because our lives of obedience unto death are taken up into the sacrifice of Christ, and this is made possible only by the action of the Holy Spirit.

Our more mundane needs are not left out of the prayer. The rabbis used to say that we can pray for today's food or for tomorrow's; but praying for food further in the future shows a lack of trust in God's providence. Nelson borrowed and adapted a saying of St Ignatius of Loyola when he said before a battle, 'We must pray as if everything depends on God, and fight as if everything depends on us'. Practising our dependence on God through prayer helps us to allow God to be God in our lives; and absolutely nothing is too big for God to accomplish or too small to merit his concern. However, we must remember that he will give us all we need to accomplish our vocation, but may not give us all we want. 'Thy will be done' has priority.

'And forgive us our trespasses as we forgive those who trespass against us'. This is central to the teaching of Jesus. In Luke's Gospel, Jesus reads the proclamation of his mission, using the words from Isaiah:

> The Spirit of the Lord is upon me,
> because he has anointed me
> to bring good news to the poor.
> He has sent me to proclaim release to the captives

and recovery of sight to the blind,
to let the oppressed go free,
to proclaim the year of the Lord's favour. (Luke 4.18)

The Jews were very conscious that God had rescued them from slavery in Egypt, that God is a God who wants people to be free. At the same time, they knew nothing of a society without slaves, and poor people often had to sell themselves into slavery to pay their debts and to support their families. As a kind of compromise between their faith in a freedom-loving God and hard, economic facts, the Jews instituted the 'year of the Lord's favour', every seven years and, later, every fifty years. In that Jubilee year, all debts were cancelled and all slaves set free. They were warned not to be reluctant to lend when the Jubilee Year approached. Those slaves who did not want to be freed had an ear nailed to a doorpost as a sign that they were now slaves in perpetuity. This ignominious treatment reminded people that, if God wants to make us free, we have the obligation and responsibility to accept freedom.

This is the background of the text from Isaiah and of Christ's proclamation in the synagogue at Nazareth. The good news, the gospel, is that God is granting a general amnesty to those who have committed offences against him. Jesus teaches that this is because God is a loving Father: he manifests his nature by practising his *hesed*, his mercy or loving kindness. As God is God, this obliges us to accept God's forgiveness ourselves and to forgive everyone else their debts against us. Jesus does not distinguish between those who offend us and those who owe us money. As in the Old Testament, this obligation to forgive debts should not be interpreted simplistically: God is against enslaving people, not against ordinary economic transactions. Nevertheless, the prophetic stance of the Christian churches that demand the release of the poorest countries from their debt burden is in keeping with this petition. Individuals or countries that are caught in a poverty trap must be liberated from it because this is the will of God. This is no voluntary decision by those who believe in the biblical God; it is an absolute obligation.

St Matthew has the parable of the unforgiving debtor which illustrates this petition. St Peter asks Jesus how many times they should forgive their enemies, perhaps seven times? 'Seven' is a general word meaning any precise number. Jesus answers, 'Seventy times seven', which means that we should always forgive. He illustrates it with a parable: a man owed a king ten thousand talents, an enormous amount; and because he pleaded with him, the king forgave him the debt. After leaving the king's presence, the debtor met someone who owed him a hundred denarii, a relatively small amount. In spite of the man's pleas, he threw him and his family into prison. When the king heard of it, he was extremely angry and turned the debtor over to the torturers until he had paid the whole ten thousand talents.

The human race has marginalized God so that we do not take naturally to the offer of divine sonship that God offers us. Jesus came to convince the world of sin because people without any relationship with God can never appreciate sin's enormity. We need to be poor in spirit in order to appreciate our sin and mourn; and this is necessary if we are to have Christian sanctity because it differs from other types in that it does not divide us from the worst sinners, but unites us to them. St Augustine was walking with his friends when they came across a notorious sinner. St Augustine remarked, 'There but for the grace of God, go I'.

The first lesson in this parable is that we have all been forgiven by God an enormous amount. We shall only truly forgive our neighbour if we are aware of this fact. Forgiving our neighbour is the outward behaviour of those who have a true relationship with God; and not to forgive our neighbour is the outward sign that our relationship with God is inauthentic.

'**And lead us not into temptation, but deliver us from evil**'. Perhaps this is better translated, '**And do not bring us to the time of trial, but rescue us from the evil one**'. We are asking that the trials, the persecutions and the temptations that we experience should not prove too much for us, because we know that we are struggling not just against flesh and blood, but with the devil and his angels.

Our temptations take place between two great 'times of trial': Jesus suffering his passion, and the trial at the end of time, when the world as we know it will pass away to make way for a creation transformed into Christ. Jesus prayed in Gethsemane that the cup should pass from him, just as he instructs us to do. He is not one for spiritual heroics and he does not expect his disciples to be. When Peter tried to express such heroism before the passion, Jesus told him that he would betray him three times. Spiritual heroics smack of spiritual egoism. We have already prayed that God's will be done, as Jesus did in the garden. He wants us to rely on God rather than on our own courage and humbly to seek deliverance from the time of trial, leaving to God how he answers our prayer.

The definitive battle on the cross between humble obedience and the devil's pride and power means that ultimate victory is assured. However, the kingdom has only been inaugurated and the whole of creation has to pass through death to resurrection. Meanwhile, the devil and his angels still have tricks up their sleeves. They cannot resist the power of a life lived in Christ because a Christian is a tabernacle of the Holy Spirit. Their power is largely the power of illusion, false desires that don't satisfy, false promises of happiness, false fears, false ambitions: they tempt by deceiving; but we are easily deceived. Hence, deliver us from the evil one.

We can squeeze more meaning out of the Our Father, and see that the whole prayer is about the kingdom, if we interpret it chiastically:
'**Hallowed be thy name: Deliver us from the evil one**'. This theme is suggested in Psalm 8, 'O Lord, our Sover-

eign, how majestic is your name in all the earth ... you have founded a bulwark because of your foes, to silence the enemy and the avenger (or 'rebel'). 'Enemy', 'foe', 'avenger' or 'rebel' are all words that can be applied to the 'evil one'. In apocalyptic thought, God's name will be definitively glorified because it will become visible to all when the 'prince of this world' is overthrown and God's kingdom is established.

'Thy kingdom come: Deliver us from the time of trial'.
This more clearly identifies the time of trial with the fiery ordeal which precedes the coming of the kingdom. I suppose that Purgatory, in so far as it is a negative experience, is the personal participation in the time of trial of those who enter heaven before the Parousia, the bringing to perfection in us of that process of dying with Christ that allows us to live with him in heaven.

In apocalyptic literature, there is a river flowing from the throne of God in heaven which will irrigate Jerusalem and its surroundings when God's glory becomes manifest in the Parousia. It is both fire and water. As fire, it destroys all that opposes God and purifies all that is unclean; as water, it is bubbling with life. It irrigates the dry land, turning it into a garden. This river is the Spirit of God. When Isaiah confesses that he is a man of unclean lips, they are purified with fire from the coals from the altar of incense. In one extra-canonical work, the angels dip their mouths into the river of fire so that their praises may be worthy. The theme of the Spirit as water is found in St John's Gospel, while in Hebrews, God is described as 'a consuming fire'. God's presence in an imperfect world is always bad news for unholiness and good news for all that is holy, death to what is untransformable, and resurrection for all that can be transformed. The whole of Temple worship was preoccupied with the dual effect of God coming closer to us. Thus *korban* or sacrifice involved both death and life, flesh destroyed and blood, which was life, being poured on the altar. When God's kingdom comes, it is both destruction and salvation, and hence it is a time of trial. We ask that it will be for us an experience of salvation: of purification and life, rather than destruction. We ask this, not only on the Last Day, but also when we approach Almighty God in the Sacred Mysteries. It is a warning to us to take God seriously: God is no 'sugar daddy'.

'Thy will be done on earth as it is in heaven: Forgive us our trespasses as we forgive those who trespass against us'. The second of these petitions is asking that we may be forgiven in heaven as we forgive others on earth. The outstanding characteristic of God's kingdom and of those who are to live in it, is loving kindness by which sin is forgiven. It is identified with the will of God. We saw, when we interpreted the Beatitudes chiastically, that 'mercy' or loving kindness is the most visible characteristic of the person who is poor in spirit and puts into practice the other beatitudes. Here, we see that it is the outstanding characteristic of the kingdom. When we are a community that forgives our enemies and only wishes them well, then the Christian Church is visible in the world because Christ is visible in our actions. When we are a community that feeds on our tribal hatreds, then we make Christ invisible in our situation and the Church becomes like salt that has lost its taste. One of the strongest weapons in the devil's armoury in the twentieth century was ethnic conflict, between Catholics and Protestants in Northern Ireland, and between Orthodox Serbs and Catholic Croats and Muslim Albanians in the Balkans. The teaching of Jesus is quite clear: God loves all and everybody, and when we fail to reflect that love even to our worst enemies, we are no longer following Christ. The kingdom is made visible by our practice of *hesed* or loving mercy and cannot function on earth as in heaven when we fail to forgive our enemies from our hearts.

'Give us this day our bread of the Coming' is left as our most important petition: Give us all we need to fulfil our vocation as members of God's kingdom. It expresses our hunger and thirst for righteousness; it asks that we may receive life from every word that comes from the mouth of God; it asks for the Holy Spirit and for the bread of the Eucharist; and it places our mundane needs in God's hands so that we dedicate our attention simply to doing God's will.

The priest goes on to expand on the final petition of the Our Father and this ends with everybody saying: **'For the kingdom, the power and the glory are yours, now and for ever'.** This is a doxology which is found in some ancient texts of the Our Father. Almost certainly it is a liturgical appendage, used in some ancient churches when they prayed the Our Father in common, as we do here.

The Sign of Peace

We saw in our study of 'Blessed are the peacemakers' that 'peace' in a Christian context means much more than ordinary tranquillity; it is the tranquillity that comes from an authentic relationship between God and ourselves which results in a new relationship among ourselves. This tranquillity is a gift of God only for those who practise the Beatitudes. It is synonymous with salvation experienced. It is the peace that the world cannot give because it can only come from Christ. It is the peace that was on the faces of the martyrs as they went to their deaths in ancient Rome. It is the peace that no one can take from us, and that only sin can banish. This is offered to us at this point in the Mass, and we receive it only in so far as we receive Christ with purity of heart.

The priest says a prayer for peace, to which the people answer, **'Amen'.** Then he says, **'The peace of the Lord be with you always'**, and the people answer, **'and also with you'**. This peace comes from Christ who is represented by the priest. The people then offer the peace to each other at the priest's invitation.

Theologically speaking, this is a good place for the sign of peace, because it is not principally the reconciliation of estranged people that is being offered, but the peace which comes from union with Christ in his sacrifice.

However, psychologically and dramatically, it is in a bad place. In South America and in Africa, the people are very demonstrative. They are not content to give the peace to their immediate neighbours as the rubrics enjoin, because everybody wants to give the peace to everybody else. It becomes a major operation and lasts a long time. The sense of reverence and holiness that was there during the eucharistic prayer is interrupted by neighbours greeting each other, and it is often difficult to return to a proper spirit of recollection in time for communion. This is especially true if a great number of the people are children. Sometimes there is a lapse into general conversation, all with the best intentions, of course. There is a good case for putting the kiss of peace back before the eucharistic prayer, as is done in the Eastern rites and with the Neo-Catechumenate. When the people lack a good theological appreciation of its significance, which is most of the time, it introduces another theme right in between consecration and communion and becomes an interruption. It is much better to allow the people to greet each other as much as they want as an introduction to the eucharistic action. Such friendly enthusiasm has its place in the Eucharist, but not between the eucharistic prayer and communion; and the kiss of peace before the eucharistic part is in keeping with our Lord's instruction that we should only offer sacrifice after we have made peace with our neighbour.

Breaking of bread

This is one of the characteristic eucharistic actions of Christ. Although originally it was a simple preparation of the loaf for distribution, it has been seen as a symbol of Christ's brokenness on the cross and the completeness of his self-giving at communion. If priest and people can receive from the same loaf, this is to be encouraged, because it strengthens the symbolism of sharing. The least that a priest can do is to break up his large host and put some of the particles in the ciborium for distribution. If the hosts have been consecrated at that same Mass, we are being more faithful to what Jesus told us to do, but this is sometimes not practical.

The choir or people are instructed to sing the **'Lamb of God'** all the time that it takes to break up the consecrated bread, repeating it as long as it takes. However, this is impractical because the third 'Lamb of God' ends with 'grant us peace', thus bringing it to a natural end, even though this petition no longer precedes the sign of peace which was the original reason for singing it.

Communion

After making his private preparation, the priest genu-flects and, raising the host above the paten, says: **'This is the Lamb of God who takes away the sins of the world. Happy are those who are called to his supper.'** The people then say with him, **'Lord, I am not worthy to receive you, but only say the word and I shall be healed'.** Both the priest's proclamation and the people's reply are adapted biblical texts. The priest's announcement is a combination of two: that of St John the Baptist in St John's Gospel, when he said, 'Here is the Lamb of God who takes away the sin of the world', is combined with 'Blessed are those who are invited to the marriage supper of the Lamb', from the Apocalypse. Then priest and people make their own the prayer of the centurion in the Gospel of St Matthew, 'Lord, I am not worthy to have you come under my roof; but only speak the word and my servant will be healed.'

The priest receives his own communion and then gives communion to the people. He says to each one: **'The body of Christ'.** The communicant says, **'Amen'**, and receives the host either in his hand or on his tongue. The sign is more complete if the communicant also receives the chalice. Even though we receive Christ fully when we receive the host, something is lacking because in the Eucharist we are not only receiving Christ; he is also telling us something through signs. The blood of Christ, given in the chalice, symbolizes the covenant with his Father which we are participating in by receiving communion, a relationship of blood brotherhood with Christ: the idea of covenant relationship is underplayed when we receive the host only. It also conveys the festive aspect of the marriage feast of the Lamb. If Christ wanted to give us communion with bread only, he would have done so. I really do think that we should give the chalice as often as the bishops' conference permits. One day, I hope, it will become normal. The priest or assistant says: **'The blood of Christ'**. The communicant answers, **'Amen'**.

While communion is being given out, it is normal to sing a hymn or a psalm with its refrain. This should be of a kind that aids the people to participate in the communion.

We receive the risen Christ himself and, through him, we are united to his Father who is our Father because we are one body with his Son. We are also united to the angels and saints, and to all on earth who are similarly united in this bodily union with Christ, made possible by the Spirit for those with faith. This new set of relationships with the Father, through the Son, in the unity of the Holy Spirit is eternal, and is the substance of eternal life.

As we pass through the veil which is Christ's flesh, we become 'bones of his bone and flesh of his flesh', sharing in the marriage banquet of the Lamb, becoming one body with him. We are exercising our priesthood before the Father on behalf of ourselves and of the whole world, being one with the blood which pleads more strongly than the blood of Abel. The Byzantine Liturgy talks of our receiving communion for ourselves and for the people. The ministerial priesthood, acting as instrument of Christ, enables the whole community to exercise the priesthood which we received at baptism, because we can only exercise it as members of the Church and in submission to Christ who activates our baptism through the Spirit.

This participation in the 'world to come' is the true source of our unity as Christians on earth. Differences and divisions caused by nationality or geographical distances or political allegiance are insignificant beside our unity in Christ which we attain in the Eucharist. Thus, St Thomas Aquinas says that the *res sacramenti*, the purpose of this sacrament, is the unity of the Church.

Only when we appreciate what happens in the Eucharist, and especially at communion, does the full scandal of Christian disunity become apparent. We are taken up into unity with Christ's body in heaven. If the whole purpose of the body of Christ on earth is to bear witness to the world of this divine dimension of things which has been transformed by Christ, reflecting heavenly realities by the way we live our lives on earth, then we fail to do so to the extent that we do not acknowledge on earth those with whom we are united in heaven.

Cardinal Ratzinger has said that the Orthodox Church is wounded because of its disunion with Rome. This is perfectly true; but we are wounded too. The situation is complicated because we are divided by what we believe to be God's will, and this cannot be compromised. We are incapable of uniting while serious questions are not resolved; but that means we continue to be wounded by division. Every time the Patriarch of Constantinople celebrates Mass with his flock, he is made one with us in Christ; and we are made one with him whenever we celebrate. This is done not by us but by the Holy Spirit. Let us pray that the same Spirit will resolve our differences.

Silence

If ever there was a time for silence it is now. The people have all gone back to their places, the priest returns to his chair, and each person continues his communion with the Lord. Without a time of silence, the temptation is to skate along the surface of the rite without deepening our relationship with God. This is not a time for giving out notices, because all our attention should be concentrated on him whom we have received.

Prayer After Communion
The priest goes to the altar or stands at his chair, and says or sings: **'Let us pray'**. Then he ends the communion rite with a prayer, to which the people answer: **'Amen'**.

After this prayer, the priest or someone else may read the notices. Then the **Blessing** is given, which can be the usual short one or it may take a more solemn form on Sundays and feasts. This is followed by the **Dismissal** which can take several forms.

Chapter Twenty-six

Good Liturgy: Bad Liturgy

I cannot accept that the quality of our liturgy depends on the way the priest is facing when he celebrates. The view is often expressed that it is bad liturgical practice for the priest to face east with everybody else when celebrating Mass. This means that, for most of the Church's history, and in all the Eastern churches apart from the Maronites, facing east is somehow mistaken. That it is often said that 'the priest celebrates Mass with his back to the people', shows that those who make the criticism remain victims of the very theology they wish to eradicate. They are the first to say that the Mass is a celebration of the whole Church in which the priest has a ministerial function. In such a theology, the fact that the priest has his back to the people is no more significant than that the people in front of the assembly have their backs turned towards those who are behind. In fact, the practice demonstrates his oneness with the people as their leader.

Facing east is a perfectly valid expression of the eschatological nature of the Mass because all are facing towards the heavenly Jerusalem. 'But you have come to Mount Zion and the city of the living God, the heavenly Jerusalem, and to innumerable angels in festive gathering, and to the assembly of the first-born who are enrolled in heaven, and to God the judge of all, and to the spirits of the righteous made perfect, and to Jesus, the mediator of a new covenant, and to the sprinkled blood that speaks a better word than the blood of Abel'. (Heb. 12.22–4) The advantage of this position is that there is a liturgical 'place' for God, not because he is confined to any particular place but because that is the way we imagine things. There is no danger of marginalizing God because everybody is facing towards this sacred spot in the liturgical drama. In ancient Syrian churches there is an empty niche in the east wall of a kind that would house a statue in a pagan temple. It was adopted by Moslems who all pray facing towards Mecca. In other parts of the Church, the priest or bishop faced the empty chair which he vacated to stand at the altar. This is God the Father's place in the imagery of the Apocalypse. Facing some place in the church which stands for God's presence is a very good liturgical practice. If this still were the liturgical norm, some of the temptations we shall mention below would never have arisen.

On the other hand, after a long time during which the eschatological dimension of the Mass, so important to the Judaeo-Christian and patristic understanding, was consigned to the dustbin of academe and after centuries when the theology of the Mass was interpreted from the point of view of the clergy, it became necessary to kick-start a process by which the Mass came to be seen as an essentially communal activity of the Church, indeed the means by which the Church is repeatedly constituted by God, and realizes itself as Church as it sits down to feast with the risen Christ, the angels and the saints. Turning the altar around seemed a good way of doing this. I believe that it has succeeded.

Changing the relationship between priest, altar and people has involved adopting a different paradigm or governing model to help us understand the Mass. Emphasis is given to the Eucharist as a communion sacrifice, as a sacred memorial meal, in which Wisdom gives the bread and wine to her children, and God lays out succulent food before his people. The altar is more and more referred to as a table. I see no harm in this as it is an obvious consequence of the new, yet traditional paradigm. Jesus Christ as host of the meal, and the Eucharist as a foretaste of the feast with Abraham, Isaac and Jacob in the kingdom, are becoming increasingly common in our explanations of the Mass. The new layout not only puts emphasis on the Eucharist as the source of our unity on earth: it is also a celebration and a foretaste of the marriage feast of the Lamb. It not only puts emphasis on the togetherness of the celebrating community; it is also a new way to emphasize the eschatological nature of the Mass, one that is perhaps more graphic for us than the old way. The Church discerned that it was necessary to do something new in order to recover important elements in our own Eucharistic patrimony. The Eastern traditions have not had to do this because their history has been different.

More important than the way the altar is facing is that those who celebrate the rite do so with an adequate understanding of what the Mass is about, and that care is taken to express that meaning as clearly as possible. The main weakness of the modern liturgy is a consequence of one of its strengths: it is very adaptable to different circumstances, but one circumstance was not adequately taken into account. It was assumed that all priests, and those who organize the celebration of Mass, have a real understanding of what they are doing. It was taken for granted that those who read the documents of Vatican II would understand and remember them and would not supplement them with their own agenda. The problem is that in the new rite, if a priest has a distorted view of the liturgy, this will result in a distorted celebration. Let us look at a few basic principles.

Who is the most important participant in the Mass? From what we have said, it is very clearly God. Hence, good liturgy will make that clear, and bad liturgy will obscure it.

A very simple rule which should be obvious is that, when we are praying to God, it should be clear that this is what we are doing. I have been present at Masses where the priest keeps eye-contact with the people all the time and, by his gestures and outward attitude, seems to be talking to the people all the time, even when the words he is actually saying are addressed to God. In fact, the people are so conscious of him and he is so conscious of the people that there is little room for God. When we pray to God we should be clear but also recollected. There is no harm in concentrating on God when the words are addressed to God.

Moreover, it is not the priest's job to project himself towards the people: he is humbly putting himself at God's disposal to be used as his instrument, and this should be clear by his way of celebrating. St Thomas Aquinas said that the priest is an instrumental cause of the sacraments and this is usually illustrated by the function of a pen in the writing of a letter. In this case the 'writer' is Christ and the 'pen' is the priest. It would be a strange state of affairs if someone who received a letter were more conscious of the pen than of the person who wrote it. St Paul was so aware of being a mere messenger, a vehicle of the Spirit, that the Corinthians thought he was weak. With the priest facing the people there is a danger that he rather than God becomes the centre of attention, and this must be combated by the priest in all humility. Of course, humility is a necessary condition for a fruitful participation in the Mass for everyone; but the self-effacement of the priest makes the difference between good liturgy and bad liturgy.

The Letter to the Hebrew says:

> Therefore, since we are receiving a kingdom that cannot be shaken, let us give thanks, by which we offer to God an acceptable worship with reverence and awe; for indeed our God is a consuming fire. (Heb. 12.28–9)

Awe is considered so pre-Vatican II by some that one translation of this passage in a Latin American Bible replaced it with 'tenderness'! Modern liturgy, they believe, should be informal and easy going, and awe is Old Testament, which means they haven't read the New Testament very carefully. As Rudolf Otto showed in his *The Idea of the Holy*, awe is the natural emotion of human beings when faced with the Other, the *mysterium tremendum et fascinans*. If awe is eliminated from the liturgy – and this has happened too often – then we are dehumanizing it. In the presence of God, awe is the most natural thing in the world. One of the best descriptions of it that I know is found in Kenneth Graham's *Wind in the Willows*. The fact that it is completely pagan doesn't matter because we are dealing with a natural emotion:

> 'This is the place of my song-dream, the place the music played to me,' whispered the Rat, as if in a trance. 'Here is the holy place, here, if anywhere, we shall find him.' Then, suddenly the Mole felt a great Awe fall upon him, an awe that turned his muscles to water, bowed his head, and rooted his feet to the ground. It was no panic terror – indeed he felt wonderfully at peace and happy – but it was an awe that smote and held him and, without seeing, he knew it could only mean that some august Presence was very, very near. With difficulty he turned to his friend, and he saw him at his side, cowed, stricken, and trembling violently ... 'Rat' he found breath to whisper, shaking, 'Are you afraid?' 'Afraid?' murmured the Rat, his eyes shining with unutterable love, 'Afraid of him? O, Mole, never, never. And yet – and yet – O, Mole, I am afraid.'

I want you to picture a concrete church with a corrugated roof in a village not far below the Equator in Peru. It is full of peasants who are talking among themselves. A few are praying in front of statues, touching them and crossing themselves. The sisters have been practising hymns with the congregation while they waited for the priest. On the altar is a guitar which the sister has been using, and a bottle of pop to refresh the priest when he arrives. The young priest enters, smiles at everybody, dumps his bag on the altar, drinks the pop and begins to vest. The sister tunes up once more. When everybody is ready, they sing the first hymn and the Mass begins. Twenty-five minutes later, the priest unvests, puts his vestments in his bag which once more he has placed on the altar, and leaves.

Unfortunately, this scene is very common where over-worked priests go from one place to another under a tropical sun. Where is the reverence and awe? Where is there a sense of the presence of God? The priest is mainly conscious of doing his job; he is 'confecting' the sacra-ment. The heat, the dust and the mosquitoes can all fairly be blamed; but he isn't even aware that there is anything missing. No reverence is paid to the altar which is used like any other table. The only people who show reverence are the peasants with their statues. Many know they are being short-changed. With the proper motivation and a little organization, this kind of celebration need not happen. It is by no means universal; but it is all too common.

There are parts of the Mass where the main movement is from the Church towards the Father; and there are other parts where the main movement is from God to the people. Another simple rule is that nothing should be done to obscure these movements.

I once went to a parish where the Mass was celebrated in a way that, until then, I thought only existed in the fevered imagination of members of the Latin Mass Society. The introductions of the commentator were longer than the lessons; and she really came into her own at the Presentation of Gifts. The offertory procession had nothing to do with the bread and wine nor were the offer-ings gifts in any real sense. Instead of being the moment where we give our five loaves and two fish to Christ, it was a sort of class using 'symbols'. One by one, the people brought a candle, signifying Christ, a Bible, signifying the Word, a bowl of seeds which signified life, and grapes and bread, which signified the Mass. The monitor gave a commentary as each of these 'gifts' came up to the altar. Anything of value was returned to the people afterwards: they were not giving them away. Few people went to communion so that, if you had blinked, you would have been excused for thinking that there had been no communion at all. As soon as the last person communicated, about two or three minutes after the priest had received the chalice, a woman stood up in the sanctuary and started devotions to Our Lady of Perpetual Succour. After that came the notices, and, after the notices, the postcommunion prayer and blessing. Thus the meaning of both Presentation of Gifts and Communion were obscured by activities which had nothing to do with the Mass. In fact, the whole meaning of the Mass was obscured. It was all words, words, words and no silence. The more important the feast, the more words were used, the greater the opportunity to teach the people by 'symbols' and explanations.

I am convinced that to abolish awe is liturgical suicide. It is achieved by putting something or someone else in place of God in the liturgy, or by domesticating God in an unrealistic fashion, or simply by not understanding what the Mass is about. There are several causes, none of which has anything to do with the reformed rite as such.

1) There is the influence of some spiritually-damaging ideas which come from a decadent form of Protestant pietism. Fear, any form of fear, is realistic, before conversion to Jesus, but has no place in the Christian life of someone who has been converted. After conversion, all is sweetness and light. Choose Jesus as your Saviour and you have arrived. Sign on the dotted line and you have everything that God has to offer. Hence awe is out and a kind of happy confidence is in. It is what Bonhoeffer called 'cheap grace'. Of course, it has nothing to do with the New Testament. Unfortunately, there are Catholics who have been tainted by this attitude, and it is presupposed in some celebrations of the Mass.

2) Then there are those 'liberals' who use the mentality of modern secular man as the standard by which the New Testament and Christian practice are interpreted. The secular mentality becomes the mould in which the Christian message has to fit. Anything that the modern world does not appreciate is cut out or forgotten, and anything that is important to the modern world is made central to the Christian message. As secular people have no recognizable experience of God or of any form of Ultimate Reality they are incapable of awe; hence, a really modern celebration will concentrate on human relationships within the Mass community, and the *mysterium tremendum et fascinans* is pushed to the background. No wonder people look to the Eastern religions and witchcraft to find what is lacking in the practice of their own faith.

3) There are two basic patterns of Eucharistic celebration: the Protestant one and the Catholic one. In the Protestant pattern, the word speaks to us while we respond in faith. Even the sacraments are the Word addressing us: the only really significant movement is downward. In the Catholic pattern, God speaks to us and we speak to God; and Christ is the means by which both the downward and upward movements are made. Thus, in the Swedish Lutheran Church, the words of institution are sung to a Gospel tone because they are addressed to us, while they are words spoken to God in the Catholic Mass. Under Protestant influence, the Mass is often completely centred on the congregation and there is no sense of being lifted up into the presence of God, and hence, no awe.

4) Often, those who re-organize the liturgy are teachers or ex-teachers who cut their teeth on Masses for children and on youth Masses. They know that what they did in those circumstances was very much better than what had happened beforehand; and they mistakenly transfer what they did in that situation to the ordinary Sunday Mass, often with the young people's approval. They are unaware that adults are capable of and need to express a wider and deeper spirituality. For instance, I suspect the

American sister who organized the Mass in my last example had been an infants' teacher. Children cannot sit still for long and have to be kept active. Making up for them things to do during the Presentation of Gifts is allowable and even desirable; but introducing these activities into normal Masses goes directly against the stated aims of the Vatican II reforms that abolished secondary symbolisms in order to make the primary ones more visible. Again, teenagers are often less capable of awe than other people because the world is their oyster, and the problems that chiefly concern them are not about God as such but about their own place in the world. Youth Masses help them to address their problems within the context of the Church. They are successful for young people precisely because they are geared to their problems and speak their idiom. Masses for the whole community should be different.

5) These deviations would simply not be allowed if priests did not, at least unconsciously, use validity as their only real standard in celebrating Mass. After all, they often know that the celebration is not as it should be. However, they think that none of these things really matter so long as the right words are said. But the Mass is much more than that! God is taking up his abode among us, and we are being brought into his presence just as truly as was Moses on Mount Sinai. As instrument of Christ, the priest is enabling the congregation to exercise their priesthood by entering through the veil of Christ's death into the kingdom of his resurrection, with the angels and the saints before the throne of God. All this is reduced to and absorbed by a mechanical approach by which, if the priest begins at the beginning and goes on to the end, Mass is celebrated validly and everything else is relatively unimportant.

At a time when the social supports have collapsed and people need to be put into touch with the reality of the kingdom about which Christ taught and which he makes present, this very reality is among us, but too often disguised by the way the Mass is celebrated. No wonder people are voting with their feet.

Another simple rule is that there must be a balance between communal participation and the interior life of those taking part. At one time there was no external participation beyond the presence of the laity who stood up, knelt, and sat down together. Now it has swung the other way and all the emphasis is too often on communal participation alone.

It is the theme of this book that each person has a one-to-one relationship with God, as well as a communal one, and that they are inter-related. You cannot abolish one in favour of the other. Good liturgy will fulfil the needs of both; and bad liturgy will ignore one in order to emphasize the other. Good liturgy will form community by respecting the interiority of each person in his relationship with God and with the rest of the assembly; bad liturgy will form a crowd by insisting only on the maximum amount of external conformity. An overemphasis on external conformity is an over-reaction to the time when the priest celebrated 'my Mass' while the faithful concentrated on private devotions. That is now such a long time ago for most people that it is silly to go on reacting against it. We must aim at balance.

The Church is the communion of Christian persons in the one body of Christ, as God is the communion of three divine Persons in one divine Nature. In the Church, the Holy Spirit works inside each person, even as he unites us together in one body. Good liturgy will take this into account; bad liturgy will ignore it. As the Cistercian Fathers used to say, there must be a balance between togetherness and solitude.

It has been said that, 'the medium is the message'. This means that most people are more influenced by the message implicit in what stimulates their senses, what they hear, touch, taste, smell and see, than by theoretical analysis. Hence, a priest who gives the impression that the relationship between the people and himself is the central fact of the Mass really does marginalize God. The same happens when the liturgy is centred round human relationships, and where everything is directed at the congregation. When a priest simply reads through the Mass without devotion and when a Mass is ill-prepared, God's presence is trivialized. The 'new Mass' puts a tremendous responsibility on the shoulders of the priests who celebrate the Eucharist.

It is most important that the outward form of the Mass expresses its inner truth as found in Scripture and Tradition; that what people see and hear and what they do helps them to enter deeply into the Christian Mystery they are celebrating. Everything must be judged by that. If anything is done or sung which obscures the meaning of the text or distorts the meaning of the Mass, it must be rejected.

In Negritos, I prohibited 'Lamb of God, you take away the sins of the world' sung to a jolly ditty, even though the people liked it. Why? If you spend half an hour meditating on the meaning of the words in their scriptural and liturgical context, you will know why. Liturgical music must come out of the words, as Michelangelo's statues were carved out of stone. For this, the composer must make the text his own and then turn it into music. Beauty in art allows us to taste the God-given truth of things, and liturgical music helps us to taste the truth of the Mass. If it doesn't, it is no good, however catchy the tune, and however popular it is.

I am not saying that people should not sing in their own musical idiom. Byzantine chant is very closely related to Greek folk music, and mediaeval drinking songs were not far removed from Gregorian plainchant. But Byzantine chant is not Greek folk music, nor is plainchant suitable for drinking. The difference is that in the liturgical music there is a relationship between the music and the words.

We have said that there must be a balance between interiority and participation. If it is possible to form a choir, then it is good to give an opportunity to the people simply to listen. The rubrics allow the Gloria to be sung by a choir. Here the people can listen and participate by turning what they hear into interior prayer which has been inspired by the beauty of the music. Other possibilities are during the offertory or the communion. The only stipulations I would make are that the music be conducive to prayer and be relevant to the Mass; and that, if it is during the communion, the choir have the opportunity to communicate: first things must always come first.

When the liturgy is centred on the community rather than on God, then worship often gives way to entertainment; and what people like becomes the chief criterion for what is acceptable. We have seen this happen among our liberal Protestant brethren over a long period of time; and we have also seen that, in the long run, it doesn't work. Many of the experiments we have taken part in as though they were the latest and most effective device were tried in the Protestant churches in the nineteen-thirties, and were found wanting. The problem is that the Mass cannot compete as entertainment over a long period with watching television and visiting the pub. What good is singing 'Lamb of God' happily, if the happiness does not derive from the words and the music disguises what the words wish to say? What good is being joyful at Mass if it is because people like a good singsong? When the Mass becomes primarily a source of entertainment, you may get instant success; but only at a superficial level. A paradox is at work. You get maximum external participation, while the music they enjoy can act as a block which prevents them entering the Christian Mystery they are celebrating. It is possible to have a true text and sing it to a lie.

There is much good liturgical music being composed, and there is a wealth of good hymns in English. Taizé is a source of high quality music which is easy to sing. Vibrant Christian communities like Sant' Egidio in Rome and the Jerusalem Community in Paris use Russian chant which is very pleasing to the modern ear in a liturgical context. The great success of the recordings of the monks of Silos, even among non-believers, and the constant flow of visitors to monasteries, show that Gregorian Chant is still very attractive, and some of it is not too difficult for ordinary congregations. There is much to choose from: all it needs is the will.

What we have said in this chapter amounts to one plea: that the attitudes, gestures, music and actions in the Mass should correspond to what we know by faith is happening in the Mass. That was the intention of Vatican II in calling for a revision and it is the motivation behind all the directives that have been published since. The modern secular world is in great need of theophanies, and we take part in a theophany each time we go to Mass but, too often, this is not recognized because of the way we celebrate it.

However, we participate in the theophany of the Mass so that we too will become theophanies: that was the meaning of 'sons of God' in the time of Jesus. We are to be the means by which people come into contact with Christ, so that all may enjoy the harmony between God and humankind which is salvation. This is what is meant by our vocation to be 'peacemakers'. The communion with Christ that a eucharistic community enjoys is only as profound as is allowed by the 'purity in heart' of its members. Whether we become members of a movement or not, whether or not we are inspired by the success stories of others and strive to copy them, whatever model we use for the celebration of Mass, whatever way the priest is facing, we need an authentic liturgy which truly expresses our Catholic faith, and an authentic spirituality which is in harmony with what we celebrate. To concentrate on renewal of liturgy without also emphasizing a renewal of spirituality is to make a superficial change, while to have a spirituality which bears no relationship with the liturgy is simply not Catholic.

There are many different spiritualities in the Church and we are free to adopt any one of them. However, all have one thing in common. Although they differ enormously in shape and emphasis, they all bring us on to the royal road to joy which is given us in the Beatitudes. Individual people have different starting points. Some begin the journey with sorrow for sin and the quest for salvation; some are inspired by compassion for those in need; some seek the joy of contemplation. Nevertheless, as they progress, they are all led by the Spirit to follow the same road of the 'poor in spirit'. The combination of an authentic liturgy and an authentic spirituality will result in communities that will reflect Christ's presence in the modern world, 'so that the world may know that you have sent me and have loved them even as you have loved me'. (John 17.23)

Chapter Twenty-seven

Ite Missa Est

You will receive power when the Holy Spirit has come upon you, and you will be my witnesses in Jerusalem, in all Judea and Samaria and to the ends of the earth. (Acts 1.8)

After the crucifixion and resurrection of Christ and before his ascent into heaven, the disciples were solemnly told that they would be his witnesses. This was not so much an obligation that they should be his witnesses: it was a promise that they would be. This was a consequence of the coming of the Holy Spirit. The Holy Spirit did not come on each one of them privately, but as they were gathered together in the upper room and, by so doing, made them the Church as we know it by uniting them to Jesus in heaven. They became witnesses to the risen Christ precisely because, as Church, they were united to him and shared his life.

We have seen in the commentary on the Mass that we are the body of Christ because we share the one bread and the one cup. The Eucharist is our Pentecost. In it we share in the Christian Mystery as truly as those who took part in the historical events and, like the apostles, we are united to Christ and share his life. Like the apostles, we eat and drink with the risen Christ through the power of the Holy Spirit who comes down on us, and we too become witnesses to the risen Christ in the world. 'Go, the

Mass is ended' means that we are sent, commissioned and enabled to witness to Christ among our neighbours.

Why is this so much theory? Remember, Christ didn't only say we must witness: he promised us that we would be witnesses. What difference does the witness of the Catholic Church make in the secular world? We go to Mass and then we go out and start witnessing, and this ought to make some kind of impact. I am sure that it makes more impact than we are aware of. Nevertheless, if Pentecost happens in our parish or community every Sunday, it ought to be more visible. I am convinced that we do not have an impact by liturgy alone nor by spirituality alone, but that a combination of the two, an interpenetration of the two, allows us to receive the Holy Spirit in a way that is truly explosive in its effect. This is true in the various movements which that same Spirit has given the Church during the last fifty years. Merely copying their external features will not lead to anything of importance. What we need to do is combine liturgical renewal with spiritual renewal, and that is why living the Beatitudes goes hand in hand with liturgical celebration.

There is a reciprocal relationship between the Mass and the Beatitudes. By following the Beatitudes our lives are at one with the Mass we celebrate, because both Beatitudes and Mass are ways of sharing in Christ's death and resurrection. In the Beatitudes we have an inner change of attitude, and move from an ever-deeper poverty in spirit, through practising steadfast love in Christian community, until we arrive at purity in heart. In the Mass we move from hearing the Word of God, through sacrifice to communion. The two movements are complementary. Without practising the Beatitudes, what in our lives can be transformed into Christ in the Mass? Without celebrating Mass and becoming Christ's body together, how could the promises that Jesus made in the Beatitudes be fulfilled? The reality behind the Eucharist is our participation in the risen Christ through death to self in obedience to the Father. We can take part only in so far as we are in truth 'living victims' in solidarity with Christ in our actual lives, and this involves living according to the Beatitudes.

According to the great mediaeval Cistercian writer William of St Thierry, 'In a church at certain times, the sacraments of the Christian religion are dispensed visibly and in figure, while in cells [of hermits] as in heaven the reality which underlies all the sacraments of faith is constantly celebrated'.[1] What he says about hermits in their cells can logically be applied to any serious Christian life. By living according to the Beatitudes we are constantly sharing in the Christian Mystery that we celebrate in the Eucharist.

God has spoken to us in the Liturgy of the Word, and we have ascended through sharing in Christ's sacrifice to be united with him in heaven. We have passed through the veil that separates the ordinary historical world of cause and effect from God's presence and have talked directly to the Father. Because we are striving to live according to the Beatitudes, and our attendance at Mass is not an interruption of a completely secular week but rather the climax of a week trying to do God's will in all things, our communion with Christ has been deeper than we know. Now it is time to return to the secular world.

However, it is no longer a secular world for us because we have plumbed its deepest secret. We return to our mundane affairs united with him who is 'the image of the invisible God, the firstborn of all creation, for in him all things in heaven and on earth were created, things visible and invisible ... all things have been created through him and for him. He himself is before all things, and in him all things hold together'. (Col. 1.15–17) Behind every thing, every event, every situation, every person or group of persons, there is the presence of the risen Christ. It is not a presence in history because he is now eternal, but we live in historical time and he can take part in history through us when we respond in faith. We are the body of Christ and he wishes to work in and through us. In so far as we are pure in heart, we have become 'peacemakers', so that Jesus now lives in us and we in him, and the light we shed around us is the light of Christ. It is for this that we were chosen before the creation of the world; it is for this that we have been baptized and have shared in the Eucharist. However, we do not exercise our function as peacemakers by calling attention to ourselves, or by telling people that we represent Christ. A peacemaker is very conscious of his own need for Christ. In this he is the same as the worst sinner. He looks for Christ wherever he may be found and, because the peacemaker is pure in heart, he sees Christ everywhere.

As de Caussade said, the duty, attraction or cross which every moment brings is but a shadow by which the power of God, the Holy Spirit, conceals itself in order to bring Jesus Christ to souls. Outwardly, the ordinary events of our lives are no different from those that happen to anyone, but our faith enables us to discern in them the invisible element which is nothing less than 'God himself performing great works'. God manifests himself to our faith in both the ordinary and the extraordinary, the humdrum and the exciting, the dramatic and the boring. Thus, de Caussade speaks of every moment that we live the Christian life in Eucharistic terms: 'O bread of angels, heavenly manna, the pearl of the Gospels, the sacrament of the present moment!'

Our ability to identify duties, attractions and crosses with Christian realism depends on our poverty of spirit and especially our purity of heart. To the extent that we are unconverted, we shall interpret our duties according to secular values, confuse the attractions of grace with our own desires or ideals, and take up only those crosses which win us the world's approval or add to our comfort. We need an Abrahamic faith which is ready to step out in obedience into the unknown even without understanding why or knowing where we are going. Without it, our Christianity becomes either a conversation with ourselves, or a non-Christian message expressed in Christian language. If we are to be authentic Christians, the Gospel must interpret the world about us and not the other way round. This will happen only if we live according to the Beatitudes.

There are many examples in history of causes which were identified with the Gospel by those who supported them, but which we now know had very little to do with the workings of grace. For example, there is an intoxicating and lethal mixture of nationalism and religion, where all too-human loyalties are given the absolute character that belongs only to our loyalty to God, and have turned patriotism into a form of idolatry. We have witnessed Catholics and Protestants in Ireland. We have seen Orthodox Serbs and Catholic Croats in the Balkans looking at each other with hatred, without the slightest intention of forgiving one another for the sins of the past. Ethnicity has become an idol and old people, women and children have been sacrificed to it during years of ugly war. One of the Greek fathers said that Orthodoxy without charity is the religion of the devil, and we have seen Christ's own teaching on forgiveness forgotten in Christ's name by people on both sides.

The only antidote is purity in heart, and this is acquired by those who hunger and thirst for God's will in spite of their own natural feelings. We should have enough humility, enough solidarity even with the worst, to suspect and reject our tendency to judge others. We should know that the neighbours whom we dislike are there, in part, so that we should love them; for if we love only those who love us, what is there extraordinary in that? Above all, we should seek God in all things and on all occasions. Jean Pierre de Caussade says that we should abandon ourselves to God's Providence. Our will must be made one with that of God through faith. We become one with God when we fulfil the duties that he has laid upon us through circumstances, and when we accept all that happens to us as either willed or permitted by him.

In St John's Gospel, Christ's ministry is divided into two

distinct parts, one part symbolized by daylight and the other by night.

In the first part, Christ works and does so freely in spite of the many attempts to stop him. He is in complete control. When he cures the blind man on the Sabbath he says, 'We must work the works of him who sent me while it is day; night is coming when no man can work'. When he is about to go and raise Lazarus his disciples remind him that he is going into danger. He replies, 'Are there not twelve hours of daylight? Those who walk during the day do not stumble because they see the light of this world. But those who walk at night stumble, because the light is not in them.' At the Last Supper he says to his Father, 'I have glorified you on earth by finishing the work you gave me to do'. At the same Supper Judas goes out, and it is night.

If St John emphasizes Christ's freedom to work against all opposition during the daylight, he is the only Gospel author to say that Jesus is bound when he is arrested. When he is before Pilate, he is asked, 'Do you not know that I have power to release you, and power to crucify you?' Jesus answers, 'You would have no power over me unless it had been given you from above.' On the cross, he cries out, 'I thirst!' He who had preached and performed his signs freely and without hindrance during his ministry, is now bound and becomes a prisoner. He who said that all power had been given to him in heaven and on earth, is now under the power of Pilate. He who had said that all who are thirsty should come to him, is now thirsty himself. He is bound, powerless and in need of other people's help. Before, he was the active subject in the Gospel scenes of his public life, doing the Father's works. Now he is the passive object, accepting what is done to him.

St Seraphim of Sarov tells us that the Christian life does not consist in copying the externals of Christ's life, but in offering our own lives to God. These two phases in Christ's life correspond to the two forms of abandonment to Divine Providence: the active, by which we perform the duties of our state in life; and the passive, by which we accept the circumstances of our lives which we cannot change, whether positive or negative, as being in God's plan for us. This is the whole of the Christian life. We are reminded of the classical Jesuit prayer:

> Lord, grant me the courage to change what I can change,
> the patience to accept what I cannot change,
> and the wisdom to know the difference.

As the poor in spirit accepted persecution, so we must accept all that happens to us as willed or permitted by God and, like the meek, we must accept whatever work that God's Providence gives us, and react positively to every encounter with Christ on a day-to-day basis. Thus we offer to God our lives, and this offering becomes included in Christ's offering in the Mass. This is our essential participation in the Eucharist.

I believe there is a tendency to confuse what is necessary in the life of the Church with what is essential. A parish priest in Peru may have anything from fourteen thousand to over a hundred thousand people in his care. In the Andes, one parish may include several towns that are between two to five hours' distance from one another. In Tambogrande there were one hundred thousand parishioners in one town and over a hundred and thirty villages, with only four priests, then three, and afterwards two. Now there is only one secular priest, and the parish has grown. To do all that is necessary is beyond the priest's powers, and he has to choose, not between necessary and unnecessary activities, but what necessary things he is going to do and what he is going to leave undone. This makes it even more important to concentrate on the essential; otherwise he will become disillusioned and disheartened by his failure to do all that is necessary, and he will cease to try. Without an inner relationship with

Christ, both the priest who has continually to leave undone necessary tasks and the people, who are so inadequately served by the priest, would lapse into indifference. 'Without me you can do nothing', said the Lord and, in Peru, it is only too obvious.

After Vatican II, we have concentrated on liturgical changes that were necessary. It was necessary that the Eucharist should be the action of the whole community, and not just celebrated for the community by the priest. It was necessary to enrich the participation of the people, and to give them more and better texts according to the best liturgical models. However, perhaps there has been too much emphasis on external participation, and too little on our interior participation, too much head and too little heart. Without the Beatitudes, the best liturgy that we can hope for is one that celebrates a superficial togetherness with superficial joy because our daily relationship with Christ will be skin-deep. I am sure that, for many people who lapse from the Church, their participation in the Mass was shallow for a long time before they stopped going. Such a Christianity will never make us peacemakers, salt of the earth and light of the world, and we never shall be witnesses that Christ is alive, nor shall we be instruments in his mission to the world.

The essential function of the Christian, whatever his or her particular vocation, is to be so filled with Christ that others may meet Christ in and through us. It is not a matter of having the right words or having a good organization. These are desirable but not essential. What is essential is that our outer eucharistic celebration as the Church should reflect, not only Christ's relationship with his Father, but also our own inner relationship with Christ. The rest will follow. The end product is a community of 'peacemakers', people who illuminate the world around them with the light of Christ. 'Peacemakers' do not go around saying, 'Look at me!' They reflect Christ in so far as they forget themselves and see Christ in others and in every situation. We have used the example of

Mother Teresa of Calcutta. There are many things that
are extremely desirable for us to do if the Church is going
to make an adequate response to the challenges of twenty-
first-century secular society, but there is only one thing
absolutely essential: that we take the road to joy, the way
of the Eucharist and the way of the Beatitudes. Unless we
do this, all our planning, all our policies, all our singing
and rejoicing will be a waste of time.

In my commentary on the Mass I have made a number
of suggestions as to how we should celebrate it. Some of
these are controversial. However, we should not exagger-
ate their importance. The best parish priest I ever met
was totally tone deaf and could not have celebrated in the
way I suggested, even if he had wanted to, but his humble
love of God and his neighbour shone through his celebration. That is what we need: eucharistic celebrations
where the spirituality of the participants shines through.
This brings us back to the Beatitudes.

The most important duty that our pastors have towards
their people is to provide a Eucharistic liturgy that allows
them to participate in the deepest possible way in the
Christian Mystery, and we must discover means to guide
ourselves and others along the path mapped out in the
Beatitudes. It is because of this conviction that this book
has been written.